Advance Praise for

Class Matters

One of the biggest myths of US corporate culture is that America is classless: we are supposedly all middle class. Betsy Leondar-Wright not only shatters this myth, she gives us inspiring stories and practical tools to heal the wounds of class inequality in our society.

— Dr. Kevin Danaher, cofounder, Global Exchange

Betsy Leondar-Wright offers a compelling look at the issues that confront activists in going face-to-face with class. Recognizing that class in the United States is often viewed through other prisms, *Class Matters* does not reduce its subject to simple economics or to two-dimensional characters. Instead, the book forces the reader to confront the very real issues that are involved in addressing the interplay of class, race, gender, and sexual orientation in the struggle for social justice.

— Bill Fletcher, Jr., president, TransAfrica Forum

Class Matters is a living, breathing document full of joy and tears. Betsy Leondar-Wright has managed to bridge the gap between theory and practice and point the way beyond identity politics to a more inclusive movement for social justice. *Class Matters* is one of those indispensable books that give us a glimpse of democracy's next evolutionary step.

— Robert Fuller, author of *Somebodies and Nobodies: Overcoming the Abuse of Rank*

Class Matters is a breath of fresh air. It uses the voices of
people who have worked the grassroots to address the most difficult
problems facing the progressive community. It throws off dogma and
pc-thinking to ask how can we really be effective in a country badly
divided and separated by class. In fact, this is one of the few
books around to really speak honestly about class. Progressives are
reverent about all manner of oppression but show only a
passing interest in the challenges facing white working class
Americans — without whom progressives will always be
marginalized. Betsy Leondar-Wright has had the courage to
organize against the odds, and here she shows the courage
to knock down convention and barriers to build cross-class
alliances. We all need her to succeed.

— Stan Greenberg, pollster and author of *The Two Americas:
Our Current Political Deadlock and How to Break It*

CLASS
MATTERS

CLASS
MATTERS

cross-class alliance building
for middle-class activists

Betsy Leondar-Wright

NEW SOCIETY PUBLISHERS

Cataloging in Publication Data:
A catalog record for this publication is available from the National Library of Canada.

Cover design by Diane McIntosh.

Printed in Canada.

Paperback ISBN: 0-86571-523-8

Inquiries regarding requests to reprint all or part of *Class Matters* should be addressed to New Society Publishers at the address below.

To order directly from the publishers, please call toll-free (North America) 1-800-567-6772, or order online at www.newsociety.com

Any other inquiries can be directed by mail to:

New Society Publishers
P.O. Box 189, Gabriola Island, BC V0R 1X0, Canada
1-800-567-6772

New Society Publishers' mission is to publish books that contribute in fundamental ways to building an ecologically sustainable and just society, and to do so with the least possible impact on the environment, in a manner that models this vision. We are committed to doing this not just through education, but through action. We are acting on our commitment to the world's remaining ancient forests by phasing out our paper supply from ancient forests worldwide. This book is one step towards ending global deforestation and climate change. It is printed on acid-free paper that is **100% old growth forest-free** (100% post-consumer recycled), processed chlorine free, and printed with vegetable based, low VOC inks. For further information, or to browse our full list of books and purchase securely, visit our website at: www.newsociety.com

NEW SOCIETY PUBLISHERS   www.newsociety.com

To the late, great Bill Moyer

Class Matters

Cross-Class Alliance Building for Middle-Class Activists
By Betsy Leondar-Wright

Table of Contents

Overview

Working Definitions

Class in the US is a confusing and slippery topic. The definitions that make sense to one person may not make sense to another. The following definitions are offered in hopes of starting a discussion with shared language.

What do we mean by class?

Class is relative status in terms of income, wealth, power and/or position.

What do we mean by working-class, low-income, middle-class, and owning-class people?

The US has no hard-and-fast divisions between class groups. Income and wealth are both on spectrums, and most of us move a little up or down the spectrums during our lifetimes. Some people grow up in one class and as adults live in another.

For immigrants, there's another layer of confusion, as their class status in their country of origin is often different from their class status in the US

Nevertheless, it can be useful for understanding class dynamics to clump people roughly into the following groups:

WORKING CLASS: People with some or all of these class indicators, and their family members:

* little or no college education, in particular no BA from a four-year college
* low or negative net worth (assets minus debts), usually modest income
* rental housing, or one non-luxury home long saved for and lived in for decades
* occupations involving physical work and/or little control in the workplace.

Lower middle class: These families are somewhat more prosperous and secure, but they have much in common with working-class people, such as no BA and/or less control over their work and/or fewer assets than professional middle-class families. If they own a small business, it can only survive by the proprietor's hands-on work.

Class Self-Identifications

It's not true, as sometimes is said, that almost all Americans call themselves "middle-class." That's only the answer when the choices presented are lower, middle, and upper class. Few people want to call themselves "low class."

However, when "working class" is one of the options, then many people identify themselves as belonging to the working class.

Class self-identification:

	1998	1972-1998 (avg.)
Lower class	5%	5%
Working class	45%	46%
Middle class	46%	46%
Upper class	4%	3%

Source: National Opinion Research Center, available at www.norc.uchicago.edu, cited in Jack Metzgar, "Politics and the American Class Vernacular," *Working USA*, Summer 2003.

Working-class and lower-middle-class people are varied in race, culture, values, and political beliefs. They are mostly white, but compared to the composition of the whole population, a disproportionate number of them are people of color and women. Working-class and lower-middle-class people are more likely to have strong ethnic and religious identities than middle-class people.

POVERTY CLASS: A subset of working-class people who chronically can't get income sufficient to cover all their basic needs.

Signs that someone might belong to this class can include:

* substandard housing or homelessness

- long-time use of public benefits, such as welfare, or charity
- chronic lack of health care, food, or other necessities
- frequent involuntary moves, chaos, and disruption of life.

Poor people are varied in race, culture, values, and political beliefs – although a disproportionate number of them are people of color, women, children, and people with disabilities.

Because some low-income people see "poor" as a negatively loaded term, many activists use "low-income" to be more respectful.

PROFESSIONAL MIDDLE CLASS: College-educated, salaried professionals and managers and their family members.

Signs that someone might belong to the professional middle class can include:

- four years of college, especially at private and/or residential schools, sometimes a degree from a professional school
- secure homeownership, often with several moves up to bigger houses in a lifetime
- more control over the hours and methods of work than working-class people have, and/or control over others' work
- more economic security than working-class people have (although that difference is eroding), but no way to pay bills without working
- social status and social connections to help the next generation remain in the same class.

Middle-class people are varied in race, culture, values and political beliefs; they are disproportionately white.

Upper middle class: These families have more in common with owning-class families, such as more luxuries and travel, than most middle-class families, but still depend on salaries, not investments, to pay bills.

OWNING CLASS: Investors and their family members with enough income from assets that they don't have to work to pay basic bills. A subset have positions of power or vast wealth that put them in the ruling class.

How Big Is Each Class?

About two-thirds of Americans are working-class, low-income, or lower-middle-class. Fewer than one in ten Americans remains in the poverty class for a generation or more, although many working-class people spend part of their lives in poverty. About three percent of Americans belong to the owning class. Almost a third of all Americans are in professional middle-class families.

Signs that someone might belong to the owning class can include:

- an education at elite private schools and elite colleges without student loans
- large inheritances
- luxuries, multiple homes and international travel
- social connections and financial knowledge to help the next generation remain wealthy.

However, people who live modestly on investment income also belong to the owning class.

Owning-class people are disproportionately white; they are varied in culture, values, and political beliefs.

Reality Check
Who has how much money

Many Americans guess wrong about how their income and assets rank among the population as a whole.

THE DISTRIBUTION of WEALTH IN THE UNITED STATES EXPRESSED AS PEANUT BUTTER in a SANDWICH

Compare Your Income

Household income in 2002

Lowest fifth	$ 17,916 or less
Second fifth	$ 17,917 to $ 33,377
Middle fifth	$ 33,378 to $ 53,162
Fourth fifth	$ 53,163 to $ 84,016
Top fifth	$ 84,017 or more
Top 5 %	$ 150,002 or more

Source: US Census

Compare Your Wealth

Average (mean) household net worth in 2001

Lowest fifth	negative (more debts than assets)
Lowest 40% (as a whole)	$ 2,900
Middle fifth	$ 75,000
Fourth fifth	$ 215,300
81st to 90th percentile	$ 490,300
91st to 95th percentile	$ 937,400
96th to 99th percentile	$ 2,453,000
Top 1%	$ 12,692,000

Source: Edward Wolff's analysis of Federal Reserve data

"Like Parent, Like Child"

Recent studies find that there is less income mobility from one generation to another than previously believed.

Parents' Income Quintile	Chance of children attaining each income level
Top fifth:	
Top fifth	42.3%
Middle fifth	16.5%
Bottom fifth	6.3%
Middle fifth:	
Top fifth	15.3%
Middle fifth	25.0%
Bottom fifth	17.3%
Bottom fifth:	
Top fifth	7.3%
Middle fifth	18.4%
Bottom fifth	37.3%

Source: Thomas Hertz (American University), cited in Alan B. Krueger, "Economic Scene: The apple falls close to the tree, even in the land of opportunity," *New York Times*, November 14, 2002.

The data challenge the notion that the United States is an exceptionally mobile society. If the United States stands out in comparison with other countries, it is in having a more static distribution of income across generations with fewer opportunities for advancement. — Alan B. Krueger

Marilyn Humpries

How Did I Come to Write Class Matters?

Betsy Leondar-Wright

Picture a meeting of 20 women in a scruffy movement office. I've been working with them for three intense years, struggling to save the welfare safety net. The welfare recipients present their demands to the middle-class anti-poverty advocates. When we don't agree to all the demands, some low-income mothers raise their voices. Their staff declare the coalition dissolved and abruptly end the meeting. I mourned the loss of that coalition for years.

Now picture me in Seattle at the 1999 globalization protests, joining 500 beefy guys wearing blue shirts in the Steelworkers March. Down a hill towards us come 300 students of all races, pierced and tattooed, mostly wearing black, who feed into the march. As I look down the line of alternate blue and black clothes, I have a flash of exultation: "This is my movement!" But now picture me back in Boston watching the local globalization coalition shrink, with no-one from unions attending meetings anymore. My elation deflated into discouragement.

The despair I feel at these class rifts is not a new feeling. It's familiar from childhood.

The despair I feel at these class rifts is not a new feeling. It's familiar from childhood. When two second-grade girls share a giggle, what happens next? Do they have play-dates and sleep-overs? In my experience, the answer was yes only if we both had college-educated fathers and single-family houses. If the other girl lived in an apartment or had a dad who worked with his hands, then our affection was expressed only at school. We never entered each other's homes.

How did this social distance come to pass? No adult told us not to play together. There was just a nameless uneasiness that kept us from inviting each other home.

At 14, I had a boyfriend at camp, the first boy I really kissed. He was thrillingly tough and streetsmart. We swore we'd stay in touch. Two weeks after camp, he took a train from his city, where he lived with a large Italian family in a small apartment, and came to visit me. We kissed in the train station. After dinner at my house, he and I went for a walk, and he didn't kiss me, didn't talk much. He got back on the train, and I never saw him again. I felt rejected. I was 30 before it occurred to me, "He felt freaked out by my house!" My family had just moved into a huge, 15-room house on a hill.

Sage Soifer

In that house, I began to associate wealth with loneliness. My parents weren't getting along, my dad and I were fighting, and we all retreated to different parts of the house. The amount of family conversation probably dropped by half when we moved there. When I think back on my high-school and college years, I think I got a taste of owning-class life experience in an otherwise middle-class life.

My father spoke of America as a "meritocracy," in which intelligence and hard work determine success. His dearest wish was that his daughters go to elite schools. In 1974, I went to

Princeton, which was a shock to my system. It was obvious that something other than meritocracy accounted for some admissions. The attitude later called "slacker" was evident among some "legacy" students, whose fathers and grandfathers had gone to Princeton. Their social life centered around eating clubs, some of which selected members by asking class-laden interview questions like "What does your father do?"

I was nauseated by this minority of snobbish students. At the same time I was inspired by the minority of radi-

grass arguing about what a post-revolutionary society would look like. My visions were decentralized, nonviolent, and ecological. So when a Movement for a New Society (MNS) speaker came to campus and described a similar vision, I dropped out and moved into the MNS community in Philadelphia.

I arrived just when working-class MNS members were staging a revolt. The founders were mostly gutsy white working-class veterans of the recent Civil Rights and anti-Vietnam-War movements. A wave of people like me,

to be on the staff of economic justice organizations since 1987.

Recently I was talking with a friend who was considering working on economic issues, but she said she didn't think she had the appropriate experience since her entire life had been spent among professionals. It made me realize how different my life has been. I've worked with admirable activists across the range of the class spectrum. Just three examples:

- For a few years while I was living with low-income friends in a low-income neighborhood, my job was organizing low-income tenants, and I served on the board of a low-income organization.

I suddenly got it that there were structural causes of social problems. I dropped my liberal activities – registering students to vote, interning at Planned Parenthood – and joined the radicals sitting on the grass arguing what a post-revolutionary society would look like.

- I've been involved in some movements that were over-whelmingly middle-class, such as those against nuclear power and Central American intervention.

cals. The South Africa anti-apartheid movement was heating up, as was the anti-nuclear-power movement.

I remember one moment that felt like being hit by lightening, when I was transformed from a liberal to a radical. I was helping raise money for the famine in the Sahel. A campus radical told me that multinational corporations were still exporting grain from the Sahel. I suddenly got it that there were structural causes of social problems. I dropped my liberal activities – registering students to vote, interning at Planned Parenthood – and joined the radicals sitting on the

middle-class ex-students, had recently flooded the organization, and the founders found many of us flighty, self-indulgent, and oblivious. In working-class speak-outs, they told us of the disrespect and deprivation they had faced growing up. My 21-year-old open heart was imprinted by their words, and I resolved to be an ally.

I reached out hopefully to make working-class friends. Leading classism workshops, I enthusiastically urged other middle-class people to speak up for working-class people. I steered myself towards economic issues and have had the good fortune

- My job at United for a Fair Economy includes getting media coverage for members of the Responsible Wealth project, people in the richest five percent who speak out against the rules being tilted towards the wealthy.

Over 25 years of activism, every experience has given me insights into and questions about class. I've been chewing over these questions, reaching out to others preoccupied by class issues, turning my insights into classism workshop agendas – and now, with *Class Matters*, writing about steps towards better class dynamics.

Writing *Class Matters*

After some painful rifts along class lines in the 1990s, I began looking for resources about cross-class alliances. Fred Rose's and Linda Stout's wonderful books helped me – but I found no workshops to attend, no newsletters to read. Slowly I came to the conclusion that I could write something myself. In 2002, when I thought of writing for middle-class activists in particular, the ideas started to flow. Of course I welcome readers from all classes, but I have focused on what I thought might be particularly useful to middle-class activists. I hope others will write the companion guides for working-class, low-income, and owning-class activists.

Writing this book was like making a patchwork quilt. In patchworking, you cut away extra material to make a shape and then juxtapose it with other pieces to make a pattern. In *Class Matters*, I have juxtaposed my own experiences (marked hereafter with "blw") next to excerpts from 40 interviews (marked with interviewees' names) and quotations from 40 books, articles, dissertations, and websites. I don't agree with every quotation, but all come from real experience and all make me reflect on class in coalitions.

Thirteen savvy people kindly agreed to be on my Advisory Committee: Chuck Collins, Sam Grant, Sandy Jones, Paul Kivel, Jenny Ladd, Jack Metzgar, S.M. Miller, Lisa Richards, Fred Rose, Anne Slepian, Linda Stout, Dorian Warren, and Felice Yeskel. Their feedback immeasurably improved this book. Thanks also to my supportive informal advisors, Curdina Hill, Anne Wright, Doug Lipman, Kathy Modigliani, and Rafe Ezekiel, and to my beloved partner Gail Leondar-Wright, who not only gave excellent feedback, but also endured many disruptions of our family life. A month of sabbatical offered by United for a Fair Economy and a sojourn at the Mesa Refuge gave me extra time to write *Class Matters*.

The title *Class Matters* honors two writers who bridge the inner and outer dimensions of racism and classism exceptionally well: bell hooks, author of *Where We Stand: Class Matters*, and Cornel West, author of *Race Matters*.

My own life story was the hardest part to write. Books about class routinely start with the life story of a working-class person. Others start with a rich person's story. I've never seen a middle-class life story – explicitly a middle-class story – in non-fiction print, even in anthologies about class. My discomfort with writing it points to something about middle-class people's societal role: we are behind a screen, part of the machinery, impersonal. Writing my story felt like stepping out in front of the screen.

Class is a huge topic, and there are many aspects that this book is *not* about. It's not about economic systems. It's not about strategy for a cross-class movement. It's not about how to win over non-activists. In Paul Kivel's clever formulation, we all have a choice to get by, get over, or get together. This book is for those who take the "get together" path, and its goal is to help us get together better across class differences.

Betsy Leondar-Wright leading a workshop.

Activists Interviewed in Class Matters

John Anner, editor of *Beyond Identity Politics: Emerging Social Justice Movements in Communities of Color*, is Executive Director of the East Meets West Foundation in the Bay Area.

He is a man who calls himself "a garden-variety white guy with three kids and a mortgage."

Alison Bowens is the former Executive Director of Women's Institute for Leadership Development in Massachusetts.

She is a middle-class African American woman.

Brenda Choresi Carter, graduate student in American Studies at Yale, is an organizer for the Graduate Employees and Students Organization in New Haven, CT.

She is a middle-class Asian-American woman.

Carolyn Cavalier is a member of a cross-class women's group in the Bay Area.

She is an owning-class Jewish white woman.

May Chen is Vice-President of UNITE and Manager of Local 23-25, which represents thousands of garment workers in New York City.

She is a middle-class Chinese-American woman.

Woodrow Coleman is a member of the Planning Committee of the Bus Riders Union in Los Angeles.

He is a working-class African American man.

Manuel Criollo is a staff organizer of the Bus Riders Union in Los Angeles.

He is a Latino man who grew up working-class.

Attieno Davis is the former Racial Wealth Divide Education Coordinator at United for a Fair Economy in Boston.

She is a working-class African American woman.

Barbara Ehrenreich is the author of *Nickled and Dimed*, *Fear of Falling*, and other books and articles on class.

She is a white woman who grew up working-class.

Theresa Funiciello, author of *The Tyranny of Kindness*, directs the Caregiver Credit Campaign in New York City.

She is a white married woman who was a low-income welfare mother for many years.

Wendy Gonaver is a graduate student at the College of William and Mary in Williamsburg, VA.

She is a lower-middle-class white heterosexual woman.

Sam Grant teaches Ethnic Studies, Social Science, and Graduate Psychology at Metropolitan State University in St. Paul, MN, and works as a consultant to the university on community-based initiatives.

He is a working-class African American man.

Gilda Haas is the Executive Director of Strategic Actions for a Just Economy (SAJE) in Los Angeles and teaches at the UCLA Urban Planning Department.

She is a middle-class white woman.

Michael James directs the Institute for Popular Education at the University of California at Berkeley.

He is a working-class Japanese-American/African American man.

Paul Kivel, author of *Uprooting Racism, You Call This a Democracy?*, and other books on oppression, lives in Oakland, CA.

He is an owning-class white Jewish heterosexual man.

Jerry Koch-Gonzalez is a diversity trainer in Western Massachusetts.

He is a Cuban immigrant who grew up working-class and is now middle-class.

George Lakey, author of *Powerful Peacemaking* and co-author of *Grassroots and Nonprofit Leadership*, directs Training for Change in Philadelphia.

He is an older working-class white gay man.

Cameron Levin is a Strategic Thinking consultant with social justice organizations in Los Angeles.

He is a young middle-class white man.

Penn Loh is the Executive Director of Alternatives for Community and Environment in Roxbury, MA.

He is a middle-class Chinese-American man.

Pam McMichael is an activist and writer in Louisville, Kentucky, who co-founded Southerners on New Ground (SONG).

She is a working-class white lesbian.

Nell Myhand, diversity trainer, is the author of the forthcoming *Harvest the Tree of Justice: Women Cross Class.*

She is a lower-middle-class African American lesbian.

Raúl Quiñones Rosado is co-director of ilé: Institute for Latino Empowerment/Instituto para la Conciencia y Acción in Caguas, Puerto Rico.

He is a working-class Puerto Rican man.

Rachel Rybaczuk is a graduate student at the University of Massachusetts in Amherst.

She is a young low-income white woman.

Susan Remmers was the Executive Director of the McKenzie River Gathering foundation in Portland, OR.

She is an upper-middle-class white lesbian woman.

Natalie Reteneller is the Director of the Louisville Youth Group.

She is a young working-class white lesbian.

Lisa Richards is active in Sisters Together Ending Poverty in Marlborough, MA..

She is a low-income white heterosexual woman who is the mother of five children between age one and 13, four of whom are biracial.

Barbara Smith, author of *The Truth That Never Hurts* and editor of *Home Girls: A Black Feminist Anthology*, lives in Albany, NY.

She is an African American lesbian who grew up working-class and is now lower-middle-class.

Preston Smith, associate professor of Politics at Mt. Holyoke College in South Hadley, MA, is on the Interim National Council of the Labor Party.

He is an African American man who grew up in a lower-middle-class Air Force family.

"Ellen Smith" (name changed at her request) works as a staff member with a community organization where she was a grassroots leader for four years.

She is a young bisexual working-class white woman.

James Spady is a graduate student at the College of William and Mary in Williamsburg, VA.

He is a middle-class white heterosexual man.

Laura Stern is an activist in the Bay Area, CA.

She is a lower-middle-class white Jewish lesbian.

Linda Stout, author of *Bridging the Class Divide*, is Executive Director of Spirit in Action, based in Western Massachusetts.

She is a disabled white lesbian who grew up low-income.

Roxana Tynan is Accountable Development Director at the Los Angeles Alliance for a New Economy.

She is an upper-middle-class white woman from England.

Ahbi Vernon is a member of a cross-class women's group in the Bay Area.

She is a middle-class white Jewish heterosexual woman.

Dorian Warren, a graduate student in Political Science at Yale University, is based in Chicago.

He is an African American man from a working-class background.

Barbara Willer is the Lead Organizer/Director of a community organization that works to increase parent leadership and power in public education.

She is a middle-class white lesbian who grew up working-class.

Billy Wimsatt, co-author of *How to Get Stupid White Men Out of Office* and author of *No More Prisons* and *Burn the Suburbs*, is the director of Indyvoter.org.

He calls himself a "cool rich kid": a young upper-middle-class white man.

Shirley Yee is a consultant with the Todos Institute in the Bay Area.

She is a first-generation young lower-middle-class Asian-American woman.

Felice Yeskel, Executive Director of the Stonewall Center at the University of Massachusetts at Amherst and co-director of Class Action, does training and consulting on issues of class.

She is a white lesbian who grew up working-class and is now middle-class.

Why Do We Need Cross-Class Alliances

blw

The labor movement, the civil rights movement, antiwar movements, the women's movement – over and over again Americans have risen up and organized to transform their society. Each major movement has won significant reforms, satisfying the pragmatists aiming for limited concessions by power-holders. But each one has disappointed the visionaries who dreamed of deeper structural change.

Why have movements failed at their larger goals? Among other things, because all have had bases too small to shift the fundamental balance of power. Everyone who dreams of a fairer society would do well to aim to broaden our movements to include a larger percentage of the American people. But the American people have historically been too divided by race and class for a mass movement to cross many demographic lines.

Racism has been used repeatedly to divide and conquer potential allies for change. Many books document this use of racism, and many anti-racist organizations challenge it. There are also many analyses of past movements that see their limitations as a result of tactical mistakes, geopolitical contexts, economic forces, and other causes. All these explanations contain a piece of the truth. The crucial role of class in splitting and weakening movements, however, has too often been overlooked.

The antiwar movement of the 1960s hastened the end of the war, probably preventing nuclear weapons from being used in Vietnam, and deterred later US administrations from open military invasions for more than two decades. But Students for a Democratic Society's vision of participatory democracy, in which people have a say over the decisions that affect their lives, didn't come true – nor, for that matter, did the hippies' vision of the Age of Aquarius materialize. One reason was that vast reservoirs of potential support were never tapped. Opposition to the war was in fact higher among lower-income than among higher-income Americans. Yet the movement was dominated by students and other members of the middle class, whose attitudes towards working-class people varied between romantic idealism and prejudices against "hard-hats." Counter-culture markers like long hair and flamboyantly ratty clothes were often used to define the borders of the movement, which left out many potential supporters from other subcultures. The GI movement of antiwar soldiers and the student movement formed some alliances but could have combined forces more powerfully.

The Civil Rights movement won an end to legal segregation through a mixed-class mobilization of African Americans and their allies. It was both the most class-diverse movement of the twentieth century and the most successful movement. But the consolidation of its victories mostly lifted up college-educated black male leaders to national prominence, and as a result neither the "beloved community" envisioned by the movement nor the elimination of black poverty came to pass.

Earlier in the 20th century, the women's suffrage movement waged its struggle without much participation from working-class women, and the labor movement had only limited support from middle-class and owning-class allies. While the suffragettes won votes for women, the peaceful, nurturing society some of them thought would be voted in didn't materialize. While the labor movement won the 40-hour week and basic labor rights, the workers' paradise of their dreams did not come to pass. If the two movements had joined forces more, they would likely have won more reforms than they did separately.

In the 1920s, feminist groups such as the National Women's Party advocated an Equal Rights Amendment to the Constitution, without dealing with the possible loss of protective legislation for women, such as required breaks,

Racism has been used repeatedly to divide and conquer political allies for change. The crucial role of class in splitting and weakening movements, however, has too often been overlooked.

bathrooms, weight-lifting limits, and a ten-hour day. According to Diane Balser in *Sisterhood and Solidarity*, the National Women's Trade Union League and some women's unions opposed the ERA as a way of preserving protective legislation, without dealing with women's lack of legal rights. The result was that women got neither an ERA nor protective legislation. If they had combined forces and advocated for an ERA and an extension of protective legislation to all workers, how many women's lives might have been improved?

More recent movements initiated by middle-class activists have won reforms but failed to capture the imagination of the working-class majority and thus were limited in what they could accomplish. In the 1970s, the anti-nuclear-power movement successfully stopped utilities from expanding the number of nuclear power plants, but the narrow base of mostly white middle-class and owning-class support was one factor in why the dream of renewable energy went unrealized.

In the 1980s, the Central America movement won a Congressional ban on aid to the Nicaraguan contra guerrillas (prompting the infamous illegal arms sales to an official "enemy" country, Iran, to fund covert aid) and helped make possible a return to limited democracy in Central American countries. But military intervention, usually on behalf of corrupt dictatorships, continued to be a common federal policy, in part because the movement did not reach out much beyond college-educated circles and thus had limited political clout. In the polarized Cold War climate, the AFL-CIO actually sided with the right-wing dictators funded by the US

Movements initiated by working-class and low-income activists have also been limited in their accomplishments by the small amount of support

they have gotten from middle-class and owning-class people. Welfare rights organizations suffered a devastating setback in the 1990s when "welfare reform" eliminated the entitlement to a safety net, and only a tiny number of middle-class allies spoke up. If middle-class feminists had responded to proposed cutbacks in welfare rights – which are the floor on which women's workplace and family status is built – in the same way they would have reacted to an equally severe cutback in reproductive rights, welfare reform would likely not have been implemented in such an extreme form.

Organized labor, which for decades had generally been closed to community coalitions, now invites more collaboration, especially the newer service worker unions such as SEIU and HERE. But old ways of doing things still create barriers. Though the student sweatshop movement, the campus living-wage movement, Jobs with Justice, and the National Interfaith Committee on Worker Justice have formed exciting alliances, only limited numbers of middle-class people have responded to their requests for support of low-wage working people. The living-wage movement, led by unions and supported by mixed-class coalitions, has had incredible success in raising wages for employees of

municipal contractors in 110 places, but has not won over-all increases in the minimum wage, except in New Orleans. Polls show overwhelming support for higher wages for poverty-wage jobs, but that support has not translated into sufficient voter power to force state or federal minimum wage increases.

The "Teamsters and Turtles" (unions and environmentalists) who marched together in Seattle in 1999 actually managed to nonviolently shut down the World Trade Organization meetings, and there is evidence that the WTO subsequently backed off on some decisions harmful to labor rights and the environment. But within three months after this victory, the local labor-student-NGO coalitions that had sent people to Seattle dissolved almost everywhere.

The truth that we progressives of all classes have avoided facing for the last century is that we need each other. To fundamentally transform our society to be a fairer and more sustainable one, the movement we build will have to include people of every race, every age, every geographic area – and every class.

Middle-class activists in the US have a proud history of initiating, organizing, and supporting movements for progressive social change. We also have a not-so-proud history of overlooking potential allies from other classes, failing to come through for movements led by poor and working-class people and stepping on the toes of coalition partners through classist assumptions. The purpose of this book is to help middle-class activists learn to bridge class differences and put fewer obstacles in the way of effective cross-class alliances.

Protest at Seabrook nuclear power plant.

Two Stories of Cross-Class Alliances

Solidarity Works

blw

We were trying to plan a joint action by all the unions at Yale. The maintenance workers suggested a day of prayer, and the graduate student union objected: "There's no way grad students are praying." So then the clerical workers suggested a day of fasting, and someone from the maintenance workers' local said, "No way are our members fasting. The newspaper would catch a photo of someone with a doughnut."

When I heard Brenda Choresi Carter tell that story at a Working Class Studies conference, I knew I wanted to interview her about the Federation of Hospital and University Employees, a group she calls a "stunningly diverse coalition." The Yale clerical workers local consists mostly of white women, the maintenance workers local mostly of black men; the hospital workers are mixed in race and gender. The graduate student union, GESO, for which she works, is mostly middle-class; 40 percent of them are international students.

She told me that some workers were initially skeptical about working with grad students, who seemed

Marilyn Humphries

transient and privileged. But during a strike in March 2003, "GESO got rave reviews from other unions. They commented that we were on the picket lines every day despite record-breaking cold and downpours. We're young and energetic, and we brought fun to picket lines, like musical instruments and giant puppets." During that strike, she says, "we actualized our vision of Yale."

It was not easy to organize graduate students in large numbers to join GESO or the Federation: "Some students have liberal guilt, like 'other workers have real problems, not us. How can I compare myself to a custodial worker?' Some feel the other unions' contracts are not our business, that GESO should just get the best deal for ourselves. Others think unions are unreasonable.

"There's also a realistic fear of faculty disapproval. Grad students' careers depend on faculty letters of recommendation, and some GESO organizers have gotten bad letters. Some have been kicked out of labs." Given these obstacles, it's very impressive that 600 grad students participated in the spring 2003 strike.

Brenda attributes the strength of the Federation's solidarity to each group having a stake in the outcome: "The commitment it takes to pull something like this off, when the university is set on our destruction, only comes from self-interest. To organize grad students on behalf of other workers would seem like charity. The Federation is strong because we need each other to win."

The various union leaders created opportunities for human contact

---

I really value middle-class activists when they value themselves as part of the broader community.
— **Natalie Reteneller**

among their memberships, such as backyard barbecues. They sent members to tell their personal stories at each other's meetings.

Winning community support also meant reaching across differences. Brenda told me, "I went to churches to speak for GESO. Before one such meeting, I was nervous about going into a Latino Pentecostal storefront church. I couldn't imagine how graduate students' issues would play there. I just told them the truth: this is what I study, this is how much I'm paid, this is how many grad students have no health insurance. Some spend seven or eight years in New Haven, have kids, and want to buy homes, but can't. It was incredibly easy. They were appalled at our pay of $12,000 to $22,000 a year."

I interviewed Brenda only two months before another strike at Yale in September 2003. Their unity paid off in pay increases and better pensions for the clerical and maintenance workers. The university still has not recognized the graduate students' union, however.

Brenda's description of how GESO members acted as part of the Federation is a helpful model for other middle-class activists in cross-class coalitions: "One thing GESO has done well is to admit what we don't know and to ask for help from the groups more experienced in union organizing. We pitch in, do the dirty work, yet contribute what we have to give, like research reports. We haven't been know-it-alls, just because we have all this education."

Balancing Inclusion and Expertise while Developing New Experts

Gilda Haas

I'll tell you a story that has to do with class, education, and preparedness:

We had a time-sensitive opportunity in the Figueroa Corridor neighborhood in LA. One of the biggest developers in the world was planning a huge project in the neighborhood, and they needed approvals from the city. There was an election coming up, and the mayor and city council wanted to approve this project before the election. They knew that our coalition, the Figueroa Corridor Coalition, could slow things down with community opposition, so we had some clout. We had a chance to negotiate benefits for our community in exchange for our support, but only if we moved fast.

The members of the coalition include both organizations *and* individuals who are mostly Latinos working in service and garment industries and some working-class African Americans. The organizations are represented by their staff, who are mostly college-educated.

So we had to decide who would sit at the bargaining table. Would it be the people who ideally, in our vision of our organization, *should* be there – neighborhood residents? Or would it be people who because of their experience might get us a better deal? We came up with criteria: Have you negotiated with a big company before? Do you have knowledge of the content of issues on the table, such as affordable housing?

And when we applied those criteria, it was all college-educated people, not neighborhood residents. We started by saying, well, that's the breaks. But then we changed our minds. We chose people by expertise, but we also made

Graduation from Figueroa jobs development course

Gilda Haas

sure that there were community activists in the room. We had a rotating group of four local residents at the negotiations. We had Spanish translation at all times, and we called for frequent caucuses. The caucuses were to touch base with the neighborhood folks and to discuss how to react to new proposals.

And we won a lot of stuff! Including neighborhood people didn't slow us down too much, and it made us better able to prioritize what to push for.

What happened next also involved innovative ways to be more inclusive. One victory was that half the jobs will go to local residents, with a job-training program to prepare them. We could have hired a bunch of consultants to set up the program, but instead we created a course through a community college for local residents to learn how to plan a jobs program. Our group provided the students *and* the teachers. Forty people met for 15 weeks and got college credit. They went to other cities to see how they did development without displacement of local residents, and they got all fired up.

The students were a mix of Latino and African American working-class people, and the course was a chance to struggle through some cross-cultural issues. For example, they talked about their own personal experiences on various jobs. When an African American woman heard a Latino man tell a story about a garment contractor saying to him, "I don't care if you worked 65 hours, you'll just have to wait for your pay," she said, "I never had to deal with that." It started to break down stereotypes about Latino people stealing black people's jobs. There was very high-quality Spanish/English translation that allowed people to really get into discussions.

After the class, they did presentations first to the coalition, and then to the developer and the president of the community college, about how we want to do the jobs program.

So the planning itself happened in a way that developed new leaders. If we had asked people to come to meetings every week for 15 weeks, we might have had four people, but since we were offering college credit, all these people who had never gone to college before got involved. We used the teacher pay to pay for translation, childcare, and transportation.

Figueroa Corridor Coalition, presentation of jobs program

We have a long-term commitment to developing people and to creating situations where all kinds of knowledge are used. We're never going to have enough power to make change unless different kinds of people learn to work together.

I really value the dedication of some amazing white organizers that stick. — **Woodrow Coleman**

Are There Class Cultures?

blw

If having a common culture means that the people would recognize each other as similar – might laugh at the same jokes, talk somewhat alike, have a similar range of habits, etc. – then the answer to the question "Are there class cultures?" seems to be "no." We in the US experience the class system in ways so specific to our age, race, geography, religion, ethnicity, and nationality that class alone rarely seems to create that sense of kinship. If poor people from Appalachia and the South Bronx see each other as kin, it's probably as a result of some hard political work to create solidarity, not because of a close cultural similarity.

In *The Clustering of America*, Michael J. Weiss describes the Claritas Corporation's system of dividing all the zip codes in America into 62 types. The high-priced marketing consultations offered by Claritas promise to predict how the people in any zip code will tend to react to a new product or a politician's slogan, based on their neighborhood type.

For example, the suburban area where I grew up is categorized as "Furs and Station Wagons." Then I went to college and lived in a "Towns and Gowns" area, then moved to a "Bohemian Mix" city neighborhood full of counterculture folks. I've had community organizing jobs in

It's easy to fall into stereotypes about people with a particular amount of money or a type of occupation or neighborhood – easy and dangerous.

"Smalltown Downtown," "Emergent Minorities," and "Public Assistance" neighborhoods.

The 62 types are narrow enough that they each have a particular cultural flavor. Most have a predominant race, a predominant age, and/or a predominant source of income. The people in "Shotguns & Pickups" areas, even in different states, might actually recognize each other as kin. The book arranges the types in order of class privilege (by combining median income, education, and home value into a single score). Assuming that Claritas Corporation's research is sound, then it's safe to say that there are approximately 60 class cultures in the United States.

But 60 is an unwieldy number for class analysis. It's an impractical number for the purposes of having discussions about the group dynamics of a mixed group or of organizing solidarity among people of a particular class to press for social change. Two to five would be a much more practical number. But dividing up 280 million Americans into just two to five clumps means that there's going to be a lot of diversity in each clump.

So if class cultures aren't intuitively recognized by the people involved, then it makes sense to step cautiously into generalizing about them. It's easy to fall into stereotypes about people with a particular amount of money or a type of occupation or neighborhood – easy and dangerous. Working-class and poor people in particular don't need any more stereotypes of them, given how negatively they are usually portrayed in the media. Rich people are also usually villains in Hollywood portrayals. Sometimes stereotypes are based on a grain of truth unfairly generalized, but I take it for granted that "smart versus stupid" is not a cultural difference but a stereotype.

Low Income	Working Class	Middle Class	Owning Class

The romanticization of working-class people I sometimes hear on the left – they're earthy, warm-hearted people with a natural resistance to oppression – is not universal truth either. Even positive stereotypes are harmful for strategic efforts for social change because our efforts to persuade people will be based on inaccurate understandings of what motivates them. I've heard leftists celebrate economic downturns because they assume that harsher conditions will inevitably cause poor people to rise up in rebellion. That romantic stereotype leads to flawed strategy. The romanticized demonization of all privileged people as cold-hearted, uptight betrayers who collude with oppression is similarly untrue. Every class includes people whose relationship to injustice is passive acceptance, enthusiastic collusion, individual gut resistance, or collective organizing.

To avoid stereotypes, we need an experience-based approach that is appropriately cautious. So I'll attempt to stick to generalizations based in a shared experience that socializes people into a class culture.

The clearest examples of a class culture will be families with three or more generations in the same class in the United States. Recent class mobility, recent immigration, and living in the "gray area" between two classes all muddy the waters. Many – perhaps most – people's experience is of a mixed class culture. We will see culture contrasts most clearly if we compare people with long periods in the same class in the same country.

Given all these caveats, are there shared experiences that would define a number of useful class culture distinctions, i.e., significantly less than 60?

Yes, I do believe there are differences of experience that socialize most American people into one of *four* distinct cultural classes: low-income, working-class/lower middle-class, professional middle-class and owning-class. This set of four class culture categories seems to me to be based on certain material realities. And each one rings true to me from my own experience. My experience is, of course, limited (primarily to progressive activists and three northeast states), so I put the following class culture generalizations forward humbly, generalizing primarily about activists and expecting contradictory evidence from others' experience to enrich them. My goal in risking generalizations is to make visible some class-culture-based coalition behaviors and dynamics that are too often invisible.

for Low Income:	for Working Class and Middle Class:		for Owning Class:
	S T E A D Y W O R K I S		
impossible and/or not expected	inevitable and necessary		optional

Yes, I do believe there are differences of experience that socialize most American people into one of four distinct cultural classes: low income, working class/lower middle class, professional middle class, and owning class.

Differences between activists steadily employed and those who are not

One experience most people have that low-income and owning-class people do not share is this: they expect and have steady employment. Working 35 or more hours a week, 48 or more weeks a year, for 30 or more years – that's what working-class and middle-class men, and in recent decades women too, have been brought up to expect. And

I really value middle-class activists because they respect knowledge, rationality, planning, and process. – **George Lakey**

that's approximately what the majority of us experience. It's so familiar to us that we forget that not everyone shares our experience. But not everyone does.

For long-term low-income people, steady work is neither possible nor expected. They live outside what economists call "the primary labor market" of steady jobs and patch together an inadequate income from public assistance and temporary, under-the-table, part-time, and/or extremely low-paid jobs.

For owning-class people, defined as those with enough investment income to support them, steady work is optional, just one choice among many. Many are in fact employed, but during their lifetime work fewer hours than working-class and middle-class people. They may travel around for a year or two after college. They may work part-time or run unprofitable businesses doing something they enjoy. Owning-class women are more likely to take extended childrearing leaves.

The class culture of steady workers (in which I include myself) fosters pride in our pragmatism and in our disciplined work habits. And these are indeed gifts to be proud of. But lacking the expectation and experience of steady work leads people to be unconventional and to think outside the box in a way that steady workers often lose.

The very expectation of poverty from generations of low-income living can sometimes make activists bolder and more visionary. My long-time low-income friend Michaelann Bewsee, along with three other welfare recipients, founded an organization 25 years ago. She started ARISE for Social Justice without any funding, and she has stuck with it for all this time, sometimes getting paid, sometimes not. The organization focuses on whatever the low-income people of Springfield, MA, are concerned about, not shying away from controversial and unfundable issues like needle exchanges. I don't know any working-class or middle-class activists who have done the equivalent.

Chuck Collins

Marilyn Humphries/UFE

I do, however, know owning-class activists who have done the equivalent, including in my very own workplace. United for a Fair Economy was the brainchild of an owning-class white man, Chuck Collins. Chuck has been the originator of some of UFE's most original programs. He comes into the office with a dozen new ideas every week, some wacky, but some brilliant. I, a child of money-anxious Depression-era parents, come into the office every morning worrying about the length of my task list and how I'll get everything done. It's not that I'm not creative at work, but my creativity usually comes out as solving a problem, not as dreaming up something new. Chuck grew up with different expectations than I did about how constrained his life would be, and this freed him up to be a visionary. There are working-class and middle-class visionaries, to be sure, but they are going against their class culture far more than low-income and owning-class visionaries are.

Of course, most activists who don't expect to be steadily employed aren't visionaries and don't start organizations, but even so, they tend to be less bound by convention and less deterred by difficulty than steadily employed people. Often when I've felt taken aback by low-income or owning-class activists, it has been because they seem undeterred not just by difficulty, but by impossibility. Middle-class activists often take the necessity of pragmatic compromise for granted, but low-income activists often resist compromise.

When middle-class and working-class people work with low-income or owning-class people, we steady workers find ourselves frequently in the roles of the pragmatist bringing things down to what's realistic. This pragmatic role can add some helpful realism but also an unhelpful wet blanket.

In my organizing experience, the tensions between working-class and low-income people – the groups writer Barbara Jensen calls "settled living" and "hard living" working-class people – arise over issues of conventional and unconventional behavior. When I worked as a tenant organizer, there were chronic tensions between the steadily employed or retired tenants and the long-time unemployed

Constrained, Discouraged, **Low Income**	**Working Class** and **Middle Class**, steadily employed,	Entitled, **Owning Class**
more unconventional	more conventional and pragmatic	more unconventional

or erratically employed tenants on public assistance. The former saw the latter as breaking the rules and getting away with it, and frequently expressed resentment.

And as a welfare rights advocate, I often encountered hostility among steadily employed working-class people towards welfare recipients – not just among socially conservative people, but also among people progressive on most other issues, including African Americans and former short-term welfare recipients.

A lot of the confusion about class on the left comes from not understanding this class-cultural difference between long-time low-income people and long-time steadily employed people. Often anyone with less than middle-class privilege is clumped together under the labels "working class" or "poor." In part this clumping is done for the progressive goal of valuing poor people and promoting solidarity among all less-privileged people. But it doesn't serve our cause to obscure real differences and real antagonisms just because our opponents might misuse them.

Differences between low-income and owning-class activists

Perhaps it seems strange to find similarities in class groups at the polar ends. Can low-income and owning-class people really have cultural traits in common? Both are more commonly unconventional, eccentric, visionary, undeterred by impossibility, and/or impractical than steadily employed people – but what happens to their visions is

What does it do to the culture when everyone has money or lacks money? It adds or removes a sense of efficacy and entitlement.

very different because of their vastly different resources and status.

What does it do to the culture when everyone has money or lacks money? It adds or removes a sense of efficacy and entitlement. A low-income activist once told me, "Being rich means that everything works." When the car breaks down, they fix it or buy a new one. Owning-class people, especially white men, can assume that society will respond to their needs and desires.

Being poor, on the other hand, means that things don't reliably work. One thing I've learned from my colleagues living in poverty is that they spend an appalling amount of time dealing with crises and chaos: moving frequently, avoiding creditors, dealing with transportation breakdowns, crawling through the welfare bureaucracy, and dealing with sick or disabled or addicted family members, arrested and imprisoned family members, depressed or mentally ill family members, violent family members, evicted or just plain broke family members. It takes a lot of resourcefulness just to get through a day.

The psychological effects of constant crisis vary, but I've heard several poor people describe the same feeling: a discouragement that anything can change, resisted mightily but too often leeching all hope out of the spirit. I've also met angry low-income activists propelled by rage to speak out against conditions harming their families, but a sense of efficacy is a hard-won rarity. Low-income activists tend to see-saw between being lifted up into action by rage and dreams and being sunk low in discouragement over personal crises and hopelessness.

Owning-class people drive me crazy when they act like they own the planet, when they have that entitled vibe. **– Billy Wimsatt**

It's important not to romanticize poverty. I've said that in my experience low-income people are more likely to be unconventional dreamers, but most don't have the time, energy, or hope to launch their dreams in any major, outward way. More common are inner dreams – religious, romantic, artistic, or philosophical – with at most small-scale outward expressions. Buying lottery tickets may be the most common expression of a dream. Lower-income people spend more money on gambling than higher-income people, and it usually impoverishes them further. And some ways of being unconventional are, of course, destructive and illegal.

But it's also important not to assume that hardship empties people's minds and hearts. Tracy Chapman may

> *I've said that in my experience low-income people are more likely to be unconventional dreamers, but most don't have the time, energy or hope to launch their dreams in any major, outward way.*

be indulging in wishful thinking when she says, "They're talking about a revolution, standing in the unemployment line or those armies of salvation." But it's true that people waiting for buses, waiting in soup kitchen lines, and waiting out prison sentences are not zombies. They don't feel less, don't think less than people who are better off.

When owning-class people act on their visions, they have the resources to create them in a bigger way. Here's a portrait of many progressive owning-class people I've known: By carefully investing a small inheritance and living simply, they can travel around for years filming footage for the independent documentary of their dreams. Others are writing books, painting, giving away healing services,

Class Cultures Comparison

Hand-out by Barbara Jensen and Jack Metzgar at a workshop on class cultures at the 2003 conference of the Working-Class Studies Program at Youngstown State University

PROFESSIONAL MIDDLE CLASS

DOING & BECOMING
- achievement-oriented
- future-oriented
- life as transformative
- status concerns
- individualistic

UNINTENDED HOMOGENEITY
- more cosmopolitan
- weaker loyalties to persons, places, groups, institutional affiliations

BEST RESULT:
- individual achievement has positive human impact

WORST RESULT:
- the lonely individual

WORKING CLASS

BEING & BELONGING
- character-oriented
- present-oriented
- life as a tangled web of relationships
- anti-status
- solidaristic

UNAVOIDABLE DIVERSITY
- more parochial
- stronger loyalties to persons, places, groups, institutional affiliations

BEST RESULT:
- secure community

WORST RESULT:
- unachieved potential

Low Income	Working Class and Lower Middle Class	Professional/Managerial Middle Class College Graduates	Owning Class

or starting "businesses" with little likelihood of breaking even.

Contrast all these creative people with this story: An alcoholic and mentally ill woman volunteered for my affordable housing group. Her rent took up virtually all of her SSI check, so she had almost zero discretionary income. But some of it went for a pair of white sneakers and a set of washable markers. Every day she would come in with a new design drawn on the sneaker tops. Sometimes we made her day by ooh-ing and ahh-ing over her new shoe painting.

Both spending years gathering footage for an independent movie and painting a new design on your shoes every day are ways of expressing dreams that might be unlikely behavior in working-class and middle-class adults. But one has a wider audience than the other, one paints on a bigger canvas than the other.

Owning-class people may get lost and confused deciding among their options, they may do things in ungrounded ways, they may sink into addictions where their money keeps them from hitting bottom. But when they do decide to express their dream, they have a far greater sense of efficacy than do low-income dreamers, especially if they're male. There's a positive aspect to this – it would be wonderful if all human beings felt empowered to express their dreams and had the resources to do it – but there's a negative side as well.

Owning-class people can often self-fund their dreams, and so they get less feedback and have fewer external constraints from funders and collaborators. This freedom can lead to delusions of grandeur, particularly among men, a belief that one's own project is better or more important than it is, and an unrealistic expectation that others will fill one's needs. I would sum up their positive sense of empowerment and their negative sense of arrogance with the term "entitlement." Low income activists' good ideas too often

go nowhere; owning class activists' bad ideas too often don't flop.

So there are discouraged unconventional people constrained to paint on a small canvas at one end of the class spectrum, and entitled unconventional people painting on a big canvas at the other end.

Differences between working-class/lower-middle-class and professional middle-class activists

I've proposed the experience or lack of steady employment as a dividing line between class cultures. But what divides steadily employed people into different class cultures? Is there a common experience that socializes more and less privileged people differently, one that has enough of a material base to cause class-cultural differences consistent across race, religion, and geographical boundaries?

Yes. I think one life experience is key: the expectation of and experience of four years of residential college.

Going away to college is an assumed rite of passage for more privileged middle-class kids, those with parents in professional and managerial occupations. It's an experience that professional middle-class people share with owning

Low-income activists' good ideas too often go nowhere; owning-class activists' bad ideas too often don't flop.

Middle-class activists drive me crazy when they make assumptions that other people are having the same experience they are. – **Barbara Willer**

Class-Culture Aspects of Labor/Environmental Conflicts

For his book Coalitions Across the Class Divide, *Fred Rose did participatory research with union members and middle-class environmentalists and came up with a description of their cultural differences similar to that of Jensen/Metzgar and my own. Playing power politics to advance shared interests makes sense from a rooted, working-class life experience. Individuals voluntarily coming together due to their shared values in order to educate the public – this makes sense from an unrooted, middle-class life experience. From his interviews with timber workers and environmentalists locked in conflict over old-growth forests in the Northwest, he concludes:*

Loggers and environmentalists come from alien realities, and each side misinterprets the other through its own cultural framework .... Laborers must conform to work rules and the pace of production. Unions confront this external power by organizing workers' ability to deprive management of their labor.... While the working class is regulated by externally imposed rewards and punishments, the middle class internalizes the rules that regulate their lives. Personal goals and ambitions to succeed are developed early and pursued without supervision. In the workplace, outcomes are rewarded rather than tasks being monitored. People choose to work for causes that provide a sense of identity, purpose and value.... Relations with family members, peers in school and work, and neighbors tend to be inherited in working-class communities. By contrast the middle class defines itself by its activities and accomplishments.... Because of these class-based cultural differences, working- and middle-class movements have difficulty perceiving their common interests and working together.... Working-class unions and middle-class environmentalists seek change differently. The working class seeks to build power to confront external threats, while the middle class hopes to change people's motivations, ideas, and morality.

How does going away to college change someone? First and most basically, it means leaving home and spending four years with a large group of age peers.

class people, and it helps connect them in a common privileged worldview.

Others enroll in college as well, of course. But living at home, taking community college courses while working and/or parenting, is not the same total immersion experience as four-year residential college. As bell hooks, Barbara Jensen, and others have written, residential college is perceived as crossing a class boundary for many working-class and lower-middle-class kids who are the first in their families to go to college. People who have left home, lived on campus, been full-time students, and earned BA or BS degrees afterwards recognize each other as culturally similar, whether old or young, rural or urban, middle-class or owning-class, white or people of color.

How does going away to college change someone? First and most basically, it means leaving home and spending four years with a large group of age peers. It also means an immersion into abstract thinking and book learning. It means having a flexible, self-coordinated schedule with some free time. And, of course, it opens up options in professions that incorporate abstract thinking and flexible schedules.

College, whether residential or not, tends to have a homogenizing, assimilating effect. It typically means exposure to a rational secular worldview; in fact, college graduates are less religious on average than working-class people.

"Rooted" and "unrooted" are terms that sum up these differences. US-born working-class people are more likely to live where they grew up or, if they moved, to have moved as a family, not solo. They are more likely to live near extended family and to have more frequent contact with the older generations of their family – their ancestral roots. (Of course, this isn't true of working-class solo immigrants, who have been uprooted from their entire society.) There has been more geographic mobility in recent decades, but a working-class young adult is likely to have been raised and socialized by traditionally rooted people, whether stability is his or her own experience or not. Working-class and lower-middle-class people are also more likely to have strong ethnic and/or religious identities.

Besides these obvious kinds of roots, working-class and lower-middle-class people tend to have a pragmatic knowledge rooted primarily in their own experience (as opposed to book learning). They also tend to be rooted in the sense of having their time constrained by work schedules imposed by others. With fewer options, they are often rooted as in "stuck," unable to leave an undesirable job or neighborhood.

Professional middle-class people and owning-class people, on the other hand, tend to be "unrooted" because prior generations may have left behind distinct ethnic cultures. Then they unroot themselves further by leaving their families to go to college, often never returning to their hometowns. Professional middle-class work schedules are more mobile, less defined by schedules set by others. They have more options and can more easily move on to a new job or home. Professional middle-class people also unroot their minds by filling them with book knowledge that exceeds and supercedes their own lived experience.

Professional middle-class kids are each other's competitors to get into college, and then are age-segregated for four years with peers who are also competitors for professional success. Self-worth among college-educated middle-class people often rests on feeling smarter than other people – a major obstacle to cross-class alliance building!

Our movements will be stronger if they include the strengths of each class culture. Rather than reacting with judgment to activists of other class backgrounds, we should develop an attitude of welcoming gifts and giving a hand with limitations in order to make collaboration possible. Hearing each other's stories and understanding the experiences that formed each other's class cultures will enable us to become better cross-class bridgers.

However, if activists treat everyone as "equal," without recognizing institutional advantages and disadvantages, we will replicate society's class and race oppression in our movements. To be able to organize successfully, low-income and working-class activists need more of the resources they are short on: money, decision-making power, skills, and information. Middle-class and owning-class activists need to share their resources and learn to follow the leadership of those without class privilege. And we need to realize that our motivation to be allies is not some kind of nice political correctness, but rather to increase the size and effectiveness of the movements we care about.

Low Income	Working Class and Lower Middle Class	Professional Middle Class	Owning Class
Thinking outside the box, less convention-bound, but discouraged by hardship	Rooted, pragmatic steady workers	Unrooted, competitive steady workers	Entitled, unrooted, thinking outside the box, less convention-bound

Combining the gifts of all class cultures

Each of these class cultures was formed as a creative coping mechanism in social conditions that were oppressive to varying degrees, and each gives gifts and has limitations. None should be regarded as the ideal. The current class situation does not encourage the best in any of us to thrive. For the liberal assimilation worldview, the goal is to make low-income people more similar to middle-class people. But in fact, the process of humanization is just as rocky a path for more privileged people.

Our movements will be stronger if they include the strengths of each class culture. Rather than reacting with judgment to activists of other class backgrounds, we should develop an attitude of welcoming gifts and giving a hand with limitations in order to make collaboration possible.

I really value middle-class activists when they take the skills they have and use them to make the world a better place. — **Brenda Carter**

A **Successful** Cross-Class Alliance
Thanks to **Varied Class Cultures**

blw

I had an organizing job with a successful neighborhood campaign in Boston, in which a mixed-class, mixed-race organization, City Life/Vida Urbana, won back a school that had been closed by budget cuts and sold to a condo developer for $1 in 1985.

Before organizing this campaign, City Life/Vida Urbana had spent years developing neighborhood leaders and making sure that low-income people and people of color were fully enfranchised as decision-makers who felt the organization was theirs. The organizing committee met in two groups, an English group and a Spanish group, and all the materials were bilingual. The story wouldn't be such a positive one without that background.

About 50 people moved onto the school grounds for a weeklong Tent City in the summer of 1986, and about 200 people participated in daytime programs and gave crucial support, ranging from bathrooms to tents to money. We were about as cross-class as a group could be, and the gifts

CLVU

The Bowditch Tent City

of the four class cultures I've described were all ingredients in our success:

- Some homeless people moved onto the site, as the tents were better shelter than what they were used to. They knew every bakery and store that gave away leftovers, and every day we were supplied with mountains of donuts and bread. But it wasn't just their street smarts that made a difference – it was their unlimited vision. I remember a speech by the leader of the Union of the Homeless, in which she described a world without homelessness, and it made many of us cry. She brought that visionary quality to a group of hard-working activists preoccupied with plumbing and police problems.

- The working-class neighbors took charge of many logistical aspects like electricity and security. But it wasn't just their pragmatic skills that made a difference – it was their roots in the Boston community. We were, of course, doing something illegal, and I remember Irish people calling relatives on the police and in City Hall at crucial moments, and the police backing off afterwards. Their family and community connections kept us from being arrested or evicted. If we'd been all transplanted out-of-towners like me, we might have been pushed out onto the street on the second day.

- Everything went like clockwork all week, thanks not only to my detail-oriented planning as the paid organizer but also to written schedules and on-site coordination by other managerial types, mostly college-educated. Fundraising, media relations, and legal negotiations all had high-powered skills donated. But it wasn't just their professional knowledge that made a difference – it was their bohemian flair. The countercultural style of the middle-class activists made the Tent City homier and livelier; there were always young college-educated folks sitting on the ground, drumming, singing folk songs, or organizing small group discussions.

- Thanks to a couple of owning-class people who had volunteered full time for weeks preparing art activities, every day of the Tent City was a daylong arts camp. But it wasn't just their free time that made a difference – it was their limitless dreamy imagination. The arts camp was not just of the usual arts and crafts variety but had a fantastical, whimsical quality, with colorful masks and giant puppets proliferating and making the Tent City eye-catching from blocks away.

With all our gifts combined, we pulled off a miracle. Less than two years later, the city decided to turn the Bowditch school into transitional housing for formerly homeless people, which it still is today. One of my happiest memories is of the victory party, crowded together with a mixed-race, mixed-class crowd, dancing to Latin music with 60-year-old Puerto Rican men whose feet moved so fast I couldn't keep up.

I dream of someday dancing with them again at the victory party about taking back not just the Bowditch school but the whole United States.

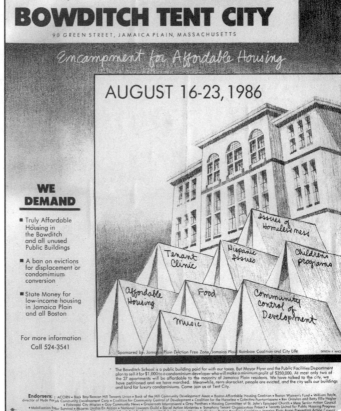

Class and Our Other Identities

Identity Politics, Race, and Class

None of us experiences class by itself. We encounter the US class system in the context of our race, gender, sexual orientation, nationality and ethnicity, religion, ability/disability, region, and other social identities and individual experiences. Yet within each identity group, the dynamics between people of different class backgrounds follow some similar patterns.

Other kinds of systemic oppression – such as racism, sexism, ableism, anti-Semitism, or homophobia – pile a double burden onto some working-class and low-income people. Yet facing one or more oppressions does not prevent middle-class or owning-class people from exercising their class privileges: it does not let them off the hook from dealing with their more privileged class position. Sorting out these intersecting identities – the responsibilities that come with being in a dominant group, the struggles that come with being in a targeted group – is not easy.

Many strategists have contrasted organizing along class lines with organizing based on identity. The following "Identity Politics and Class" section explores these issues, particularly with regard to the connection between race and class, with voices from several ethnic groups. The sections thereafter – on African Americans, women, gay/lesbian/bisexual/transgender people, and working-class white men – illustrate how those particular identities intersect with class.

Identity Politics and Class

John Anner, from *Beyond Identity Politics: Emerging Social Justice Movements in Communities of Color.*

John Anner

Ever since the 1950s and 1960s fight for civil rights gave way to the 1970s' "Black Power" and women's liberation movements, identity has been the driving force behind many US social movements. Excluded from both traditional social institutions and organizations supposedly committed to egalitarian principles, movements for the liberation of women, the disabled, people of color, and gay men and lesbians burst into the political limelight in the 1970s and 1980s, often scoring stunning successes ....

As the victories pile up, however, so do the internal contradictions of identity politics .... Does a working-class African-American family have more in common with its white neighbor or with a millionaire Black businessman? The confusion, in some cases, means that the identity interests of a group clash with the same group's other interests .... The premise of identity politics is that all members of the group have more in common than the members have with anyone outside the group, that they are oppressed in the same way, and therefore that they all belong on the same road to justice. This kind of analysis is simple and compelling, and at particular points in time it is absolutely true. African Americans in the South prior to the civil rights movement most certainly were right to use race as an organizing principle above all others.

But race is different than gender or sexuality because of the close coincidence of race and class in many times and places. It's still true in most areas of the country that the darker you are, the more likely it is that you are on the bottom of the social and economic ladder, although this is less true than it used to be.

In a political system based in principle on equal opportunity and equality before the law, lack of formal access to the system is a powerful organizing handle. Once those barriers to participation have been dismantled or lowered, however, the strategic problem changes. It becomes harder to sustain the fiction that "we all have the same problem" when some members of the group are clearly doing a lot better than others, and when the political strategies being followed clearly benefit some members of the group more than others. The result in many identity movements is a tendency towards elitism and assimilation in practice, coupled with a feigned dedication to solidarity with all the oppressed. In a sense, the dismantling of formal political barriers unhitched identity and class; identity movements can pretend that their current particularist campaigns will still raise living standards for all members of the group, but the evidence is overwhelmingly to the contrary.

Thus most of the original promise of politics based in communities of interest or identity has been diverted into middle-class campaigns for affirmation, assimilation, and "a piece of the pie." In the process, working-class and poor people of color, gays and lesbians, and others have been left behind. In some ways, the very victories of the civil rights movement created this new situation; with many of the impediments to individual mobility removed, changing the system as a whole has become even more complex ....

The issues that must be faced are those of distribution, of the right of all people to have enough to live on and develop their creative powers ....

A reinvigorated social justice Movement with a capital "m" will have to develop mechanisms of reconnecting identity politics with class issues, putting matters of economic justice on the front burner while showing how a racist, sexist power structure – now somewhat more integrated – works to deny most people the basics of a decent life .... We need to shift .... from the politics of identity to an identity as political actors. We have power in our cultures, our sense of solidarity, our love of community, our values, our families, our relationships, and our numbers. What building a social justice movement is all about is nothing less than figuring out how to claim that power and how to exercise it.

It drives me crazy when a well-off activist champions race without dealing with class.
– Jerry Koch-Gonzalez

Re-linking identity to class

In my interview with him, John Anner expanded on the themes from his book:

It's a lot easier to organize around identity than around class. People more easily identify as an ethnic group than a class. Class things run into more resistance, they're more dangerous.

There's a common argument in the revisionist left that identity politics killed class-based politics. Like, who cares if Tiger Woods can't get into a certain whites-only club, or if women can't get into the Augusta Nationals? Who cares if there are black people on the board of IBM? What about health and income being so much worse for people of color? As these movements became about identity, the universalist impulse of lifting up the worst off in society was lost. But my argument is that to put the blame on the movements themselves is disingenuous ....

Class-based movements focus on universalizing a particular social benefit. Obviously wages are one, but there's also the social wage, like health care, education, daycare, the things that in Scandinavian countries have already been won, but in our society are considered communist conspiracies.

I feel that in the end, straight-up identity politics has a very limited shelf life. There are ways of framing class issues as race issues, but most poor people in the US are white. Access to elite institutions is fine, but where's the equal attention to expanding affordable mass transit?

There are times it makes sense to describe something, for example daycare, as a feminist goal. Pick your frame by what will work.

There are class-based movements that don't self-identify that way. Look at the welfare rights movement, for example. Or the immigrant rights movement. By and large you're dealing with low-income people and working-class people, they just don't call themselves that. Or you look at the independent unions like HERE and SEIU; basically they're organizing people who make under $25,000 a year. So these are clearly class oriented.

And there's all this new grassroots organizing around the US that I reported on in the book [*Beyond Identity Politics*], that is explicitly and intelligently class identified and explicitly multiple-identity oriented. Often they're multi-racial. Instead of being about the uplift of black folks, they say, "We're advancing the broad cause of racial justice in America." You look at groups like the Center for Third World Organizing where I worked, or the organizations in the book. They are modern movements that have figured out how to re-link identity with class.

What's the Connection
Between **Race** and **Class**?

When have I seen cross-race bridging go well?
- *When the stakes are low – for example, among people who just met at racism workshops*
- *With college-educated middle-class people who have learned the same lingo about oppression*
- *With working-class people thrown together, who resent the same boss or landlord*
- *At times of victory, when an organizing effort wins a reform*

In all these situations, the people tend to share the same class background or class level. I haven't seen many real, solid relationships built or conflicts resolved across both race and class differences. And some degree of hope seems like a necessary ingredient.

I asked the question "What's the connection between race and class?" in almost every interview, and almost everyone had a vehement answer. Here are a few of them:

Some people of color come from middle-class backgrounds. When there is an alliance between middle-class white people and middle-class people of color focusing on the race dynamic, often they're not focusing on the class dynamic or the tensions around priorities. I ask how race-focused are we going to be versus how class-focused. As hard as race is, it's something we know, we're passionate about it. The class dynamic is much less clear. For the person of color who's championing race and who comes from an upper-class background, on class they're not a victim, they're part of a dominant group, and no-one wants to feel that. There's an avoidance of taking responsibility. For white people taking on race, you can get strokes for that. But to champion issues around class, it's more uncharted territory, and you

get no strokes for it. It takes more self-searching. Let's start taking it apart. Let's try to get to the truth.

—Jerry Koch-Gonzalez

Preston Smith

Why have class issues lagged so far behind race and gender? In this country race has been a proxy for class. In our imagination, race subsumes class. African Americans didn't have to confront class as much until there was some socio-economic progress which undergirded intraracial stratification. Often in the process of engaging in racial conflict, it has brought class conflict, both in and outside of black communities, into fuller view.

It's now more acceptable to say "trailer trash" because whites can't make the usual racial insults in polite company. Interestingly, in this regard white Jerry Springer guests become proxies for black people because they represent black stereotypes, which are in turn class stereotypes.

—Preston Smith

There are two contradictory things to look at. First, people conflate race and class, assuming whites are middle-class and assuming black and Latino people are poor. And it's true that a middle-class black person usually has a whole lot less financial back-up than a white middle-class person. But on the other hand, if you include black middle-class people in an organization, that doesn't mean you've dealt with class diversity. Dealing with race doesn't mean you've dealt with class.

White middle-class activists drive me crazy when they forget the race analysis, when they try to equate race and class. In the US, even poor whites can never forget their white privilege.
– Raúl Quiñones Rosado

LAANE

Addressing class means adding the issue of rebalancing resources. Dealing with race in a mixed group usually means working on how white people can act less entitled and arrogant. But with class, there's another layer: how are people charged for services, how are people paid.

Class is most invisible when I'm with all white people, because poor white people tend to be so marginalized within white culture that it's assumed everyone is more middle-class. But black and Latino communities know they include poor people. In any cross-class grouping there are people who are passing, but it's more intense for poor white people. In white culture, there's more stigma against poverty. There's more generational and geographic distance from poverty. In black and Latino cultures, there's more acceptance of challenging middle-class people, often by calling them white. You can call on racial solidarity there. Poor white people don't have that base to stand on.

—Paul Kivel

Low-income white people sometimes feel like, "me, too – but if I say so it's going to look like I'm feeling defensive about white privilege." White middle-class activists tend to be much more up for paying attention to race, at least on a surface level, so white working-class people get lost in the shuffle.

—Linda Stout

Racial solidarity, particularly the solidarity of whiteness, has historically always been used to obscure class, to make the white poor see their interests as one with the world of white privilege. Similarly, the black poor have always been told that class can never matter as much as race. Nowadays the black and white poor know better. They are not so easily duped by an appeal to unquestioned racial identification and solidarity ....

Nowadays it is fashionable to talk about race or gender; the uncool subject is class ....

Class matters. Race and gender can be used as screens to deflect attention away from the harsh realities class politics exposes. Clearly, just when we should all be paying attention to class, using race and gender to understand and explain its new dimensions, society, even our government, says let's talk about race and racial injustice. It is impossible to talk meaningfully about ending racism without talking about class. Let us not be duped. Let us not be led by spectacles like the O.J. Simpson trial to believe a mass media, which has always betrayed the cause of racial justice, to think that it was all about race, or it was about gender. Let us acknowledge that first and foremost it was about class and the interlocking nature of race, sex and class. Let's face the reality that if O.J. Simpson had been poor or even lower-middle-class there would have been no media attention.

—bell hooks, *Where We Stand: Class Matters*

.... Identity politics are why liberals are losing elections. We've gone over to that completely. We're marching for ourselves, and no one's really extending. We're not basing our policies on also changing the lives of people who don't agree with us.

—Sherman Alexie, interviewed in *Spare Change News*, August 2003

Class matters. Race and gender can be used as screens to deflect attention away from the harsh realities class politics exposes. Clearly, just when we should all be paying attention to class, using race and gender to understand and explain its new dimensions, society, even our government, says let's talk about race and racial injustice.

— bell hooks, *Where We Stand: Class Matters*

I've been trying to let go of the idea of basing my politics on the good of a small group. I've become less and less Indian-centric as the years have gone on ... I talk about poor people, I talk about disadvantaged people, and that sort of covers everything I need to cover. It becomes not about race, region or country, but about a particular group of people sharing the same circumstances. I talk about the universal condition of the poor, and thinking and talking about it that way helps eliminate the negativity of tribalism

---

Identity politics are why liberals are losing elections. We've gone over to that completely. We're marching for ourselves and no one's really extending.
— Sherman Alexie

I got a call ... from a reporter at *US News & World Report* who was working on an article about what they were calling "the white underclass." The reporter had found through demographic studies that Southie [South Boston] showed three census tracts with the highest concentration of poor whites in America .... The magazine's findings were based on rates of joblessness and single-parent female-headed households. Nearly three-fourths of the families in the Lower End had no fathers. Eighty-five percent of Old Colony collected welfare. The reporter wasn't telling me anything new – I was just stunned that someone was taking notice. No one had ever seemed to believe me or to care when I told them about the amount of poverty and social problems where I grew up.

Liberals were usually the ones working on social problems, and they never seemed to be able to fit urban poor whites into their world view, which tended to see blacks as the persistent dependent and their own white selves as the provider. Whatever race guilt they were holding onto, Southie's poor couldn't do a thing for their consciences. After our violent response to court-ordered busing in the 1970s, Southie was labeled as the white racist oppressor. I

I really value white middle-class activists when they are in the anti-racist tradition of John Brown, committing class suicide. **— Woodrow Coleman**

saw how that label worked to take the blame away from those able to leave the city and drive back to all-white suburban towns at the end of the day.

—Michael Patrick MacDonald,
All Souls: A Family Story from Southie

Latinos and class

In Laredo, on the border in Texas, it's all class. The rich landowners are "Hispanics," and everybody else is "Latinos." In high school I knew this kid who always wore a sweatshirt that said "Brown." I thought it meant he had a lot of Chicano pride. He let me think that, then years later told me that all his sisters and brothers went to that college. I had never heard of the Ivy League.

—Tomás Aguilar

The staff at the Bus Riders Union is mostly college-educated people of color, though most of them grew up working-class. Sometimes there's resentment of them by certain Latinos on the buses, particularly of Chicanos whose Spanish isn't as good. "Who are you to come here educated and not speaking my language?" is the attitude. It's a teaching moment about the history of how they lost their Spanish fluency. Class tension comes out as ethnic tension.

Latino college students sometimes come as interns. Often they take a very ideological anti-government stance. They point out the history of broken promises to Latinos and ask why the group negotiates with officials who have harmed the community in the past.

—Manuel Criollo

In an analysis of oppression in Puerto Rico, in relationship with the US, colonialism is the extension of

racism across borders, implemented through military force and economic policy. Race and class are intimately linked.

—Raúl Quiñones Rosado

Asian-Americans and class

Third day of the new semester, new school, new city, new people. I happened across a group of Asian students, and a Filipina, like myself, was among them. We greeted each other and exchanged a few introductory remarks. "Are you here on EOP [Economic Opportunity Program]?" the Filipina asked me. "No," I responded. "Then you're a preppy," she declared. I was angry and confounded at the same time. Hot air spun circles in my head. If a white person tried to put me down, I immediately shot back a counter. Instead, I was silent. I asked myself, "Is something wrong with me?" The Filipina and I never became friends. I avoided her. Whenever I saw her during our time together in school or since, our

Jeannette Huezo leading United for a Fair Economy workshop on global economy

original confrontation was the first thing that came to mind.

—Virginia R. Harris and Trinity A. Ordoña, "Developing Unity Among Women of Color," in Gloria Anzaldúa, ed., *Making Face, Making Soul = Haciendo Caras*

My dad came from China, my Mom from Tokyo. I grew up in an upper-middle-class white suburb and always felt I was supposed to be a way I'm not. Partly it was US/Asian issues. Me and my friends had different lifestyles. I worked five days a week throughout the year at my dad's restaurant starting in 7th grade while my friends did summer camp and sports.

I'm really interested in immigrants and children of immigrants and why they left. I grew up hearing my mom's

CLVU

story of growing up in Tokyo. She was five when the US dropped the bombs, and she saw houses burning and dead people's feet sticking out from under blankets. I wonder what are the privileges I often take for granted having been US born? And what are the costs of immigration?

—Shirley Yee

In 1982, Chinese garment workers in New York went out on strike. The community groups such as the benevolent societies – the leadership in Chinatown – have members who belong to the union, and the union has worked hard on our relationship with the community. About 90 percent of the garment shop owners are Chinese, so that makes disputes in the workplace very sensitive. When there's a campaign against a big retailer, then the community rallies together.

The Chinese teachers in Chinatown have children of garment workers in their classrooms, and they expressed an interest in helping the striking families. They already knew many of the parents and felt concerned about kids not getting much attention because their parents worked such long hours.

But it's not the same with Chinese people who live in the suburbs. They generally don't get involved in Chinatown issues. They come to Chinatown for voter registration and politics, that's about it. There's even some a lot of anti-union feeling. The Asian Labor Group has worked to diffuse some of the impression of unions as corrupt white thugs.

—May Chen

Marilyn Humphries

White middle-class activists drive me crazy when they lose the centrality of racism in our country, putting everything as class, and they don't confront US history of racism. **– Manuel Criollo**

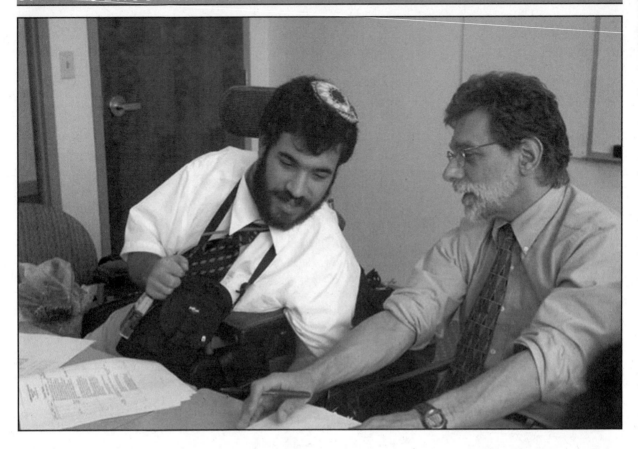

Jews and class

I am the daughter of immigrants. In 1933, my father had to leave behind his wealth in Germany. He was from an upper-middle-class background, being groomed to be a judge, when one of his mentors told him, "It's gonna be bad." He had to leave family, friends, and profession behind and make his way. My mother's family was upper middle-class. Years later my folks realized that they came on the same boat, her upstairs and him in steerage.

I have class vertigo in my life, with European bourgeois attitudes but not much money. My brother went up

and my sisters and I went down class-wise. I was raised in Alabama in the 1950s. There were 50 Jewish families in town, none but ours with European parents.

I was very aware of racism and anti-Semitism, and the huge class dynamics in the south. My ride to school passed mansions with columns, maids, and gardeners, and houses on blocks of cement falling apart. The mystery of my childhood was bearing witness with an outsider's eye to huge differences, the constellation of anti-Semitism, racism, and class.

In 5th grade I had a friend whose father I found out later was in [the white supremacist group] Posse Comitus. One time she and I

bought boxes of grape and cinnamon gumballs and wanted to sell them for one cent more to make some money for more candy. The storekeeper called her dad before we got back to the house and he forbid us to sell the candy and lectured us on the international communist

---

My ride to school passed mansions with columns, maids, and gardeners, and houses on blocks of cement falling apart.

— Ahbi Vernon

conspiracy. I went home and said, "I think that's capitalism, not communism." There was this learning that if they [white folks] did it, it was the American way, but if I did it, it was a Jewish conspiracy.

—Ahbi Vernon

I'm Jewish, and that's where it begins. My consciousness about justice comes from the Jewish traditions of asking questions and being aware. Tzedakah (which means justice and is the term used for how Jews give money to others) and tikkun olam (translated as healing the earth).

I grew up only among Jews and don't remember being in a gentile's home until I was an adult. I grew up noticing injustices in who had money and who didn't. We were lower middle class and lived among many middle class and upper middle class people, with the social standing of middle class but not the money. My mother grew up working class, my father lower middle-class. If I wanted to go to camp, it had to be paid for from my babysitting money since my family could not afford to send me on their own. I got jobs at age 15 to

buy my own clothes and pay for college, which was different than most of my friends. I always looked at

My consciousness about justice comes from the Jewish traditions of asking questions and being aware.

— Laura Stern

what I didn't have, not at what I did have.

—Laura Stern

THE WORLD STANDS
ON THREE THINGS
· · ·
· ON · TORAH ·
· ON THE SERVICE OF GOD ·
· AND ON ACTS OF LOVINGKINDNESS ·

Pirkei Avot   פרקי אבות

Marilyn Humphries

Middle-class activists of color drive me crazy when they don't acknowledge their privilege and that it's a class-based thing. **— Penn Loh**

African American
Class Dynamics

Interviewing African American activists for Class Matters *was a remarkable experience for me, a white woman. I heard common themes in interview after interview. When two people brought up the slogan "Lifting as we climb," one as a positive example and one as a negative example, I knew something interesting was happening. I had obviously tapped into a deep, ongoing conversation in the Black community about class and race. The section headings that follow are lines I heard in more than one interview.*

Class Is Different
for African Americans

Class identity in the Black community is complex and often confusing. It cannot be evaluated by using measures identical to those used for whites. If the white upper class is made up of captains of corporations,

Barbara Smith

there is no black equivalent. You might have the person who runs the black insurance company, but that's not the same as Ford Motor company.

During segregation, education levels did not result in the income level you'd expect. So class had more to do with values and behaviors. I describe myself as coming from a working-class family, based on income level and occupation. Most people in my family were well-educated but did manual and domestic work, not the kind of work their training was for. So your job title didn't necessarily correlate with your relative status in a community that is economically and racially oppressed. We were lower middle class by education and status, even while we were working class by income.

There were also people who were genuinely middle class in the Black community, black business owners and doctors. The true black bour-

geoisie I find problematic, as alien to me as I perhaps am alien to someone working as a hospital orderly. They are generally not radical, because the system worked for them, and when the system works for you, you often don't question: "I can make it, my family made it, what's so bad about living in the US?"

—Barbara Smith

Historically, most black workers were servants and laborers. Even some with middle-class status were personal servants, Pullman Porters, or elevator operators. Their class status came from the fact that their clientele were upper-class whites and the work was cleaner than manual labor. The industrial black working class first appeared during World War I, which triggered the Great Migration to cities and the North. After the Second World War with black participation in the defense economy, there was an elevation of the black working class in terms of skills and income, and a modest expansion of the middle class. By the 1960s, a black middle class grew significantly with professionals, clerical workers, and small business owners. Through Civil Rights and Black Power activism of the 1960s and 1970s, the black baby boomers got into college and graduate school. I benefited from that activism and the fruit of those struggles: affirmative action. Now there are black CEOs, though disproportionately fewer than in the white population. Perhaps that can be considered progress – that the black class system is now more similar to whites than it ever was. That's what the goal of "racial democracy" is all about: having a black class structure that parallels the white class structure. Racial parity is the end goal. If you see racial injustice as the primary or only form of injustice, you are likely to think we have arrived when you see the expansion of the black professional class. I think the goal should include social democracy: less inequality overall as well as between races.

—Preston Smith

When I hear the differences between working-class and middle-class culture described as more "loyal and solidaristic" versus more "individualistic and achievement-focused," my reaction is that that model may be true for some white people, but it doesn't work for African Americans.

Since the Civil Rights movement and the rise of the black middle class, a lot of political analysts predicted that black middle-class voters would vote their class interests and not their race interests. And that hasn't been the case. Upwardly mobile black people don't vote Republican. How do we explain this continued racial solidarity in the face of class divisions within the black community? Part of the answer is a concept called "linked fate": black solidarity based on stronger loyalties to persons, places, and groups, such as black churches and black media. So even though a black middle-class family might move to a suburb, they might come back to a church that their parents have been going to over the years.

Similarly, there's a socialization process for black students that's very different from that for white students. You know the question, "Why are all the black kids sitting together in the cafeteria?" For those of us who went away to college, it's like an extended family. From the moment they got there, we would tell the freshman, "Every black person you see on campus, you have to speak to them." There's a deliberate creation of a sense of community, a political socialization that makes black students feel less individualistic.

—Dorian Warren

Qualified Linked Fate

From Cathy J. Cohen, *The Boundaries of Blackness: AIDS and the Breakdown of Black Politics*

Whether because of the economic progress achieved by some and not others, or the social mobility achieved by, in particular, middle-class black Americans, the dominant myth of a monolithic black community is tearing not only at the seams but throughout its entire fabric. Undoubtedly, many black people continue to operate within a linked-fate political framework, where the struggles of other black people are purported to represent what can happen to any of us. However, a more accurate characterization of the political positioning of most black Americans is that of a qualified linked fate, whereby not every black person in crisis is seen as equally essential to the survival of the community, as an equally representative proxy of our own individual interests, and thus as equally worthy of political support by other African Americans. The AIDS crisis, especially the limited response to this crisis in many African American communities, provides a classic illustration ....

White middle-class activists drive me crazy when they believe theirs is the default reality.
– Barbara Smith

Who Speaks for the Black Community?

There's always been a history of class conflict within the black community, at the same time as there's racial solidarity across class. When the CIO organized working-class black folks before World War II, they gave them the organizational tools to challenge the middle-class reformist organizations. In Detroit, for example, 12,000 union members took over the NAACP and made it much more radical in the 1930s and 1940s than it had been.

The NAACP today thinks of itself as representing all black Americans, although in actuality, I think we can make an argument that it is clearly middle-class blacks. There is some attention to issues impacting working-class and poor blacks, but I think most of the agenda setting and most of the power in the organization is all wielded by upper-middle-class or upper-class blacks.

There is also a politics of brokerage, where a few significant leaders broker deals for the community even though they are not being elected by or in any way accountable to that community. A lot of it is based on those leaders' threats of collective action, which they can't necessarily back up.

Let me be specific. Take Jesse Jackson. I have mixed opinions about him, but he doesn't have any kind of organizational base. In negotiating something, he can't really make a credible threat of collective action or disruption of any kind, but he doesn't need to because no-one has ever called him on it.

By contrast, an organization that actually has a membership base and is somewhat democratic can say, "Our membership is really upset about this, and we are going to cause you hell if you don't agree with these demands." And it's clear that they can. Black Workers for Justice in the South is a good example. Another would be ACORN [Association of Community Organizations for Reform

Now]. In Chicago, they are very membership-driven, and they do a really good job of training new leaders and organizing black working-class and poor communities.

—Dorian Warren

A thriving, corrupt "talented tenth" have not only emerged as the power brokers preaching individual liberation and black capitalism to everyone (especially the black masses), their biggest commodity is "selling blackness" .... Nowadays, practically every public representation of blackness is created by black folks who are materially privileged. More often than not they speak about the black poor and working-class but not with them, or on their behalf. The presence of a small number of privileged black folks who continue to work for justice, who work to change this culture so that all black people can live fully and well, is often obscured by the dominant white culture's focus on those who are fundamentally opportunistic and/or corrupt.

—bell hooks, in *Where We Stand: Class Matters*

Dorian Warren

When I was a member of the Laborers and Hod Carriers Union, the union reps had big expensive cars. Poor black people like to see their leaders living good. Churchgoers like their ministers to dress fancy, drive big cars. Athletes, every dollar they make takes pennies from poor people, but black people look at it as progress. When Jackie Robinson made it, my cousin said, "Come on, the door's open now."

—Woodrow Coleman

Blacker Than Thou?

Class is sometimes used among African Americans as a club to beat someone with. As a Black feminist and out lesbian, I get accused of being middle-class simply because being lesbian is a "white disease." Amongst Black people, there's a question of "what's a 'real' Black person? What kind of music does a real Black person listen to? How does a real Black person talk?" It's blacker than thou. There are as many ways of being Black as there are Black people on the planet, as far as I'm concerned ....

In the new introduction to *Home Girls*, I wrote about the accusation that Black feminism is middle-class and therefore irrelevant. I write about how many poor and working-class Black women not only support tenets of Black feminism, but actually live them. But I also write about how not consistently working across class has been a detriment to our political growth.

—Barbara Smith

Critical Faculties Turned off

There's a problem of authenticity for anyone who is not, say, sufficiently poor and black. I've seen it play out in this way: Some white middle-class foundation officers are not critical at all of certain black organizations or black working-class leaders. Whatever they do, the foundations support because they are an "authentic voice." Some program officers here in Chicago fund some really bad community organizations because the leaders of those organizations put themselves out as the authentic black working-class voice. The foundation person refuses to question that, doesn't ask, "Why are you working on this and that issue?" Authenticity ploys and games are everywhere.

Saying that someone is more oppressed than someone else is used in an opportunistic way. Like if I raise something at a meeting, someone who disagrees may say, "Well, you go to Yale," as a way to win. It's ubiquitous. So I guess I would not want anyone to relinquish skills of critical analysis. It can be hard, but it at least has to be struggled through.

—Dorian Warren

What stood out most strikingly about Malcolm X, Martin Luther King, Jr., Ella Baker, and Fannie Lou Hamer was that they were almost always visibly upset about the condition of black America. When one saw them speak or heard their voices, they projected on a gut level that the black situation was urgent, in need of immediate attention. One even gets the impression that their own stability and sanity rested on how soon the black predicament could be improved. Malcolm, Martin, Ella, and Fannie were angry about the state of black America, and this anger fueled their boldness and defiance.

In stark contrast, most present-day black political leaders appear too hungry for status to be angry, too eager for acceptance to be bold, too self-invested in advancement to be defiant.

—Cornel West, *Race Matters*

Black middle-class activists drive me crazy when they assume the black middle class needs to "save" the black working class. And I'm frustrated when they look at progressive politics only in racial terms and don't take on working-class issues. — **Preston Smith**

"Lifting as We Climb"

"Lifting as we climb" was the slogan of the National Council of Negro Women. Three of the African Americans I interviewed brought it up when I asked about dynamics between middle-class and working-class black people:

My sister and I were raised to maximize our talents and potential for the greater good of all. "Lifting as we climb" says it all. The goal was not just a nice life for yourself; you have a responsibility to give something back. Now young middle-class Black people are raised to be individualists. Often they don't grow up in Black communities and are not so racially conscious. I was raised to know about Black heroes and sheroes and role models. My family looked up to teachers, social workers, the helping professions, ministers.

—Barbara Smith

I see a paternalism in the slogan "Lifting as we climb." It's positive that black people feel a sense of obligation and responsibility for each other in the face of institutionalized racism. It's better than just climbing and not lifting!

But the paternalism applies when someone feels "I know what's best for you." In real social equality, the working-class person has as much say as the middle-class person. Instead, there's an assumption that we, the black middle-class, are still going to be ahead even after you're uplifted, that it's natural for us to be ahead within the race. The test comes with policies that threaten your social or economic superiority. As a black middle-class person, do you support those policies, such as the unionization of black owned businesses or the building of affordable multi-family housing in your neighborhood?

The Urban League* is an example of this paternalistic racial uplift organization, along with other black middle-class organizations. Because of their racism, whites thought all blacks were the same. In response, African Americans felt that they had to adopt a certain kind of public decorum. They could not be loud, boisterous, demonstrative, or expressive. It was a way to tell whites we're not all alike, to overcome stereotypes, we're not like

Marilyn Humphries

bell hooks

the poorer black people who both you and we think fit your stereotypes.

The recent manifestation of this thinking has been the "role model" ideology. It's assumed that if you're higher than someone else on the class ladder, you're a role model for them. It doesn't matter what your actual character is. One's apparent achievement in the marketplace becomes the only criterion of value. The implicit message is that poor black people need their behavior corrected. I reject the idea that the middle class belongs in all leadership positions and has the answers for the race as a whole. It goes back to Booker T. Washington and W.E.B. DuBois' "talented tenth."

—Preston Smith

*In the early 20th century, the Urban League went door-to-door in Chicago, welcoming black migrants from the South with leaflets about cleanliness, sobriety, citizenship, and respectable behavior in public places. (blw)

I told Barbara Smith that Preston Smith sees "Lifting as we climb" as being at times paternalistic. Here's her response:

I don't hear it that way at all. You have to fully understand the degradation and horrors of life in the post-Reconstruction south. When they said "Lifting as we climb," they were saying it's not enough for themselves to have this little frame house, they have to think about rural poor people who have nothing. The black women's clubs were trying to rescue people in extreme poverty, the young women coming up from the south and ending up in prostitution, drug addiction, and early death. If that's "lifting as we climb," then let's lift as we climb.

There has always been elitism in the black community. There may have

---

I really value middle-class activists of color when they are organizers who organize working-class people to demand things for themselves. **– Dorian Warren**

been some women in the black women's club movement who considered themselves a better class of woman. Some may have looked down at the poorly dressed, uneducated poor black girl. There is a reality of leadership by lighter-skinned women. But to say that these efforts were driven solely by elitism is not seeing the full picture, not understanding how bad it was during that period when those organizations were forming.

—Barbara Smith

The distinction I want to make is between uplift ideology, such as the black club women, and a more democratic vision that a good organizer should have. These democratic principles say that people can decide for themselves and act for themselves, both individually and collectively. And that there should be some accountability.

A group can elect representatives to represent them, but the process of figuring out the issues should be a col-

when white supremacy began consolidating itself again. The planter class in the South tried to get the closest thing they could to slave labor, and so we see the retrenchment of black civil and economic rights in that period. That's when we really get to see uplift ideology in action. It was a strategy to survive Jim Crow.

And there was also a broader cultural trend in American politics, a noblesse oblige. We see it in the reformers, especially the progressive reformers at the turn of the 20th century: "These poor workers, these poor immigrants, we have to cultivate them and give them the right etiquette (and in some cases, the right working conditions). They clearly can't do it for themselves, so it's our duty to do it for them." I think we should take a step back and understand that historical context, that there are a lot of well-intentioned people who believe this particular ideology. But I think at this particular historical moment, there's no excuse for it.

communities that broke through the dominant uplift model.

—Dorian Warren

One of the things that caught me off guard when I first starting teaching here was the deep conservatism of many of my middle-class African American students in my course on class. (I suppose I carried stereotypes of blacks as more likely to be liberal, and was surprised to find that my most vehemently conservative students were usually black.) It took me a while to figure out that the conservatism was a product of being raised in upwardly mobile families (which was less common amongst white students whose family history tended to be more stable). Most of these folks (or their parents) had experienced being unemployed or living on welfare and had now moved on to more stable middle- and upper-middle-class jobs. They had compelling and insightful stories about family members and close friends involved in welfare fraud, reckless behavior, drug dealing, etc. Their family, though, moved out of all that. The lesson they often took away from that experience was that hard work and responsible living produced positive results. Consequently, they were largely unsympathetic to the plight of many poor people, thinking that middle-class liberals were naive about the realities of poverty. There was often tension in class between poor/working-class students and middle-class students, regardless of race. It was a real challenge for me to adjust my teaching to acknowledge the grain of truth in what they had experienced, but to place it in a larger and more complicated context.

—David Croteau

My visceral reaction to "Lifting as we climb" is that it's a nasty middle-class ideology. But, taking a step back, I think it's important to look historically where this comes from. — Dorian Warren

lective process. Then you can have representatives who say "This is what the group, through a democratic process, has agreed are the issues." That's very different than people appointing themselves to speak for the group.

My visceral reaction to "Lifting as we climb" is that it's a nasty middle-class noblesse-oblige ideology. But, taking a step back, I think it's important to look historically where this comes from, to the post-Reconstruction era

I think SNCC [Student Nonviolent Coordinating Committee] played a major role in breaking through the uplift model because they were going south and intentionally leaving southern black communities with actual organizing skills to organize themselves. As opposed to the "great leaders," King and others, coming in and doing something for the community. Ella Baker was also in this more radical black tradition of empowering

Sisterhood and Solidarity

blw

The wave of feminism that started in the late 60s was widely perceived as a middle-class movement. That perception was in some ways accurate, and in some ways inaccurate.

The focus on breaking limits – the first woman astronaut, the first woman Senator, etc. – obviously shone a spotlight on elite women. Women also broke into blue-collar trades, though to less fanfare. Breaking out of traditional feminine constraints – claiming comfortable shoes and assertive behavior – was a priority especially for the white, class-privileged women for whom the feminine roles were the most restrictive. Certainly ditching the housewife role wasn't a priority for the majority of working-class women who had always worked for wages. The vast surge in the number of employed women in the 1970s was due to the rising cost of living as well as to feminism. But the rallying cry "The personal is political" tackled problems like domestic violence, abortion rights, and rape that were even more pressing for women with fewer resources to protect themselves.

Women's groups sprang up by the thousands in the 1970s, and some were explicitly for working-class women, such as Women Employed in Chicago and 9 to 5. Others organized black women and other women of color, or women on welfare. But the groups that ended up with funding and media coverage were mostly white middle-class groups.

It's important to remember that our images of 1970s feminism may be distorted by the way the media trivialized "Women's Lib." The term "bra-burner" came not from some campaign obsessed with underwear but from a protest at the Miss America pageant over demeaning public displays of women's bodies, and housewife magazines and pornography were thrown in the trashcan along with bras. Class-privileged women were working to change very harmful images of and restrictions on women.

But in the absence of connections with working-class and low-income feminists, more privileged feminists did sometimes veer into the trivial. One low-income group asked their local NOW [National Organization for Women] chapter to join a coalition against cuts in Medicaid coverage for women on welfare, and was told no, the NOW chapter had picked their campaign for the year: a local department store that charged more for hemming women's pants than for men's.

Middle-class feminist groups have been challenged vigorously by women of color, with historic conflicts at National Women's Studies Association conferences. Groundbreaking anthologies by women of color, beginning with *This Bridge Called My Back*, sometimes framed their critiques of white feminism in class as well as race terms. The resulting changes made feminist organizations somewhat more inclusive of working-class women. The new *Ms. Magazine* covers welfare reform and service-worker organizing far more than the old *Ms. Magazine* did. NOW made an organizational commitment to protecting the welfare safety net, though most of its members didn't follow.

But times have changed only so much: now in the 00's, the young feminist leaders most visible in the media are still college-educated and still concerned more with the representation of women than with childcare and wages.

If the working-class archetype of a blue-collar white man weren't distorting our vision, we would see clearly that most women are working class, that most working-class people are women, and that feminist organizing and class-based organizing need to overlap to succeed.

Middle-class activists drive me crazy when their sense of entitlement leaves them so narrow-minded they can't see other people's issues. — **Roxana Tynan**

Working-Class Women
Seeking **Allies**

My tip for middle-class feminists is to stand in low-income women's shoes. Everything that happens to you happens to them, only worse, because there's no money to do anything about it. You've raised a child, you know it's work, you had a mother, and you know she worked. Listen. Hear while standing in their shoes.

—Theresa Funiciello

Historically, women shirtwaist workers in the early 1900s were helped a lot by suffragette women of the middle and upper classes. Trade union support organizations made alliances of those progressive women with workers to improve working conditions through health and safety laws.

—May Chen

The middle class have professionalized women's groups. Now they are just professional groups of paid professionals. They don't even pretend to have a grassroots involvement anymore and it has kind of co-opted the feminist movement, even the battered women's shelter movement.

Working-class women started up these shelters, and often they were in leadership, but once they started getting boards, the boards were middle-class people with money; then they wanted middle-class, degreed, college women to run things. Every time the grassroots group became institutionalized as a professional organization, it lost the multi-class basis and it lost its grassroots involvement.

—Woman interviewed by Claire Cummings for "Class Lessons: Women Creating Cross-Class Coalitions in a Welfare Rights Movement"

If you look at the mission statement of any women's studies department in the country, they talk about "gender, race, and class." That became the holy trinity of the feminist movement. But the consciousness-raising process used so effectively by the early women's movement has been extended to race but not to class. Women talked about their experiences growing up in a gendered society as girls and the differential experiences of males and females. And when the issue of race was raised, feminists started to meet in same-race groups, with consciousness raising for white women about white privilege. One National Women's Studies Association conference was entirely about race, and every single participant spent a lot of time in a small group to examine their lives from a race perspective. There were groups for Latina women, African American women, Jewish women, etc. And yes, our gender identity does impact tremendously on our experience of the world, our race identity does impact tremendously on our experience of the world – and our class identity does as well.

Marilyn Humphries

"Yes, this is a two career household.
Unfortunately I have both careers."

[T]he dilemma we so often read about today, over whether women can combine careers with child raising, is freighted with implicit class assumptions: that women have careers, as opposed to mere jobs, and that they have the wherewithal to abandon these careers without condemning their children to penury ….

Several years ago I attempted to pitch a story on women in poverty to the editor of a glossy national magazine (which, in the interests of my future career, will remain unnamed). We were at lunch, always a high point in the life of an impecunious freelancer, and I made my case through the mesclun with parmesan shavings and polenta-crusted salmon while the editor yawned between bites. Finally, over the espresso and death-by-chocolate dessert, he rolled his eyes and said, "OK, do your thing on poverty. Only make it upscale."

—Barbara Ehrenreich, in *Fear of Falling*

There were also times when homophobia had its day, when everyone was examining their sexual orientation privilege. But it has never happened in any widespread way about issues of class.

The feminist movement does include class in the phrase "gender, race, and class" and talks about it on the theoretical and structural level. But there's hardly any dialogue on the personal level. There hasn't been a women's studies conference devoted entirely to class where women all broke up into class-of-origin groups and talked about the impact of class on our life, our relationships, and our choices. The kind of thorough examination starting at the personal level, looking at the curriculum, the reading lists, and the mission of the enterprise, has happened in a serious way around those other issues, and I don't believe to this day has happened around the issue of class.

—Felice Yeskel

Gender equity efforts in many organizations focus on glass ceiling issues that mostly benefit white professional and managerial women. Naturally, women of color and working class women tend to be skeptical of their opportunities for advancement in this context …. [But] working-class women and professional women may be able to work together on child-care issues if the agenda for change is defined to meet the needs of women through all hierarchical levels in the organization."

—Evangelina Holvino, "Class: 'A Difference that Makes a Difference' in Organizations," *The Diversity Factor*, Winter 2002

I really value middle-class activists when they bring their commitments and abilities to the causes of workers. — **May Chen**

Middle Class Feminism
in the Eyes of **Women of Color**

I'm grateful that my experience [with women's issues] began with the Third World Women's Alliance on the West Coast. Some black women in SNCC had published a newsletter called *Triple Jeopardy*, which inspired the founders of the Third World Women's Alliance. The newsletter outlined that racism, sexism, and class were at the heart of our struggle. So we were struggling with issues like infant mortality in black and Third World communities in the US This was one of my first understandings of the class question. Unlike the white women's movement, which was battling over lifestyle-related issues, we were battling over our rights to equal access. We didn't care if we could take our bras off or not. My mother had been a union worker at Raytheon for 43 years before she retired. We were struggling to work and for equitable pay, as workers.

The cross-class alliance in the women's movement was problematic from the beginning. It was dominated by white middle-class women who had a different agenda. Our issues were tied into access to jobs, education, etc. But instead, the movement stayed focused in things like rape crisis, which is important, but isn't the heart of the struggle as it affects working-class women. We weren't June Cleavers. The class restrictions that kept white middle-class women inside the kitchen didn't shape our lives. Poverty, race and sexism did.

—Attieno Davis

[T]he previous (white) women's movement had attempted to create an empowered sisterhood through erasing our differences as women of color under the "unifying" category of "women", a category which was given its particular meanings in opposition to the category "men." The privileging of the binary opposition, however, made invisible important differences within each of these categories. Thus racism was unthinkingly perpetuated in the name of liberation. The "common ground" which was to comprise the sisterhood of the women's movement was constructed so it forced a false unity of women, a unity which worked to

Attieno Davis

erase and thus oppress the lives of many women …. Eventually, the dominant women's movement began to falter under a proliferating multitude of ideological differences with unexpected "enemies" and "friends" emerging from every side. We Third World feminists do not take this lesson lightly, as we realize that for us there will be no simple, utopian route to sisterhood.

—Chela Sandoval, "Feminism and Racism: A Report on the 1981 National Women's Studies Association Conference," in Gloria Anzaldúa, ed., *Making Face, Making Soul = Haciendo Caras*

White middle-class women profit in several ways from the exclusion of upwardly mobile women and women of color from the ranks of academic equals in their universities, from the pages of women's studies journals, from positions of power in professional associations, and from a central place in feminist theories. Foremost among these advantages is the elimination of direct competition for the few "women's jobs" in universities; for the limited number of tenure-track and tenured jobs; for the small number of places for women among the higher professorial ranks; for the meager number of pages devoted to research and writing on women in the mainstream professional journals; and for the precious limited space in women's studies journals. White women, struggling for acceptance by male peers, a secure job, and a living wage in the academy – especially since many are forced to work part-time or in a series of one-year appointments – may not "feel" that they are in a privileged position. Indeed, in many ways and in many cases there is little privilege. However, their relative disadvantage in comparison with white men should not obscure the advantages of race and class that remain.

—Maxine Baca Zinn, Lynn Weber Cannon, Elizabeth Higginbotham, and Bonnie Thornton Dill, "The Costs of Exclusionary Practices in Women's Studies," in Gloria Anzaldúa, ed., *Making Face, Making Soul=Haciendo Caras*

Working-class
Feminist Memories

Claire Cummings, from her dissertation "Class Lessons: Women Creating Cross-Class Coalitions in a Welfare Rights Movement":

I joined my first women's consciousness raising [CR] group through [a Women's] Union. I still vividly remember an attractive airline hostess in my first CR group being laughed at by the middle-class women for saying that she did not feel exploited as a woman in her job. In that "coffee, tea, or me" time when "stewardesses" were required to wear ultra short minidresses, high heels, heavy make-up, and heavily sprayed bouffant hairdos, she felt compensated by her travel, health, and salary benefits. For the radical feminists in my group, she was the epitome of the exploited woman. With such attitudes and treatment prevalent, it is clear why few working-class and Black women identified with or wanted to join women's lib groups and organizations. Their cultural values of responsibility and group solidarity, their economic and family needs and interests, clashed with the free-wheeling, individualist feminists who seemed to have little responsibility for anyone other than themselves ….

[T]ogether with another woman, I launched a daycare center as a feminist project …. The group I formed set out consciously, and perhaps a bit idealistically, to create an environment where the children and we would be free from hierarchies of, and socialization into, sexism, classism, and racism. The amazing thing about our experiment was that it worked on every level: we were an egalitarian collective where we rotated every position in the organization. Everyone changed diapers, wrote grants, cooked, built climbing structures, signed checks, and controlled

---

White middle-class liberals are not willing to make sacrifices. They are not seriously committed to much of anything. Their comfort comes before justice. **– Barbara Smith**

the money. Everyone taught, did administrative work, and was politically active in grassroots childcare advocacy work …. We were a group of women and men, younger and older, Black and White, Asian and Hispanic, educated and uneducated, upper, middle, and working-class, and welfare mothers, operating under consensus as a feminist collective openly dedicated to providing the kind of daycare whose sole focus was to free working mothers. Our wild success was to be short-lived; we were evicted after four years and forced to disband when we were unable to find a comparable space.

In retrospect, it is clear to me now that with all its trials and tribulations, tensions and conflict, pride and glory, I came away with a model and an important lesson: cross-class coalitions are worth the struggle. That said, the experience was not without pain. The injuries of class are a pervasive force and dealing with the pressing issues of grinding poverty on little baby bodies and their desperate mothers is no walk in the park …. Tensions surfaced when the old pattern of White middle-class domination reared its ugly head. Differences in opinion as to what was an appropriate structure and leader emerged as the root of most dissension and were a recurring threat to our group cohesion. Two

White middle-class women and one White upper-class woman were uncomfortable sharing power with welfare mothers and wanted a permanent director, an end to consensus-based decision making, and a more "normal," meaning hierarchical, organizational structure. After much campaigning for this change, they called for a vote, which they promptly lost. The disappointed trio of classist women were surprised by the enthusiasm and pride taken in our chosen forms of interaction and structure, and failed at some naked attempts to grab power when reporting us to the welfare department on their way out worked to no avail. And I learned another important lesson: when people get a taste of collective empowerment that works, when they learn that submitting to consensus can meet needs as well, if not better, than majority rule and hierarchy, they will support it ….

The consequences to the women's movement and to feminism of excluding poor and working-class women's voices, ideas, experiences, values, and contributions are many …. [I]gnoring class differences creates a movement which expends too much of its energy and resources on feminist theoretical achievements, safe reforms, and bureaucratic organizations which tend to diminish the resources, power, and historical ability of the working-class to disrupt. This type of women's movement tends only to extend the privileges of a minority of middle-class women rather than to achieve widespread political actions that fundamentally challenge, threaten, and ultimately change the sexist, racist, and classist status quo.

Ellen Shub

GLBT and C

blw

Why focus on gay, lesbian, bisexual, and transgender (GLBT) people and

class? Not just because it's a huge movement that is winning major victories at a time when many issues are moving backwards. But because it's one of the identity movements in which class privilege has both distorted the image of the constituency and distorted the substance of its political stands.

The most common media image of GLBT people is well-off white gay men. Portrayals of gay men's culture in particular are linked to elite culture and expensive consumer goods, as evidenced by the TV show *Queer Eye for the Straight Guy*.

Right-wing homophobes frequently pull out average income numbers that show gay people to be much wealthier than the average American. Their sources include the marketing materials that gay publications show to advertisers to entice them to buy ads, so the privileged image stems from attempting to appeal to corporations.

In fact, GLBT people are part of every class and race. Not surprisingly, lesbians, as women with no men in the household, have lower median incomes than other women. Transgender and other "gender-queer" people who are far from conventional gender norms sometimes find themselves stuck in poverty. But surprisingly, according to some surveys, gay men also tend to have slightly lower average incomes than other men.

However, it's not a media myth that the biggest-budget GLBT organizations have been dominated by professional middle-class white gay people. Some of them, notably the Human Rights Campaign, have been resistant to including class and economic issues in their platforms or to prioritizing the needs of poor queers. But other GLBT activists, including some I interviewed and quote below, have been bridge-builders who connect GLBT and class issues.

The media image of homophobes tends to be that of working-class thugs. In fact, most decisions to discriminate, especially in big institutions, are made by college-educated professionals or the ruling class. Class propriety has kept many people from tackling AIDS, as talking about sex and destitute, sick gay men is sometimes taboo in polite society.

continued on bottom of next page

Marilyn Humphries

Middle-class black LGBT activists drive me crazy when they don't try to change the systems that oppress them and many others — for example, when they're concerned only about getting on the boards of white gay organizations — **Barbara Smith**

Working-Class Queers, Middle-Class Queers

The Louisville Youth Group runs a support group for GLBTQQ [Queer and Questioning] and straight-ally youth. I was a teenager myself when I helped start it, and now, 13 years later I'm paid staff.

Natalie Reteneller

I try to give priority to the least privileged kids. Because they have fewer resources, they're more in need of a hand up. Some statistics for homeless youth show that between a quarter and half are homeless because they have been rejected at home for being gay, lesbian, bisexual, or transgender.

People are coming out at younger ages. It used to be college, now it is high school or middle school. Sometimes they get kicked out of their homes. We get quite a few young people from the foster care system, which has a disproportionate number of GLBTQQ young people.

When someone's considering coming out to their family, I ask them to assess their risks of being thrown out or cut off from their basic needs. Not to stereotype, but physical abuse seems more prevalent in lower-income young people. But it is important not to assume some of these same risks aren't there for wealthy young people too. I'm not as worried about their basic needs, but I'm actually more concerned about their isolation. They, too, are at risk of high-risk behaviors.

Because they often have more to lose financially – like a car or the prospect of college – they are less likely to come out. Many of these young people stay in the closet and go on to college, but have trouble reconciling that part of their lives with their families.

In our group meetings, youth leaders pick the discussion topics, like coming out, school issues, and relationships.

I go to many different meetings around Louisville related to youth, and I make sure I introduce myself as someone from a GLBT group. I don't let being a lesbian or being younger hold me back from allowing others to see me for who I am.

—Natalie Reteneller

Homophobia and classism have sometimes been intertwined. Black churchgoers had an image of gay and lesbian people as "lowlife." Lowlife meant criminals, adulterers, prostitutes, people who didn't keep their property up. But pre-Stonewall, being gay or lesbian also qualified. I was concerned

continued on next page

GLBT and C, continued from previous page

But it's not only in the media that there is some correlation between class privilege and gay tolerance. It's a topic that is difficult to talk about without falling into stereotypes. Homophobia has been steadily melting away from public opinion at all income levels. But in the 1980s and 1990s, it seems to have eroded faster among more privileged people. Religion is a major bulwark protecting homophobia, and working-class people are more likely to have religious affiliations and to be in denominations with stricter religious rules. Colleges and universities were an organizing base for the GLBT movement, and millions of people came out at college. Meanwhile, in the most common socializing institution for working-class young adults, the military, it became more dangerous to come out. Working-class queers and allies have often had to buck more institutional hurdles and more rigid gender norms than their middle-class equivalents.

However, there's a natural alliance between queers and working-class people, if only we don't let homophobia or classism get in the way.

about that because I was raised to maximize my talents for the greater good; I wasn't supposed to turn out to be lowlife.

There's a class difference between black LGBT people who moved from their hometown and those who stayed where they came from. In Albany, NY, middle-class LGBT people of color frequently came there from somewhere else, to try their wings and start a life far from their families, and so they tended to have fewer problems with being out of the closet. But working class LGBT people of color were more likely to have grown up there, and still lived near their families and childhood neighbors, so they tended to be completely or partially closeted, or to experience tension and conflict about coming out.

—Barbara Smith

I know that I have been hated as a lesbian both by "society" and by the intimate world of my extended family, but I have also been hated or held in contempt (which is in some ways more debilitating and slippery than hatred) by lesbians for behavior and sexual practices shaped in large part by class. My sexual identity is intimately constructed by my class and regional background, and much of the hatred directed at my sexual preferences is class hatred – however much people, feminists in particular, like to pretend this is not a factor. The kind of woman I am attracted to is invariably the kind of woman who embarrasses respectably middle-class, politically aware lesbian feminists. My sexual ideal is butch, exhibitionistic, physically aggressive, smarter than she wants you to know, and proud of being

called a pervert. More often she is working class, with an aura of danger and an ironic sense of humor.

—Dorothy Allison,
*Skin: Talking about Sex,
Class and Literature*

As I became older, I became increasingly attracted to theories of class struggle. These gave me hope that poor people of color would ultimately unite against rich white people. While I still work hard to end class inequality, my view has changed some. Finding a queer community made me more compassionate about the humanity of rich people and white people. I've fallen in love with white men who have died of AIDS. I have befriended rich men and women who share the fear of violence and the humiliation of the closet. There are those who call me an Uncle Tom for calling rich white gay folks my people, but I can't help myself. We have too much in common, and the burden of ending oppression is too big. I am now open to allies and friends wherever I can find them.

—Scot Nakagawa, *Queerly Classed:
Gay Men and Lesbians
Write About Class*

When the Fischer meat packing workers went on strike, some of us in a gay rights group, the Fairness Campaign, proposed that the group back them up. It was a mostly white

middle-class group, and there was a volatile conversation, with some members saying it was off the point, not our issue, it would detract from what we were doing. But we said that you can't separate discrimination from workplace safety and wage protection. You need to back your natural allies and have their backing. We are not enough in numbers to go it alone, and you can't get there just on good will. Some members of the Fairness Campaign had awful stereotypes of unions.

But even without the whole group's support, a few of us participated on picket lines with the strikers. It made queer people real to the union members.

Marilyn Humphries

We brought up class analysis in Fairness Campaign trainings, how it's connected.

And when our anti-discrimination proposal came up for a vote, the union stepped forward, they came to City Hall and spoke up, and that helped us. We didn't win right away, but eventually our legislation passed. And we had union support all along the way. And we continued to be on the front line with them.

—Susan Remmers

I really value middle-class activists when they are open to understanding me and letting me understand them, when they're open to being vulnerable and building trust. — **Linda Stout**

Classism and the **GLBT Movement**

Pam McMichael

Southerners on New Ground (SONG) had an intentional 3-year plan to include a class analysis at the National Gay and Lesbian Task Force's annual Creating Change conference. A few of us, black and white lesbians, began SONG in 1994, following the 1993 conference. Congress was debating NAFTA, and the NGLTF acting director had proposed a position against it at the conference, which was focused on race and class. Many people asked, "Why are we talking about NAFTA at a gay and lesbian conference?" In part, SONG grew out of answering that question, to continue the conversation about how economic issues and race touch everything.

SONG led the pre-conference institutes in '95, '96, and '97. That third year the conference was in San Diego, near the border, and SONG took 30 queer organizers across the border to talk with maquiladora workers.

SONG deliberately connected with poor people's groups, like the Kensington Welfare Rights Union, because lesbians and poor people are both blamed for society's ills. We worked with the Highlander Center and KWRU on organizing the North-South Dialogue on Poor People's Movement Building. We helped send southern LesBiGayTrans activists who worked on both economic justice and LGBT issues to the Poor People's Summit.

We organized a retreat with the Highlander Center, the Center for Democratic Renewal, and the Women's Project to help groups to deal with homophobia in their organizations. In many cases, the constituency was actually ahead of the leadership. The leaders would say things like, "Oh, our group isn't ready for that." They were holding back people who were ready to move. The retreat was on the tools to take on homophobia within their social change organizations.

—Pam McMichael

Plastic Flowers

William Mann, from "A Boy's Own Class," in *Queerly Classed: Gay Men and Lesbians Write about Class*:

"That's unfortunate," said a friend, gesturing to a small house with a neatly trimmed yard .... Along the edge of the house were planted pink and blue plastic roses .... "Plastic," my friend said. "Can they not afford *seeds?*"

The geraniums in the window boxes on the side of my mother's house were [also] plastic. "I wanted something really bright over there," she explained .... Once, I thought there was nothing wrong with plastic geraniums. There was an entire aisle of plastic flowers in Woolworth's that I would parade down as a boy – Princess Anne on her wedding day .... Artificial flowers entice a young gay boy's imagination – but I came to

learn they offend an adult gay man's sensibilities ....

"How the hell did you ever wind up here, kid?" I've asked myself, time and again. From the little factory town where I was born ... how did I end up sharing a house in the tony west end of Provincetown, every summer for the entire summer, year after year?

It's simple: I'm gay. Had I not been gay – had I been my brother, for example – I would never have discovered the access that led me to a different place. My brother and I attended the same college, a state university .... But only I ventured into a world my parents had never known .... A visiting gay lecturer took me to dinner and later introduced me to well-known activists and writers ....

Had I not been gay, I wonder, would I be like my brother, secure in his class, happy to be a Knight of Columbus chugging beer on a Friday night ... taking his wife to the annual Spring Fling ...? There's a beauty in that, of course, a simple but nonetheless profound beauty. Had I not been gay, that could well have been me, and I might not have been unhappy.

But that's not me .... The first gay people I knew were not working-class: in fact, I've known precious few, even now. Perhaps that's because to be working-class – or at least, to show the signs of it – is anathema to a particularly dominant part of gay male culture .... To admit that one's mother displayed plastic geraniums would be "unfortunate" ....

The schism between the classes is very real, and it is likely even more

apparent among the gentrified world of the gay elite .... [O]ther gay male friends, when pushed, admit to a certain pressure to hide their particular classed culture .... How many of us have so deeply hidden our origins that even a sincere attempt at beauty like planting plastic flowers becomes "unfortunate"?

The **Queerness** of the Working Class

Joanna Kadi, from *Thinking Class:*

Working-class people's responses to queers vary widely. Some are radically supportive, some are mildly supportive, some don't care much one way or the other, some hate queers viciously and say so to our faces, some stand outside queer bars with baseball bats.

These responses parallel those of the middle and upper classes. Among these groups, some are radically supportive, some mildly supportive, some liberally tolerant, some hate queers viciously and say so. The most homophobic usually don't carry weapons; they've got other ways of maiming and killing us that don't involve anything as "dirty" as physical assault ....

The word *queer* captures not only my sexual identity but my class identity as well. It accurately positions me on the margins of the class hierarchy, without any chance of being "normal," that is, middle-class .... Figuring out my "queer" working-class identity helped me understand radical acceptance from working-class people. If contented working-class people share a gut feeling of queerness, it's not a total shock when a son comes out as gay. His sexual identity fits with our experiences as "queer" in relation to

Joanna Kadi

rich people. My aunt didn't freak out when I said, "I'm a lesbian. I live with my lover." She immediately asked if Jan treats me well, and if she takes care of me. When I reassured her, she said, "That's wonderful." End of discussion ....

Within working-class families where members love and respect each other (and I'm not saying this describes all working-class families), caring for kin is linked to a deep distrust of "the system" – the capitalist system that exploits us and benefits the rich. Our love for each other is tempered and steeled by our exploitation and our need to stick

---

Some middle-class LGBT activists don't see how homophobia is entwined in systems of oppression. It's not just about negative attitudes. **– Barbara Smith**

together. We're all we have, so we must stay connected ....

While experiencing the pleasure of deep love and radical acceptance from some family members, I've also gone through the anticipated displeasure of vicious queer hatred from other family members, most notably my parents. The night I broke my big news, they said it all: "You're sick. You ought to be locked up in a mental hospital." ....

Working-class homophobes like my parents carry a lot of bitterness which stems in large part from capitalist oppression. They don't accept their lot in life. They want more money, more stuff, and more status. Yet they don't agitate for change; they sit with other like-minded working-class people in resentful anger over the little they've been allowed to acquire.

This bitterness pops up when these people react to "difference," which they despise and fear in the family, society, themselves. Back to my parents. My father, a dark-skinned Arab, hates being set apart from white norms. He and my mother hate being set apart from middle-class norms, and have no desire to experience "queerness" in relation to those norms. They'd rather make it in the system established by rich people; they'd love to assimilate and be welcomed into the fold .... So it makes sense that they'd let loose with

My father, a dark-skinned Arab, hates being set apart from white norms. He and my mother hate being set apart from middle-class norms, and have no desire to experience "queerness" in relation to those norms.

— Joanna Kadi

homophobic condemnation when I come out and embrace one particular form of queerness ....

Classism permeates every level of the queer movement .... Queers and poor people share common agendas. Central concerns of working-class/working-poor people have recently been taken on by AIDS activists — nationalized health care and protection from unemployment .... However, to date the queer movement has focused on alliance-building with rich people .... When I flew to D.C. for the 1993 Queer March on Washington, I thought I would throw up if I heard one more TV interview with an earnest, middle-class queer explaining, "We're just like everyone else. This march will prove that." For the phrase, "everyone else," read middle-class, white, monogamous, heterosexual couple. Don't read poor Chicana single mom ....

Working-class and working-poor queers who found each other in urban centers in the 1950s and 1960s ran the gamut from kiki to drag kings and queens to butch-femme couples to bull dykes. They toughed it out on the streets and did the best they could to resist extreme brutality and social scorn. But these folks weren't accorded leadership roles, let alone respect, in the larger movements for queer liberation that formed in the 1970s and 1980s. Sometimes they couldn't get in the door. When they managed to, they didn't have a powerful role in shaping the movement and neither did younger working-class queers. Instead, middle-class and upper-middle-class queers shaped the strategies and actions of the past three decades. I'm disturbed by the push for alliance with the corporate board room and not the union hall, by the invisibility of working-class queers, by a refusal to take class seriously ....

I want the queer movement to articulate a clear agenda of ending heterosexist/homophobic oppression, of integrating and welcoming all queers into the movement, of supporting liberation movements for disabled people / people of color / working-class and working-poor people / women .... The queer movement needs an integrated analysis of all oppressions.

Working-Class White Men

Straddling
Two Worlds

David Croteau

I was born into a type of family that became a cultural stereotype shortly before it became an endangered species: the "traditional," white, "ethnic" blue-collar family.... [M]y father worked in a paper mill for forty-four years ....

As long as I can remember, I was determined not to work in the mill .... Education was going to be my ticket out .... Neither of my parents had attended high school, let alone college, so I was left rudderless in choosing schools. [A] guidance counselor suggested to me that perhaps, despite my excellent grades, welding would be more "practical" for someone with my "background"....

From the very first day, my college education brought with it a new awareness of how different cultures could be. I have a vivid memory of the awkwardness and discomfort on my parents' faces when they met my assigned roommate and his obviously wealthy parents ....

After college I went to work for the national office of a "peace-and-justice" organization in New York

City where I continued to be acutely aware of class issues .... While I had a strong respect and affection for my fellow activists, it became startlingly apparent to me that many of them within this part of the Left often had no concrete referent in mind when they talked about "the working class" .... [A]ctivists' notions of "the working class" tended to fall at extreme poles: either workers were the gloriously idyllic proletariat (who one day would smarten up and start doing their revolutionary duty) or they were stupid, fascistic hard hats for whom there was no hope (and who were the easy target of ridicule). Either way, their working class bore little resemblance to the working class I knew ....

Having been socialized into two different classes, I was constantly aware – sometimes painfully so – of the differences between these cultures .... The issues I was learning to analyze and address were not the issues of primary concern to my family and friends. The issues that did concern them were either only vaguely addressed or completely ignored by the middle-class Left's agenda. More important, the idea that politics was a sphere of life worthy of extensive involvement and accessible to people like themselves seemed inconceivable to them .... I was confronted with the undeniable reality of a class divide that separated the cultures of the working-class world from which I had come from that of the middle-class, political Left to which I had traveled.

I really value middle-class activists when they're respectful and not patronizing.
– Gilda Haas

The River, by Bruce Springsteen

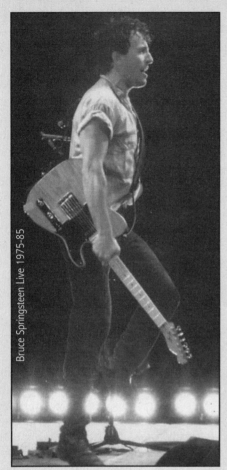

Bruce Springsteen Live 1975-85

I come from down in the valley where, mister, when you're young
They bring you up to do like your daddy done
Me and Mary we met in high school when she was just seventeen
We'd drive out of this valley, down to where the fields were green
We'd go down to the river, and into the river we'd dive
Oh down to the river we'd ride

Then I got Mary pregnant, and man, that was all she wrote,
And for my nineteenth birthday I got a union card and a
    wedding coat
We went down to the courthouse and the judge put it all to rest
No wedding day smiles, no walk down the aisle
No flowers, no wedding dress
That night we went down to the river and into the river we'd dive
Oh down to the river we did ride

I got a job working construction for the Johnstown Company
But lately there ain't been much work on account of the economy
Now all them things that seemed so important
Well, mister, they vanished right into the air
Now I just act like I don't remember, Mary acts like she don't care
But I remember us riding in my brother's car
Her body tan and wet down at the reservoir
At night on them banks I'd lie awake
and pull her close just to feel each breath she'd take

Now those memories come back to haunt me
They haunt me like a curse
Is a dream a lie if it don't come true, or is it something worse
That sends me down to the river, though I know the river is dry
That sends me down to the river tonight
Down to the river, my baby and I,
Oh down to the river we ride

Working-Class Men as Good Allies

I was on a super-diverse advisory council for a statewide union local in Pennsylvania. We all identified as workers and all wanted the local to succeed.

When I was running for office, some white council members said that there were rural places in the state I shouldn't go alone as a black woman. So these two white guys offered to go with me when I was campaigning. One was tall and thin, and the other looked like a Hell's Angel, rough and tough but with a big heart. I had these two bodyguards with me on the road! That's my idea of allies.

—Alison Bowens

"But Aren't they All **Bigots**?"

blw

For activists who think of ourselves as struggling to end the "isms" – sexism, racism, etc. – adding classism to the list means opening up our definition of oppressed people to include working-class white men. This makes many women and people of color nervous. They think of white men as the most privileged group, and it galls them to hear that there's some way that the majority of white men are actually oppressed.

In some movement groups, I sense that people oppressed by racism, sexism, and/or homophobia can have a certain hip status that white working-class men just don't have.

And on a deeper level lurks a fear that working-class white men are more sexist than other men and more racist than other white people. This fear, which holds many activists back from reaching out to working-class white men, is a mix of accurate perceptions of a minority of them and unfounded classist stereotypes of the majority.

Working-class white men sometimes get a bad rap for racism and sexism that actually pervade our society. People of color report finding racist attitudes among white class-privileged people and women as well – but sometimes expressed in a more subtle way. Opinion polls show racist and sexist attitudes gradually diminishing in all demographic groups. The decisions that perpetuate institutional racism and sexism, on the other hand, are not made by working-class white men, but by big employers, landlords, government officials, HMOs, etc.

We don't do our movements any favors by buying into the myth that white working-class men are more likely to be prejudiced than they actually are. This classist myth has lent support to employers and policymakers who have used divide and conquer tactics. Working-class organizing has been weaker in the US than in other industrialized countries in part because race has been pitted against race for centuries. We perpetuate this division if we presume that working-class white men are closed to progressive movements.

The more helpful attitude for middle-class activists to hold towards grassroots white working-class men is to assume they're our potential brothers in the movement unless proven otherwise. Some will, in fact, turn out to have more multicultural experiences and bridging skills than we do. Some will have prejudices – but hey, so do we. A little humility is in order.

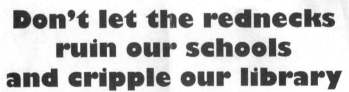

Don't let the rednecks ruin our schools and cripple our library

There are people — even in Winchester — who don't see much value in quality public schools.

There are people — even in Winchester — who don't care if the town has to fire librarians and drastically cut back on library hours.

They don't care if residents are barred from borrowing books from other libraries. Who needs books!

Maybe it's just selfishness, but they don't even care if the town has to fire police officers.

But these are some of the important things that make Winchster the high-value, desirable town it is.

Don't let the rednecks win. Vote YES for an override to pay for Winchester quality.

Don't need no schools, anyway!

Vote OverrideYES March 26

Flyer posted all over Winchester, Massachusetts in 1999

Middle-class activists drive me crazy when they use "redneck" as an insult meaning stupid and racist. Where I come from, it's a badge of pride that you're tough and you work outside.
– Southern white man I met in Central American movement

Where Did the **Archie Bunker**
Stereotype Come from?

How Did It Come to Be That So Many Activists Expect White Working-Class Men to Be Especially Racist and Sexist?

blw

US history includes both right-wing use of classist stereotypes for political ends *and* real examples of blue-collar men's racist violence, such as Southern lynch mobs and Chicago Neighborhood Associations blocking fair housing. These violent racists have been a tiny percentage of white working-class people, but they have been a potent force in US politics.

Living in Boston, I've sometimes seen real racism and sometimes had my stereotypes burst. Boston had some of the most painful racial divisions in the North during the 1970s busing controversy. Seared into the minds of Bostonians are the ugly images of South Boston and Charlestown racists stoning buses full of black children. I have to admit that when I moved here in 1982, the sound of working-class Boston accents brought images of those stone-throwers to my mind.

Then in the mid-1980s, I worked as a research assistant for Boston College sociologist Bill Gamson on *Talking Politics*, a book about how working-class people form political opinions. I facilitated focus groups about topics including affirmative action. One evening I facilitated a white group in South Boston. The group got very heated during the affirmative action discussion. No-one said anything negative about people of color or in favor of violence. Their anger was instead class rage directed at the judge who ordered school integration. They were angry that the judge and liberal busing supporters lived in the suburbs or sent their children to private school. They were angry at the dilapidated and overcrowded schools in their neighborhood and in the black neighborhoods to which their children were being bused. They were angry that there were so few scholarships available for them or their children. I was an outsider and they were obviously eager to show me that their point of view had merit and wasn't racist – so perhaps I was getting the sanitized version and privately some of them had more prejudices. But their class analysis impressed me. They thought that liberals cared about poor black people and not poor white people.

Barbara Ehrenreich, in *Fear of Falling: The Inner Life of the Middle Class*, writes that the working class was "discovered" in the 1970s by academics, the media, and politicians. The Nixon administration commissioned a task force on blue collar workers. In 1970, the Ford Foundation switched its funding from black community activism to groups serving white ethnic groups. The working-class "Middle Americans" being "discovered" were portrayed as white men, even as the working class was in fact rapidly shifting to more women and people of color. The purpose of this "discovery" was to create the illusion of a blue-collar backlash against the antiwar and Black Power movements. In

Marilyn Humphries

fact, middle-class professionals were more likely to be critical of those movements than were working-class white people. Ehrenreich tells this story:

One Poll on Racial Attitudes

In 1999, Pew Research Center asked white people to agree or disagree with the statement, "I think it's alright for blacks and whites to date each other."

- Of white people in the annual income bracket greater than $50,000, 78 percent agree with this statement.
- Of white people making less than $30,000 a year, 63 percent agree with this statement.

Two things to notice: yes, there was a difference, but at all income levels, the majority of people polled took the nonbigoted choice.

An ugly incident underscored the tensions between the working class and the professional middle class, and seemed to confirm the image of the blue-collar male as a violent reactionary. On May 8, 1970, hundreds of helmeted construction workers attacked a peaceful student antiwar demonstration in Manhattan's Wall Street district, leaving seventy students and bystanders injured. It was a terrifying event – not only to the student protesters but to the normal denizens of Wall Street ....

But the attack, which quickly became emblematic of blue-collar sentiments, was neither spontaneous nor representative of blue-collar union men. At the time of the incident, some of the nation's largest unions, including the thoroughly blue-collar Teamsters, United Auto Workers, and Oil, Chemical, and Atomic Workers, had taken official stands against the war in Vietnam. Peter Brennan, president of New York City's Building Trades Council, had not; he was a hawk and a Nixon supporter. A few members of Brennan's union disclosed to the press that the workers' attack had been planned and announced through the union in advance. Bystanders reported that the attack had

been directed by teams of grey-suited men.

Nevertheless, the rampaging construction workers were widely taken to be representative of their class and race. In no time at all, the term hardhat replaced redneck as the epithet for a lower-class bigot.

Ellen Shub

Some middle-class activists fell for this divisive propaganda.

And some fell for it again when the New Right cranked up its propaganda machine in the 1980s to hype a political alliance between big business and working people. They defined a "New Class" of intellectuals, public employees, and liberal non- profit staff and described American society as polarizing between two blocs: the parasites in the New Class and the poor (assumed to be people of color) versus the productive people in business, the rich, and Middle American working people (assumed to be white). Some activists who fall into this "New Class" have (sometimes wrongly) expected low-income people of color to agree with us politically while (often wrongly) expecting white working-class people to be our opponents on the conservative side.

Our job as progressives is to reframe the two sides: away from the right-wing "producers versus parasites" model, towards another framework: corporate and conservative wealthy special interests versus ordinary people of every race and class.

Middle-class activists drive me crazy when they fail to seek for a goal that includes everyone.
– Theresa Funiciello

Turning Bigotry Around

A Hopeful Story

blw

How to react when someone spouts racism? It can be especially tricky across class lines, a middle-class person reacting to a working-class person's prejudice. I've tried different approaches at different times, but here's one story where I feel I handled it right and made a difference.

Tom was the only working-class member of an anti-nuclear-power group I organized in a mixed-race, mixed-class neighborhood. He was a white guy who worked in a garage and still lived with his family. I really liked him; he was smart and dedicated.

On a car ride to a demonstration, Tom told me matter-of-factly, "I don't like black people, and black people don't like me." Stunned, I gulped, took a deep breath, and asked him what his experiences with black people had been. He told me about growing up in a white

On a car ride to a demonstration, Tom told me flatly, "I don't like black people, and black people don't like me."

neighborhood that gradually changed to a black one as the white families with more money moved out to the suburbs, leaving a core of low-income families like his behind in one tiny enclave. He told me about his white gang battling black gangs, and having to fight to get to school every day of high school. (Tom's childhood story, by the way, fits exactly the profile of young people recruited by white supremacist hate groups, according to Rafael Ezekiel in *The Racist Mind*.)

I just listened that first time, but later we talked about it again. He never made any negative generalizations about all black people and was never disrespectful to the few black members of our group. He just repeated, "They didn't like me, and I didn't like them," as he told me his stories of turf battles. At the end of each conversation I calmly said I had a different impression of black people and told him stories of my

Oops! An Embarrassing Confession

blw

Shortly after I wrote this section, I realized that of the 27 activists I had interviewed to that point, not one was a working-class white man! Every single working-class and low-income person I had interviewed was a woman and/or a person of color.

I had made sure that at least a third of my interviews were with activists of color. And I had created the sections on African

American, Asian and Latino class dynamics almost entirely with those activists' voices. Those kinds of racial sensitivities had been drummed into me from my earliest days as an activist.

But even though the topic of this whole book is classism, even though its goal is to get activists to take class as seriously as other differences, even though I knew that that meant adding working-class white men to our idea of

who's oppressed — it still hadn't occurred to me to find or elevate the voices of working-class white men. I immediately reached out to a few white male working-class visionaries.

My first impulse was to hide this embarrassing omission, but I figured that we all learn about classism from each other's dumb mistakes.

My apologies to my working-class white activist brothers.

friendships and activist experiences with African Americans.

A few weeks later, the group planned to spend a Saturday knocking on doors to get petition signatures. I was the one dividing up the map. I paired Tom up with a gentle, soft-spoken black gay man and assigned them a territory full of mostly elderly lower-middle-class African American homeowners. At the end of the day, I asked Tom how it had gone. "I'm a sucker for old people," was all he said. But I never heard him say anything about disliking black people again.

> *I paired Tom up with a gentle, soft-spoken black gay man and assigned them a territory full of mostly elderly lower-middle-class African American homeowners. At the end of the day, I asked Tom how it had gone. "I'm a sucker for old people," was all he said. But I never heard him say anything about disliking black people again.*

I moved away, and six months later when I came back to visit, I got together with Tom. The minute he saw me, he was bursting with a story: "Betsy, listen to what I did! This guy who worked at the garage was really prejudiced against black people, always saying nasty stuff. So one time there was a tow job, and I had to send two guys on a really long drive. So I sent this prejudiced guy along with this really nice black guy, and by the time they got back they were, like, friends, and now he doesn't say that shit anymore!" He was beaming at me. I laughed and hugged him and told him he did good.

So what did I do right with Tom that I could replicate? Can I turn this story into tips helpful to other middle-class activists?

- I liked him. I respected him as a fundamentally good person. I appreciated what he brought to the group. I never forgot that, no matter what he said.

- I listened first. I didn't jump on him or argue against him when he first said things that sounded racist to me, but drew him out and learned his story first.

- I didn't let it slide. I took it as intolerable that this energetic activist would be stuck believing harmful misinformation because of his past. I figured out something to do about it, something that gave him some credit for having some intelligence and ability to figure things out for himself.

- I gave it time. I put time into talking with him, and I waited a few weeks after his first racist comments before attempting to change his mind.

I can boil this experience down to two words: I was respectful and engaged. Something very basic, but very rare. Far more often, I've been closed and judgmental.

What Tom did right is also basic but rare: he let someone teach him something, and he took the gift he was given and gave it to someone else. I admire what he did very much.

And of course, the other hero of the story is the African American man who spent the day working with someone he may have suspected of having prejudices against him and whose charm worked the magic.

> *I can boil this experience down to two words: I was respectful and engaged. Something very basic, but very rare. Far more often, I've been closed and judgmental.*

Middle-class activists drive me crazy when they are self-righteous, especially when they become champions of other oppressions. — **Jerry Koch-Gonzalez**

The **Forgotten Majority**

blw

In *America's Forgotten Majority: Why the White Working Class Still Matters*, Ruy Teixeira and Joel Rogers break down voting records by gender, race, and class. They find that the bulk of the Republican resurgence from the 1980s to the 2000 election was due to non-union white working-class men abandoning the Democratic party, with over 20 percent of them switching, between 1960 to 2000, from being Democrats to being non-voters or third party supporters or Republicans.

By using polling data, Teixeira and Rogers debunk the myth that this represented a swing towards right-wing, conservative values. Polls show that on issues such as abortion, gay rights, and the environment, these voters, like most of the country, became slightly more liberal in the 1980s and 1990s. Nor did working-class white men become more anti-government. They did, however, become more disappointed in government, feeling that public programs had done little for them. Jack Metzgar characterizes white non-union men as those "not protected by a union, a bachelor's degree, or affirmative action [who have] lost much ground in wages and benefits over the past quarter-century, while often being culturally and politically lumped into the 'white male' power structure with whom they share little but the color of their genitalia."

Polls show that on issues such as abortion, gay rights, and the environment, these voters, like most of the country, became slightly more liberal in the 1980s and 1990s. Nor did working-class white men become more anti-government. They did, however, become more disappointed in government.

When income trends are broken down, working-class white men are the only group for which, between 1979 and 1998, the median income actually fell. College-educated people surged ahead. Non-college-educated people of color and white women gained ground, although from a much lower starting point. Hope for the future and belief in the redistributive powers of government programs have made more sense to working-class and low-income people other than white men, who actually saw a new generation earn less than their fathers. Deindustrialization, globalization, and de-unionization meant good jobs disappearing. Teixeira and Rogers attribute the change in voting patterns to bitterness at falling behind economically. They recommend that the Democratic party take up a platform that would help working-class white men as well as other

"ONE OF THE BEST BOOKS OF THE YEAR." —WASHINGTON POST

Ruy Teixeira and Joel Rogers

Why the White Working Class Still Matters WITH A NEW AFTERWORD ABOUT THE 2000 ELECTION

AMERICA'S FORGOTTEN MAJORITY

working-class people: universal health care, retirement security, and access to education.

When I told one longtime progressive activist I was writing a cross-class alliance-building manual, this reply popped out of her mouth: "We don't have to worry about those red parts of the country anymore, now that people of color are a majority." She was referring to the color code of the election map, in which the middle and south of the country tended to vote red Republican and the northern coasts and northern midwest tended to vote blue Democrat. She was also referring to a recent Census announcement that people of color now make up over 30 percent of the US population, but by 2050 would constitute over 50 percent. I had not specified white working-class people in my description of the project; it's interesting how often the words "working class" evoke a white image, and usually a white male image. And her image was not only white, but middle American and conservative. Her voice was full of scorn for white working-class people, and of relief that she now didn't need to work with them to keep the Republicans out of office. She was imagining a voting bloc made up of people of color and white middle-class liberals like herself.

Teixeira and Rogers respond to such hopes by saying that "the Democrats may be able to wait out the forgotten majority [i.e. white working-class people], as inexorable demographic trends attenuate their political influence. It could be a long wait. Extrapolating from current educational attainment trends and Bureau of the Census population projections, the forgotten majority might dip under 50 percent of voters by the year 2020. That's two decades from now and even then, we estimate they'll still comprise 48 percent of voters – a huge group that would be difficult, if not impossible, for the Democrats to work around."

Similarly, we need lots of working-class white men in our "rainbow coalition" if it's going to have clout. But beyond pragmatic political reasons, the financial worries of millions of white working-class people belong on the movement's radar screen as any urgent unmet human needs do.

When I told one longtime progressive activist I was writing a cross-class alliance-building manual, she replied: "We don't have to worry about those red parts of the country anymore, now that people of color are a majority."

I wrote a column supporting affirmative action for people of color, and the morning after it was published, there was an angry message on my voicemail. "I'm sick of you white professionals forgetting about us poor white people!"

The man had a point. When I wrote that the $120,000 median net worth for white families was seven times as great as families of color's net worth in 2001, I didn't explain that white wealth is so high in part because super-rich elites are averaged in with low-income and working-class white people, who also need government help, as do people of color. And I didn't mention my support for universal government boosts for economically struggling people of all races, as well as for race-specific programs to make up for past racial discrimination. I won't make that mistake again.

More generally, though, I learned once again that there's no way to talk about race without getting some working-class white people angry — just as sometimes it seems there's no way to talk about class without getting some people of color angry.

– blw

Middle-class activists drive me crazy when their sense of entitlement leads them to use the words "the community" to describe themselves and they don't see other interests. **– Roxana Tynan**

Some Places We Meet

Every movement has at least a little class diversity, and so individual activists from different class backgrounds could happen to bump into each other anywhere. But there are some situations that regularly bring working-class and middle-class activists into collaborations:

- Community organizing efforts in working-class and low-income communities are frequently staffed by middle-class activists.
- Unions enter into coalitions with environmental, student, religious, or peace groups to work towards common goals – or sometimes clash with them.
- Election campaigns spur activists of all classes to speak out publicly, and progressive candidates usually get elected only if voters of different classes find common ground.
- The environmental justice movement has diversified the previously predominantly white and middle-class environmental movement.
- And middle-class feminists have teamed up with welfare recipients and other consumers of human services to stop the tearing up of the safety net.

This list is not complete; it mentions just a few places where I've personally experienced cross-class collaboration or where the people I interviewed told juicy stories of successful and unsuccessful alliances.

Middle-Class Organizers in Working-Class Communities

Most social justice organizations are run by middle-class people. In some socialist utopian heaven, middle-class organizers would disappear – but hey, so would the whole social justice movement.

—John Anner

The primary principle for organizers is to empower working-class people and people of color. Don't do things *for* people, but help them to come together collectively and speak for themselves. That's the difference between uplift ideology and the democratic vision. And there should be accountability. You can elect representatives, but the process of figuring out priorities should happen democratically.

There's a difference between middle-class activists who speak *for* people and middle-class organizers who *organize* working-class people. I think organizers, across class, understand the value of people demanding things for themselves. Middle-class activists, on the other hand, feel like they can be the brokers for other people. And they think they are the best qualified to do it, because of their class status. It drives me absolutely crazy when they don't understand the value of actually organizing. They want other people to do the work. Then they can speak at the event, get the press coverage, and broker the deal. But they don't want to do the work of doing what it takes to get 200 people to the rally. That takes a lot of work. All those people didn't turn out just because they saw your name on the flyer!

—Dorian Warren

Workplace Organizing Dynamics

Jack Metzgar read this section on middle-class community organizers and e-mailed me the following paragraph in response:

The dynamics in workplace organizing are different than in community organizing. Union organizers have not usually been of a different social class from the folks they're trying to organize, and even when they are, they are much more likely to (credibly) deny it with the line "I'm just a worker like you, I just do a different kind of work." This has changed in the last decade as young, college-educated union organizers are focused on primarily low-income service workers where the class difference between organizer and workers is much more apparent. It's becoming much more like the traditional community organizer relationship. But there are still $30,000-a-year organizers of $45,000-a-year nurses, to take one current example – young, inexperienced people organizing seasoned workplace leaders. In these situations the idea that the middle-class organizer has to be constantly holding back his or her superior strength in order not to dominate or undermine people's sense of efficacy can seem entirely counterintuitive. Yeah, a good union organizer doesn't want to turn people off with an arrogant, boorish "know-it-all" attitude, but in fact the organizer has to bring a "know-a-lot" attitude to the task if they're to sell the program, to get people to believe the union really does have something to offer. Coming on strong can, in fact, be a highly effective union organizing style if the organizer, in fact, has the strength to do it. To labor organizers, the middle-class concern to not dominate the fragile esteem of low-income people can seem both paternalistic and counterproductive. Despite various insecurities and feelings of inadequacy, stable working-class people often feel formidable – and are formidable, compared with middle-class people. Not bringing all your strength to the table in organizing them is almost always a mistake. It's insulting if apparent, for one thing. And the problem with most middle-class people in working-class eyes is that they don't know what's up, and you'll just fulfill their inclination to see you as "well-intentioned but not to be relied upon."

Too many middle-class activists have an army model of organizing: a few generals come up with the plan, and the organizers are the sergeants who go out and recruit a lot of privates to follow the plan.
– Penn Loh

Dilemmas of Community Organizers

blw

I wouldn't trade my community organizing experience for the world. Nearly everything I know about poverty and urban politics, I learned from members of groups I staffed. I loved the relationships I built with people on their stoops and around their kitchen tables.

Seeing people move from being less to being more powerful was exhilarating. Here's one story. I was trying to persuade tenants at an apartment complex to come to a City Council hearing. Knocking on doors, I asked one woman,

Donna, to come; she said no, I pleaded. Finally she said she would attend but she absolutely wouldn't say a word because she was terrified of public speaking. She sat at the hearing listening to testimony, until a tenant leader mentioned the lack of sidewalks between their apartment complex and the shopping area. At that point Donna leapt up, saying, "Ooh! I have something to say about that road!" She took the mic and told a hair-raising story about how a car came within an inch of hitting her child while she was trying to get three kids down to the bus stop. The City

Council voted on the spot to appropriate money for a sidewalk – something that wasn't even on their docket of proposals. Last time I visited that city, I walked that sidewalk, grinning the whole way.

And of the five tenant groups I organized, three now own and run their own apartment complexes as permanently affordable housing, so I feel I made a real difference.

But it's a tricky relationship with many pitfalls, the relationship of middle-class organizer to working-class community.

I've encountered groups that seemed to be basically fronts for one staff person, usually a leftist white man. The low-income members were basically his mouthpieces. All their speeches were written by him; he was using their legitimacy as low-income people to spread his ideas. In the power balance between the staff's expertise and the members' knowledge of the community, those groups were way off balance.

I've also seen middle-class organizers romanticize their members. When the draconian welfare reform law passed in 1996, a staff person of a welfare recipients' group said to me, "This will just inspire our members to fight. They're outraged and they're going to rise up." Three months later her organization folded, in part due to precipitously shrinking attendance at meetings.

Grassroots members get crucial information funneled through the organizer, information they need to make decisions. The staff can convey their biases either consciously or unconsciously in how the information is presented. I remember presenting choices to tenant groups about models of tenant buy-outs – decisions that would make all the difference in the future of their homes – and trying not to let my own opinions show. If I had concrete information about why one option would be better for them, that seemed fair to share, but if it was just my own preference, I tried not to betray it. Certainly I didn't always succeed, as my doubts and enthusiasm crept into my tone of voice.

Grassroots groups usually have an open door for new members, and all kinds of people walk in. How to deal with flakes, racists, and people with axes to grind is a sensitive issue. Often the staff plays an informal role in encouraging the people with leadership potential and discouraging the problematic ones. But deciding who is what is a judgment call, and the staff's power in encouraging and discouraging people is unacknowledged and sometimes misused. It's healthier to have the whole group decide on standards of behavior that new members have to agree to. But community people have to go on seeing each other around the neighborhood, and explicit rejections can make things too uncomfortable. It can be easier to have the staff person be the "bad cop."

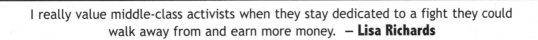

One tenant group elected as treasurer a white woman, "Janet," who I felt was bad news, but of course I had to support whoever the group elected. She seemed to look for every opportunity to set herself above other tenants. One day a nun was making a site visit for a funder. One tenant leader mentioned her neighbor "Mary." Janet exclaimed, "Mary? She's got a colored man living in her apartment!" I was very hopeful that this racist outburst, which jeopardized our funding, would be the last straw that would lead people to choose another treasurer. But to my despair, she was re-elected, and even some tenants of color and tenants who had been in the meeting with the nun voted for her. What could I have done?

Sometimes the first thing an empowered group does is to fire the organizer. Turning brand new empowerment against the nearest target is a time-honored tradition. And sometimes it's appropriate, if there's a real difference of goals or a real problem with a particular organizer. But it doesn't happen only for those reasons. The one time I was dismissed by a tenant group I had organized, their complaint against me was that I had pushed them to open up key decisions to the democratic vote of all the tenants instead of letting the steering committee decide everything. And I know people who dropped out of community organizing entirely after being mistreated by the grassroots people they organized.

In the last decade, more organizations have tried to fill organizing jobs with grassroots people from the same community. This is most feasible for bigger, better-funded groups that can do intensive staff training, so working-class people can develop the needed skills and knowledge. Working-class people from the same or a similar community who've gotten college education and/or other organizational skills and then come back to a community organizing job can be great bridge people.

What middle-class gifts did I bring? In terms of organizing skills and the specific issues I was organizing around, of course all my years of college taught me nothing. Yet my class background did give me things to contribute that were in short supply within the community. Research skills came in very handy, as did knowledge of how the political system worked, computer experience, and project coordination skills. Personal growth workshops had strengthened my traditionally female skills of empathetic active listening and conflict resolution. Speaking the language of management enabled me to be a go-between. Probably the most helpful things I brought were historical images of grassroots uprisings and ideas about diversity. Informed idealism, in short.

Given this idealism, one of the hardest aspects of being an organizer is to realize that we can't make the community be different from what it is. We dream of grassroots people uniting across their differences, envisioning collective solutions to community problems, and rising up to take action for change. But sometimes that's just not where people are. Many factors influence a community's political state. Both objective political and economic obstacles and the hopelessness of internalized classism may not be within our power to change. Sadly, our organizing efforts are not magic.

I really value middle-class activists when they stay dedicated to a fight they could walk away from and earn more money. — **Lisa Richards**

Pooling Our Different Knowledge

Gilda Haas

There are things that I as a middle-class organizer just wouldn't know. For example, my organization, Strategic Action for a Just Economy (SAJE), worked to bring banks back to inner city LA. Folks on welfare were required to pick up their checks at check-cashing storefronts, the kind that take a high percentage to cash your check. We were pushing for direct deposit in banks, but most welfare recipients don't have bank accounts. We negotiated a special welfare-to-work account with Washington Mutual.

We met with the bank to work out the terms of the bank account. The stupidest thing we could have done would be to have *me* be the negotiator, or someone like me. Not only am I middle-class, but I'm really good at keeping up my checkbook, and I don't have any unpaid debts. So I had never heard of ChexSystems. And we could have ended up with accounts that many folks on welfare just couldn't use. ChexSystems is a company with a database of people who got overdrafts or fees and didn't pay them off on time. Even after you paid them off, you'd still be on the database for five years, and if you're on it, you can't open any bank account anywhere.

So we taught the banks to look at *why* people are in the database. For example, did they pay off their debt? On the one hand, there are people who committed intentional fraud, and on the other hand, say if I deposit checks that bounce, and there's a $25 fine on every bounced check, it's not my fault. And say eventually I pay it off and I'm an honest person, should I be unable to open another account?

So we negotiated a bank account available to people who were on ChexSystems lists who hadn't committed fraud. And we negotiated terms that made it easier for people to have a bank account, because it was free, with direct deposit.

It would have been horrible without people from the community at the table. We would have found out about the check system *after* we won the accounts, and the bank would have said no to a lot of people. I had the relation-

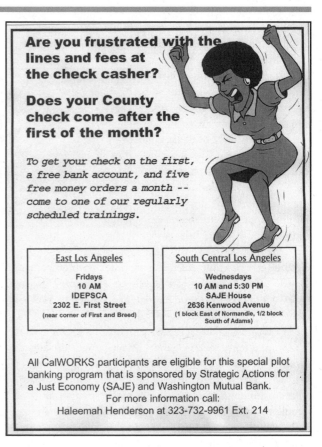

Are you frustrated with the lines and fees at the check casher?

Does your County check come after the first of the month?

To get your check on the first, a free bank account, and five free money orders a month -- come to one of our regularly scheduled trainings.

East Los Angeles	South Central Los Angeles
Fridays	**Wednesdays**
10 AM	**10 AM and 5:30 PM**
IDEPSCA	**SAJE House**
2302 E. First Street	**2636 Kenwood Avenue**
(near corner of First and Breed)	(1 block East of Normandie, 1/2 block South of Adams)

All CalWORKS participants are eligible for this special pilot banking program that is sponsored by Strategic Actions for a Just Economy (SAJE) and Washington Mutual Bank.
For more information call:
Haleemah Henderson at 323-732-9961 Ext. 214

ships to bring the banks to the table, and they knew what they needed. That was a good example of people of different classes working together.

We're not liberal or naive about what kind of knowledge you need to carry out these campaigns, and we're becoming even less naive about how long it takes to develop that knowledge. The college-educated people have one kind of knowledge, and the welfare mothers and tenants have a different kind of knowledge: the knowledge of what's going on in the community and what works in the community. There's the knowledge of experience and the knowledge of technical expertise.

Labor-Community Coalitions

Four Stories
about My Experience
with **Labor** in Coalitions

blw

When I was 23 years old and an activist against nuclear power, I was the mid-Atlantic organizer for the big 1979 No Nukes rally. At the first regional planning meetings, everyone was more or less in the same subculture: they were vegetarian, wore political T-shirts, and used an egalitarian group process.

Then at a meeting in Western Pennsylvania, 50 of these countercultural folks were in the middle of going around and introducing themselves by saying what animal they were most like, when in walks a phalanx of men in brown suits: staff and leadership from the United Mine Workers. When their turn in the go-around came, the highest ranking UMW official stood up and gave a 20-minute speech

on coal miners' support for the antinuclear movement. The others introduced themselves by saying, "I'm with him." Needless to say, they didn't specify any animals.

So I was looking down my agenda, wondering how it should change now that the union guys were here. This meeting had to get certain things done, and suddenly I was uncertain about how to make them happen. We got into small groups; the UMW guys stayed huddled together. The small groups reported back; the UMW guys passed. A spirited discussion broke out about whether to include in the platform opposition to all weapons or just to nuclear weapons; the UMW guys fidgeted. I knew we were not doing a good job including the UMW guys in the meeting, but I was at a loss on what to do.

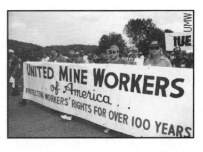

At the break, the three UMW guys approached the tallest and most impressive-looking man in the room and pledged UMW support for the rally. Then they left. And there weren't busloads of coal miners at the rally. An opportunity was missed.

In the mid-1980s, I was active in a coalition against US intervention in Central America. In my naiveté, I thought our coalition included labor. No unions were members, but we had groups with names like the Jewish Labor Guild and Labor Against Intervention. When we asked them how to get union halls for meetings, union funding, or union endorsements, they would laugh and say, "Ya gotta kiss the

Marilyn Humphries

I really value middle-class activists when they are willing
to put in many years to building an organization. **– John Anner**

ring." Calling unions, we reached clerical staff who said they'd pass the message on to the leaders – and no return calls came. I still didn't understand until I actually met with a couple of labor leaders and found out that not only did the presence of the stalwart labor members in our coalition not guarantee us the support of their locals, sometimes it was actually the kiss of death. These stalwart activists were involved in many causes without the approval of their union's leaders, without going through proper channels, and so were considered renegades. They were exactly the wrong emissaries to get us union support. After that I was more careful to learn the ropes before asking unions for support.

In the late 1980s, my job at a Boston feminist organization was to staff a coalition advocating pay equity for women employees of the city and the state. The members of the coalition were the unions representing these workers and women's groups with mostly middle-class memberships.

Our coalition did successfully pressure both the city and the state to raise the pay in some underpaid

Marilyn Humphries

women's occupations. But there were some touchy moments. When the women's group leaders needed to summarize the pay equity issue in catchy ways for a flyer or speech, they tended to say something like this: "A nurse's aide caring for ten patients earns less than a mechanic in charge of three boilers." The unions would object, saying "Are you implying that our guys are overpaid? Or that they

should make it more equitable by bringing the mechanics down?"

The way the feminists stressed the undervaluing of women's work, especially care-taking work, sounded to the union folks like classist put-downs of working-class men's jobs. In our coalition publications, we learned to discuss underpaid female-dominated jobs without putting any men's jobs on the downside of a comparison.

In 1994, when I was offered a job as the director of a human services coalition, I called up a couple of leaders of unions that represented human services direct care workers to ask how the unions regarded the coalition. I didn't want to get stuck leading an organization seen as an enemy of labor. They did have some doubts, mostly about private human service providers who got state contracts as part of a union-busting privatization drive. But they felt that the coalition had brought the two sides together in dialogue and had fairly represented the unionized workers as well as the private agencies. I took the job.

I frequently spoke to the media about welfare rights – and one quote in particular got me in trouble with a union. I was trying to describe the new bureaucratic obstacles put in the way of poor mothers getting welfare, and I said something like, "or maybe a social worker judges her for not trying hard enough to find work." The day that appeared in the paper, I got a call from the president of the union that represented the welfare department social workers, saying that members and staff were boiling with anger at my put-down of them. I had used their occupation as a rhetorical device, not even thinking that I was insulting real, hard-working people. To their credit, they invited me to come meet with them and learn more about social workers and the rules that constrained them on the job. And they forgave me for that blunder and continued to participate in the coalition.

Looking back over these four stories, I see progress both in myself and in unions, which have become a lot more coalition-friendly over the last 25 years.

Compromising
Between **Two Just Causes**

If you're entering a coalition with "old labor" – white male industrial unions – and you have time to read just one book, I recommend you read Fred Rose's Coalitions Across the Class Divide.

Fred was an activist and a researcher in two major attempts to ally labor and middle-class activists. He interviewed bridge people reaching across the deadlock between unions and environmentalists. Here is a quotation from the book about the timber wars between timber workers and old-growth forest advocates in the northwest:

From Washington State to Washington, DC, environmentalists and timber unions battled on the national stage in the 1980s and 1990s. The federal government, it seemed, faced a tragic choice between preserving timber communities and jobs on the one hand and saving spotted owls and old-growth forests on the other ....

Why was the country faced with a choice between two just causes, between the right of people to work and the right to protect the environment? Certainly other choices existed .... many compromises could be reached if both jobs and the environment were the most important policy goals. These measures would have required restrictions on the big timber companies and the redirecting of timber profits, choices that never entered the political debate ....

Fred Rose also worked on "economic conversion" projects that tried to preserve defense workers' jobs while shifting from military to nonmilitary products:

Some peace activists accuse workers at defense plants of promoting war and destruction by participating in military production. They protest at plant gates ... Defense workers, who are proud of their work, often perceive peace activists as insensitive to their economic needs and violent in their intent to destroy good jobs ....

Progressive politics in the United States depends upon reconciling the immediate needs of working people with the social, environmental, and peace-related goals often raised by middle-class movements. Conflicts over these issues have frustrated attempts to build a unified movement for change, dividing people by class, race, gender, nationality, and occupation ....

In the present period, however, coalitions between labor and the peace and environmental movements are on the rise .... Global economic and political changes have made collaboration a necessity .... Attacks on the labor movement coupled with a new generation of union leaders and the declining power of labor are feeding a broad new interest in coalitions among unions.

Sticking Together

Representatives from the Association of Washington Business called a meeting with leaders of the building and metal trades unions in Seattle in 1991 to discuss a business-sponsored bill to weaken the state's growth management law. Management had often relied on the trade unions to oppose limits on construction, and again they argued that the unions shared their interest in passing business's bill. But this time labor was also building an alliance with the environmental community around other issues important to the unions, and they refused to abandon their allies. Instead they argued that controlling growth is a quality of life issue that is important to their members. As a result, labor and environmentalists together defeated the business-sponsored bill.

—Fred Rose

Middle-class activists drive me crazy when they have a sense of entitlement to opinions about people with less privilege, like they get to judge others' motivations. **– Paul Kivel**

Reflections on Group Process Differences

One of Fred Rose's findings is that attitudes towards group process vary dramatically by class. Here are some quotations from activists he interviewed.

Union members working with peace or environmental groups:

"The peace people are too intellectual and always wanting to work on the structure of the organization. I was at a meeting recently where they talked about the structure of committees and subcommittees again. The shipyard could be closed by the time they get the structure together. The union is used to getting down to work and getting things done ...."

"Some of the issue of class is how it colors what you're used to in terms of meetings .... I'm used to Robert's Rules of Order, not consensus. And I prefer those, because if we're making a decision, then I want a decision."

"Labor for the most part belongs to a very formally structured organization in which ... it does matter who does what first and who calls whom first and that you go through the proper channels. We're kind of flying by the seat of our pants, a lot of us [environmentalists]."

"We'd try to get someone from the coalition to talk at the union meeting – well, that's fine, but you can't be at the union meeting. You have to come, say your piece, and then leave before the business starts .... The difference is the adversarial role that you play with the company, and you have to protect that at all costs. The union is quite closed. When it came time to call people to support or whatever, well, it's against union by-laws to give out home phone numbers."

Environmental activists working with unions:

"Labor groups don't process. In environmental groups sometimes you can stop a meeting and process what's going on and talk about different levels of needs and styles. I've never felt that that could happen in this coalition; indeed I thought they'd all spit up if I even suggested it."

Marilyn Humphries

Harvard Union of Clerical and Technical Workers counts its votes

Alliance
for Campus **Living Wage**

The Living Wage Campaign at William & Mary College (W&M) began in 2000. For 18 months, workers, students, and faculty held frequent meetings, pickets, and rallies. Finally W&M's president announced an increase in the campus minimum wage.

At the 2003 Youngstown Working Class Studies conference, James Spady described the campaign and articulated the principles the students tried to follow:

- *Listen and follow what the workers say.*

- *Never do for the workers anything they could and were ready to do for themselves.*

- *Do everything that we could that they couldn't, such as reserve a room.*

Wendy Gonaver was also a founding member of the campaign. She and James are now married. I interviewed them together:

BLW: What was the class and race composition of the campaign?

JS: The graduate students and faculty who started it were all white, mostly from a middle-class background, all active in the Tidewater Labor Support Committee (TLSC). We recruited undergraduate students, mainly middle-class and white, and workers, mostly African American women.

Marilyn Humphries

WG: Our mentor was Edith Heard, a local African American union activist.

JS: I would drop in on her office at least once a week to talk, sometimes help her with grievances, just learning the ropes.

BLW: You mentioned that initiating the Living Wage Campaign was a departure from TLSC's usual mode of following the workers' lead.

JS: Yeah, that's the ironic situation of the campaign's beginning. "Workers organize themselves" was our directive. But despite being sensitive to that, we tried to create a climate whereby if there was anybody interested in such a movement, they would know they had allies.

We slipped flyers under the doors of the housekeeping stations because that was a little more private from supervisors.

At first it was as if they were *our* meetings. The housekeepers would say, "*You all* should do this or that." Our goal was to shift it to an "us." And eventually, we did get to

---

I really value middle-class activists when they don't take space, but create space.
— **Brenda Carter**

that point. One key was the capacity to socialize in a natural way.

We tried to run it by looking for the general sense of the whole room. But it can be hard for academics to keep their mouths shut. We would intentionally attempt to get people to speak who don't normally speak.

It was incredibly informal, which perhaps allowed the academic contingent to lead for longer. But it also created opportunities for employees to take leadership roles. Because two months earlier, they weren't thinking about anything like this, and now they're in the midst of this campaign. There was a tendency to push too hard for too much too soon. But eventually, with some fits and starts, we found natural leaders.

WG: Twenty women came to the first meeting. But at the second and third, 50 people came, purely by word of mouth, workers inviting other workers. And so the meetings were never overwhelmed by students.

We never had written agendas. Someone would pose a question, we would break out into small groups, and one person from each would report back. Students avoided taking that role.

JS: Workers experienced the meetings as liberatory. We academics learned the degree of legitimization that we offered just by showing up. Universities are intensely hierarchical, and the pinnacle of intellectual authority is the faculty. It's empowering to have faculty ask, "What do you

all think we should do?" And if workers tell them, "We think we should do this or that," not only do faculty members agree, they picket with you.

BLW: Were there particularly good bridge people?

WG: We had a petition drive, and the driving force was the housekeepers because they had personal relationships with the students in the dorms they cleaned. That was important in getting 2,600 undergraduate signatures.

BLW: Were there disagreements across class lines?

WG: One maintenance guy was a minister. He had a beautiful voice and could inspire large groups. We instantly glommed onto him. But it was a while before we found out he had a reputation for sexual harassment.

JS: He was in his second citation for sexual harassment of a woman in the campaign!

WG: Because we were coming into their community only during these meetings, we didn't know the gossip.

JS: The housekeepers know each other, maybe carpool with each other, maybe go to the same churches. But in mixed company, they are not going to bad-mouth a co-worker.

BLW: That seems like a product of informal forms of decision-making. If there had been a vote with a secret ballot, he might have been voted down.

JS: He was chosen in an informal way in an open meeting. He spoke at one of the mass meetings, and people responded to him. To us white middle-class outsiders, that looked like legitimization.

Finally someone said to me, "Don't you ever put that guy in another position of authority again." The words she used – "Don't you ever" – spoke to a serious problem with the democratic nature of the group.

BLW: You mentioned the different reactions to the results of the campaign.

JS: The president announced that they were going to raise minimum wages – a very large raise, from $5.87 to $8.50, with benefits for everyone. To us academics, that felt like a serious victory. So it was a surprise when workers said it was not good enough. The money was too little, and it was outrageous that new hires were going to start at the higher rate while current workers' raises would be phased in over ten months.

WG: The workers came up with fun things to shout: "Eight is great, but ten would be better," or "Twelve would be better."

JS: One of the students made up a flyer saying "Living Wage Wins!" and then reproduced thousands of copies, all over campus. It was his individual interpretation of what happened, not using the sort of decision-making the campaign employed.

We had deliberately never defined what a living wage was. A principle of negotiation is never to be the first one to put a number on the table. I didn't want people arguing about a number, whether W&M could afford that much. A living wage is a principle employees can relate to, a way of calling the university to accountability for its workers' poverty.

WG: Most workers and undergraduates stopped coming to meetings. A few academics had started talking about a union membership drive, but it was a top-down thing.

JS: Once the union drive was announced, some of the supervisors began to turn against the campaign for the first time, harassing members, saying we couldn't meet on campus during work hours. Meetings got smaller and then stopped.

The union organizing hasn't gone well, even though we chose a union with a reputation for democracy and great organizers. It's tough in a right-to-work state [one where the minority of workers who don't vote for a union at a certain workplace don't have to be members or pay dues].

We snatched defeat from the jaws of victory. Be careful of what you ask for, because when you get it, it might destroy you.

BLW: *I'm so impressed with all the things you did well, but not talking ahead of time about what victory looks like – what does long-term victory look like, and what might be some small successes along the way – perhaps that hurt your campaign.*

JS: Maybe. What I'm proudest of is that we did this unusual thing, instigating a campaign and then not actually running it ourselves. And that some academics chose not to be overbearing, but to follow what the room decided.

Excerpts from an Interview by James Spady
with Four Living Wage Activists on the Williams and Mary College Housekeeping Staff

(Workers' names have been changed at their request.)

Rose: I think the thing that was the most effective was us doin the rallies ....

Jasmine: One reporter said he could hear it for miles .... The noise level around the college made people notice .... They found out what we were earning, what we want .... We even caught the president's attention and we embarrassed him.

Etta: It didn't really benefit me so hey .... I was out there participating ... got something out of it .... I got 7.62 a hour .... but people who just come in here make 8.50.

If it wasn't for them [students and faculty], we wouldn't a gotten anything anyway.

You need to go by people's years that they been here and give the people the money that they should have. Whether you're a supervisor, whether you a housekeeper, it still don't make no difference.

I think if the people woulda joined forces from the beginning, we coulda gotten what we wanted. More power. More people.

Ever since last summer .... they don't want to talk about it .... "Why don't you stop talkin about it" .... You don't have nobody to back you up any more.

Rose: What's probably gonna have to happen is another meeting, where we can discuss what we're going to do, get it started again .... That's how we got it started before.

Pearl: Once we moved out of living wage it just fell apart .... It became a union .... Well to tell the truth, Jasmine and myself and my group, we the ones that kept it goin. And once it became a union, Jasmine and me we kinda like backed away and then our people backed away ....

Rose: You could still go back to the living wage .... Even 8.50 is not a living wage.

Jasmine: There's so much more fear with the union .... You can't take no more money out of your check.

Etta: First you gotta take care of home .... get home right first. Get the pay right and the working conditions right before you move on to something big .... I think we shoulda kept it the living wage.

I really value middle-class activists when they are conscious of their patterns of communication so that they have a greater capacity to make it safe for people of other backgrounds to participate.
– Ellen Smith

Electoral Politics

Missed Opportunities

at the 2000 Democratic National Convention

When the Democratic National Convention (DNC) came to Los Angeles in 2000, a series of meetings to plan coordinated protests were attended by lots of community organizations and activist groups. Three LA activists describe how the process broke down across class and race lines:

Cameron Levin

Cameron Levin, then with Rise Up and the Direct Action Network:

For me the biggest challenge was bridging the activist world and the community-based non-profit world, because in LA there is a greater divide than in other parts of the country.

The activist groups include leftist, police brutality, globalization, and antiwar groups. Except for the police brutality group, which includes low-income youth of color, most of them are majority middle-class. The community-based organizations (CBOs) who do community organizing on economic issues really have nothing to do with these activist groups. The CBOs have a mixed-class staff, but their members and constituency are 95 percent poor working-class.

The divide is along race lines too. LA is an interesting city because there isn't a large poor or working-class white community. So the activist groups are mostly white and the CBOs are mostly people of color.

Before the Democratic National Convention, the activist groups took the initiative, but we tried to include the CBOs. In the Direct Action Network, most of us had worked for CBOs, so we knew people. I had worked at LAANE (LA Alliance for a New Economy) and two others. We talked with them, and some decided not to get involved with the Democratic convention. But some came to the meetings, including the Bus Riders Union, and we began planning a series of protests, with a different issue on each day. The idea was that we would each support each other's issues.

Woodrow Coleman, Bus Riders Union:

The Bus Riders Union saw marching at the convention as a way to send a message to the Democrats. We had particular demands we wanted from Al Gore. We went to the planning meetings, but in the end we decided not to march with the Direct Action Network. They wanted every demonstration to include direct action. Some of our members, women of color, feared retaliation from the cops. The students would leave town, and we'd still be here. We had a more long-term and strategic view than the young middle-class protestors. They wanted to smash the state, and we wanted to build the movement.

Roxana Tynan, Los Angeles Alliance for a New Economy:

Some of the young middle-class activists from LA were really thoughtful about working with the community. They were as frustrated as we were about the folks from the Bay Area who didn't respect enough the local work that was happening, who saw it as a fun party to show up and run from the cops. One example was protestors from out of town who came and smoked dope in the park – a park where the neighborhood was fighting to get rid of the drug dealers. Cameron Levin was one of the young middle-class activists who worked with us to figure out how to link it all up, how to build each other's power by trying to do things jointly.

LAANE

Roxana Tynan

Cameron Levin:

The breakdown happened at the last minute, when the Bus Riders Union pulled out. It got kind of messy. They had organized their own march, and they asked us not to turn people out for it. The issue was civil disobedience. The activist groups wanted to include a sit-in or other illegal action as part of each day. The CBOs raised the concern that civil disobedience nearby might jeopardize their members of color, who were more subject to police brutality, and especially undocumented immigrants. They pulled out and asked Rise Up/DAN not to mobilize people for it.

In the end, some of the events were done jointly, like the days focused on police brutality and education. Those were issues where the prior links were stronger between the activist groups and the CBOs. But the Bus Riders Union march happened separately. Some of them didn't trust us to keep their members safe.

The police were threatening to crack down and arrest everyone, and TV stations were showing footage of the Seattle protests and saying, "The anarchists are coming." The police chief actually went to community groups and warned them that these out-of-town protestors were coming to cause trouble. This hysteria raised the level of fear and mistrust. There was an us-versus-them mentality, with community groups saying, "This is our home and you don't respect it; we are going to have to live with the consequences."

At the end I started pushing DAN hard to drop civil disobedience connected to any legal demonstrations, to keep the community folks safe and keep our ties with them. It was one of the reasons Rise Up broke up, which was very painful for me. We had envisioned building a community/activist coalition, an ongoing relationship, and that didn't happen.

For me, a white middle-class person, civil disobedience is less risky than for a poor or working-class youth of color. The problem is the lack of awareness by white middle-class people about the different implications of the same action, which leads to an over-reliance on that one strategy. Historically civil disobedience was used as an escalation, not as the first tactic. That's how I see the class difference in using civil disobedience: for poor people it's the last resort, and for some white middle-class leftist activists, risking arrest is the first thing they do.

Community-based organizations also have to worry about their institutional sustainability, their funders, and their membership when they get involved with a movement like the globalization movement. They have to consider the long-term cost of working with ad hoc groups whose nonhierarchical nature can make them less accountable than more formal organizations. If a volunteer activist group falls apart, maybe feelings are hurt, but there are no larger consequences.

BRU

Woodrow Coleman with members of the Bus Riders Union

A coalition between CBOs and activist groups would take a lot of trust. Organizational structure can help provide accountability mechanisms and help build trust. But it's hard to create a coalition structure when some groups have constituencies and formal decision-making methods and other groups are a bunch of individuals, with no geographical or common identity.

Middle-class activists drive me crazy when they think, "We know what's best for workers."
– Dorian Warren

Class Enters the Debate
between the **Dems and the Greens**

blw

At the Presidential debate in Boston in 2000, I witnessed clashes between union Gore supporters and college-educated supporters of the Green Party candidate Ralph Nader. What appeared on TV that night was not either side's point of view, but chaotic scenes of shoving matches and shouting. This conflict exemplified some class differences in political culture and strategy.

The Nader supporters seemed to regard the conflict as a contest over intelligence and being right, and some seemed to feel superior in a blatantly classist way. When a Gore supporter yelled, "Get a job," a Nader supporter yelled back, "Get an IQ!" Some rural Green Party members came across as condescending when they yelled things like "We're your conscience" and "Don't you understand that Gore will send your job abroad?"

The taunts I heard by clean-cut union guys, on the other hand, tended to be about the nontraditional appearance of the Nader supporters: "Cut your hair, you freak!" and "Take a bath!" were depressing throwbacks to the 60s. I engaged one young ironworker in conversation and he said, "You seem okay, but why do all of *them* look so weird?"

The Nader crowd quite proudly displayed multiple causes on their buttons and t-shirts. To these professional middle-class people, activism clearly meant individual expression of their values, and the more diversity of causes, the better. The Gore supporters had only one message: "Vote union, vote Gore," and their matching union caps and shirts made visible their "strength in numbers" unity strategy.

I talked with some of the most hostile people on both sides and found an honest bewilderment at the other group's position. At least eight union members told me, "Nader may be a great guy, but he has zero chance of winning. Why throw away your vote?" I heard from several Nader supporters, "Gore supported NAFTA and the China bill. Why are unions supporting an antilabor candidate?" The middle-class strategy was based on a long-term, big-picture strategy and individual stands of conscience. The working-class position was pragmatic in the shorter term and was based on group solidarity as a tool of power politics.

THE GREEN BLUES

TO VOTE NADER IS TO HUG a Tree!

TO VOTE NADER IS TO HUG a BUSH!!

Save the PLANET

Environmental Justice

blw

For decades most of the environmental movement was made up of elite conservationists and professional middle-class ecology advocates. Then in the 1990s a new phenomenon burst onto the national scene: environmental justice. Coalesced in 1987 by the Reverend Ben Chavis and the United Church of Christ's report *Toxic Wastes and Race*, low-income people of color started organizing against the excessive share of toxic risks sited in their communities. Studies proved that polluters were fined less and cleanup moved more slowly when the health risks endangered mostly people of color.

The movement was expressly led by and for people of color from the beginning, but class only gradually emerged as an explicit issue. Several people have told me stories off the record about the Second Environmental Justice Summit in 2002. There was a major conflict over the decision-making process for the network, over whether each person or each organization would get one vote. Most of the grassroots groups there wanted one vote per group, so that no one group could pack the meeting and no group would be underrepresented if they couldn't afford to send many people. Those holding out for one vote per person

included people in leadership, who tended to be professionals of color, not people personally affected by environmental racism. The grassroots faction won after a messy fight.

Cross-class tensions as well as new collaborations grew between older white middle-class environmental groups and these newer environmental justice organizations. A participant at the first People of Color Environmental Leadership Summit in 1991, Vernice Miller of West Harlem Environmental Action, wrote in *Toxic Struggles* that she remembers "a very tense session with leaders of mainstream environmental organizations." The excerpts on the next pages all point to aspects of the dynamics between middle-class environmental groups and the EJ movement.

Environmental activism grows organically from the life experience of some professional middle-class people:

- outdoor leisure activities and wilderness travel spark our hearts to want environmental protection

- our care for our health makes us seek knowledge of toxins

- the waste from sprawl and car-dependence can become obvious to suburban dwellers

- our habits of abstract macro thinking make it conceivable to take responsibility for vast systems like climate change.

It's not classist to organize primarily middle-class people about these environmental concerns. But we have choices: whether to partner with environmental justice groups and support their work or to act in isolation as if they didn't exist; whether to include the impacts on people of color and low-income people in our materials; how we talk about population growth and immigration in terms that do or don't respect the humanity of the people involved; and whether we make our environmental organizations welcoming and accessible to interested working-class people.

Polluters were fined less and cleanup moved more slowly when the health risks endangered mostly people of color.

Middle-class activists drive me crazy when they impose their worldview on people who don't come from the same situation. — **May Chen**

EJ Voices

Our issues were being defined for us by environmental organizations. They were seeking the solutions for us. They said, "You Indian people should do it this way."

A lot of that became very divisive in our organizations. Especially when our communities don't have the resources and don't have the support ....

So you have one organization come here and they say, "I've got the answer for you," so they get a relationship with one member of our community. Another organization comes over here and develops a relationship with another person in our community. Before you know it, you have about ten different organizations talking to different people in our organization. We end up arguing over which of these organizations has the truth and has the answer to our issues. And that's a set-up.

So that's one of the reasons we organized as the Indigenous Environmental Network. With the foundation that we're recognizing our teachings, that were left with us, and the responsibility that we have as Aboriginals, as Indigenous, as First Nations, as Dakota, as Diné, as Anishinaabe. Whatever. We're doing this ourselves ....

We understood that there was a connection with racism issues but also with poverty issues ....

So down there in our environmental movement, it's not just the environment. We're talking about legal and political issues. Sometimes that's too heavy for environmental organizations and conservation groups. They say, "Whoa, wait a minute. We'll support you on a toxic issue, but we draw the line ...."

Tom Goldtooth

Some of these environmental organizations are worried that we are going to start asking for those land-trust lands back and start putting it back into our control. Nature Conservancy, Sierra Club. We're not only into just protecting these environments in parks, we're also trying to claim some of those lands back.

—Tom Goldtooth, founder and director of the Indigenous Environmental Network, from a speech at the North American Forests Forum, 1996

[The] challenge central to the environmental justice movement is to build solidarity and social capital across a multiracial public. This social capital can take two forms: bonding social capital among those suffering the most environmental negatives and bridging social capital that reaches out for support from other communities. Bonding involves building connections within a community via organizing, a task often facilitated by the immediacy of health issues and by the deep, visceral sense of evident injustice that environmental inequity presents .... [L]awyers can help communities to win injunctions, but it is a mobilized community that will ensure enforcement and thus protect the local environment.

EJ activists have also sought to build bridging social capital, working to help minority communities cultivate powerful allies in other communities. This task is facilitated by the fact that the mainstream environmental movement has made progress in recognizing the importance of environmental inequity. The task is also made easier by the general public's moral sense that the environment is a public good to which communities should have free and relatively equal access.

—Manuel Pastor, "Building Social Capital to Protect Natural Capital: The Quest for Environmental Justice," in *Natural Assets: Democratizing Environmental Ownership*

Different Approaches to
Environmental Advocacy

Penn Loh

The constituency of Alternatives for Community and Environment (ACE) is mostly lower to moderate income, and almost all our campaigns involve building coalitions with other groups. The state-wide advocacy groups with a suburban, higher-income base certainly have a different approach than we do.

Our challenge is keeping our communities driving the agenda and providing the leadership, given that there are very different levels of entitlement. In some groups, they don't have to worry about getting access to their city councilor or state rep; they just call them up. But folks here tend to think that is not possible, sometimes because they are short-changing themselves, but more often because of real life experience. It's not that people haven't tried, but that avenue hasn't worked.

Members of Alternatives for Community and Environment (ACE)

I really value middle-class activists when they are willing to support the leadership of people who have economic disadvantages. — **Paul Kivel**

Given the kind of organization ACE is, we have to be very up-front about the fact that we are working in lower-income communities and communities of color – disenfranchised communities. Our strategies are about empowerment, not just elevating one community over another, but we have to be very clear that we are fighting racism and classism that is out there. Other groups aren't so explicit.

Penn Loh

For example, we've been working with the Massachusetts Public Interest Research Group (MassPIRG) over the last five or seven years on transportation issues. We've had very good ties with their staff, folks who really believe in the work we are doing. In portraying their work to the public, they believe that if you emphasize too much the inequities of race or class, then you are driving a wedge between people you need to build alliances with. So they don't mention that. But for ACE, transportation work has to do with redressing past inequities, making sure we don't have a separate and unequal system with buses for people of color versus subways and commuter rail for white people. The MassPIRG staff understands that, but as an organ-

ization they can't wear it on their sleeve. They have a door-to-door canvass operation in the suburbs. They pitch it as "We need better transit for everybody, and we'll have better air quality." We don't disagree with that, but we have an explicit race and class analysis. Part of our work is educating the broader public about the inequities.

Another example is the groups working on sprawl and "smart growth." The Boston Society of Architects and other groups started something called the Massachusetts Smart Growth Alliance. They invited us to join that alliance, and they were going to raise big money to bring statewide advocacy groups together to work on changing state policy. But we found a lot of clashes from early on. They did a "how we live" project called the Civic Livability Initiative in which they held these charrettes [group discussions], which is what architects and planners do. They produced nice glossy materials. I don't want to denigrate it because I think it was a good conversation to have. But it didn't work for our people. For one thing, they expected people to come to these weekend-long workshops and to pay $50 to do it. We told them we wouldn't make a great effort to get low-income people there. It wasn't just the money, but it wasn't a compelling use of time. Their focus was "Let's think about what we want our communities to look like. How do we want to live?" That question doesn't resonate for people in our communities because it's so far away and impossible. It seems like a waste of their time. They haven't experienced anything that has come out the way they wanted it to. So why create our ideal vision if we have no experience winning anything? Do they have any realistic expectation that it will be achieved? You don't dangle things in front of people with no sense of how you get there.

When we organize, we have to overcome layers of defeatism. When we organized against the subway fare increase the first time, our organizers made bets with people. Of course people agreed that they were getting crappy service because their community doesn't get its fair share of investment, so they opposed the fare increase. But they asked, "What can we do about it?" So we made them a bet, that they would get involved in the group if we actually won something. And we did win a very visible victory: free bus-to-bus transfers. So then we were able to say, "Join us, because we fought this battle before and look at what we've done."

Defending
the Safety Net

The **Welfare Wars** Hit Home

blw

The breakdown in 1996 of a Boston-area welfare rights coalition, the Campaign for *Real* Welfare Reform, was one of the most painful class-based splits I've experienced.

The political context was painful enough, without any conflicts among ourselves. In our supposedly liberal state, public support for minimal cash income for poor single parents evaporated with astonishing speed. I saw a class difference in people's positions. I did dozens of speaking engagements and call-in radio shows about welfare, and while suburbanites tended to nod sympathetically (though apathetically), the hostile callers and audiences, both black and white, tended to have strong working-class accents and stories of neighbors on welfare.

There had been a successful campaign ten years before in which holding out for above-poverty-level welfare grant levels had resulted in a ten percent increase in benefits. So that was the template that welfare rights activists brought to the new fight against time limits and workfare. All

of us, but especially groups run by welfare recipients, held out for the vision of "what single mothers really need," that is, higher welfare benefits, childcare, health care, and job training. But as the threat to the very existence of a welfare entitlement became clear, as not just Republicans and conservatives but also liberal Democrats joined the "welfare reform" bandwagon, as each successive legislative proposal was more draconian, there was a class difference in how groups

responded to the new, more conservative political environment.

To advocacy and social service groups schooled by years of compromising for funders and political realities, it was second nature to support compromise bills, such as exemptions from time limits for domestic violence survivors, students, or homeless women. But to the welfare recipient groups, such compromises meant abandoning some of their members while privileging others. And for mothers who had overcome frequent impossible obstacles – for example, living on $500 a month in a housing market where the cheapest apartment cost $700 and the wait for subsidized housing was five years – the phrase

Middle-class activists drive me crazy when their idea of activism is very government-centered, like, you have to go ask the legislator to do this for you, or lobby for that, and it's not very grassroots.
— **Wendy Gonaver**

"It's impossible to get a better bill" seemed to be something to shrug off. The lifeboats offered by liberal legislators were refused, and the whole ship sank together.

The showdown came after the federal safety net was gone and neither a compromise bill nor an ideal bill was on the table. A welfare recipient group demanded that the advocacy groups promise to always follow the political decisions of the recipient-led groups. To the middle-class-run advocacy groups, this was an impossible demand that ignored the realities of their boards of directors, their funders, and their other campaigns. To the welfare recipient groups, this refusal was betrayal, a sign that they had been sold out. Some even blamed the advocacy groups for the loss of the welfare entitlement. Now, nine years later, the groups that focus entirely on welfare rights are gone or unfunded, and the grassroots groups that focus on multiple issues are still there. I think the hard line of refusing to compromise jeopardized the groups and their constituencies.

Low-income activists were so used to hearing discouraging words from always-constrained advocates and legislators – "There's no money," "We've got to compromise" – that when word of the vicious new political climate came down from the State House lobbyists, they disbelieved it as more of the same. "That was just how those middle-class advocates always talked," one welfare recipient explained to me when we looked back on the rift. Advocates were like the boy who cried wolf, too negative in times when there was progressive potential, and therefore mistrusted when we brought real negative news. The coalition dissolved when the employed pragmatists and the low-income idealists could no longer find common ground.

At other points, being visionary and undeterred by impossibility were gifts from low-income culture that strengthened the welfare rights movement. When hearings were held on Capitol Hill about the Clinton welfare reform bill, none of the national feminist or antipoverty groups organized welfare activists to come testify, saying that they didn't have the resources or that it was hopeless to try to influence Congress. It was a small grassroots group of welfare mothers in Utah, the JEDI Warriors, who contacted all the welfare rights groups in the country and organized caravans and testimony and who were later credited with improving the childcare provisions of the final bill. The low-income women saw the possibilities while the advocates saw the limits.

How Did Welfare Rights Work Fail So Spectacularly in Massachusetts in the mid-1990s?

Paula Georges, from "The Influence of Welfare Coalitions on Massachusetts Welfare Policy," dissertation, University of Massachusetts, Boston

The welfare coalition [the Campaign for *Real* Welfare Reform] did not have strong ties to labor, women, or the black community. Outside resources were critical to the uphill fight, but the magnitude of the onslaught required more than the welfare coalition was able to pull together ....

Labor unions had declined in power over the last decades with membership falling off until they now represent less than 12 percent of the private workforce. Labor still had a strong hold in the public sector, but they were under attack with Republican proposals for privatization.

In addition, with the large increase in labor force participation of women, female public sector workers became unsympathetic to the maternalist legacy of the earlier period and the right of mothers to stay home with their children.

The women's movement, particularly mainstream feminist organizations, turned their attention and put resources into legal and political struggles focused on retaining abortion rights and a women's right to choose. Black Civil Rights groups were trying to hold back the Reagan-Bush assault on affirmative action and other employment related issues in the early 1990s ....

As iterations of each welfare reform bill became more severe and punitive, the advocate partners of the Campaign encouraged [the welfare recipient group] to float winnable compromises at the State House. They were asked to be pragmatic, pursuing a strategy that called for exemptions and exceptions from the time-limits and work requirements for specific categories of recipients.

The bitter conflict over the "principled" versus the "pragmatic" strategy led to the collapse of the Campaign .... The Welfare Rights leadership within the Campaign accused the advocates of betraying bedrock principles while the advocates countered that the leaders denied the reality of national and state politics.

The combination of powerful external factors acting in parallel with the internal factors that limited the welfare coalition's leadership capacity to overcome them led to the loss of entitlement to the safety net for mothers and children in Massachusetts in 1995.

Welfare Mothers
in Conflict with Professional Advocates

Theresa Funiciello

Why do welfare recipients again and again find themselves in situations where people who won't have to live with the consequences are the ones who are defining the situation?

There's no understanding that there's a difference between a caregiver and some guy who just needs a job. Mothers really need income. It's so obvious that what poor people need and want is M-O-N-E-Y. It doesn't take a genius to figure that out. Where was the energetic organizing for more money [as opposed to jobs or in-kind benefits, which most national welfare coalitions advocate]?

All the organizing ignores the child question, except for a few groups who want more childcare. You can't make plans for college or the job market without talking about what happens with the kids. No-one waged the right to care. Welfare mothers feel very deeply about that. All they hear is, "What's wrong with you that you don't want to work for $5 an hour and not care for your children?"

Every organization was trying to get us into some kind of forced work. Trying to get college to count as work [as middle-class advocates have tried

Middle-class activists drive me crazy when they are not conscious of their privilege and the impact that has on how organizations make decisions. — **Jerry Koch-Gonzalez**

to do] is saying to welfare mothers you're not good enough, not worthy of respect as you are.

In the National Welfare Rights Organization, [professionals] decided to organize for jobs and proposed it to the mothers, who said, "No, we are organizing for the right to be who we are and to raise our children best as we can. That's not to say we won't have a job; we have worked, we will work again. But this is NWRO, for the mothering parts of our lives."

What mothers do is work. Wage work is not the only legitimate thing for an adult to do. I've never had a substantial conversation with a welfare mother who disagreed. Some feminists agree, but others don't.

I started by helping people through the maze of welfare, organizing to stop people from being beaten or raped in welfare centers. When I started being hustled by professional welfare organizers, I thought, "Oh, how nice." They helped me raise money at first, but as soon as we did-

n't turn out like they wanted, they cut us off. We won a welfare increase even though the professionals said it was impossible.

Now I'm organizing a Caregivers Credit Campaign to get a refundable tax credit for caregiving. A survey said that 95 percent of all races and classes agree with a refundable tax credit. It would be for caring for elderly or disabled people, not just children, so it's a cross-class and cross-race and cross-gender and cross-age coalition we're building.

Welfare Warriors Bridge **Class Differences**

Claire Cummings interviewed 25 women in 12 grassroots antipoverty and welfare rights organizations for her dissertation "Class Lessons: Women Creating Cross Class Coalitions in a Welfare Rights Movement." Here are some of her observations about the dynamics between middle-class (and sometimes owning-class) and low-income women:

The difference in the material conditions of the women's lives contributes significantly to the ways power is distributed. While the mainly academic and social worker middle-class member allies lead very busy lives with the demands of their professions and their own families, in general they seemed to have more time to devote to the political maneuvering necessary for having control in the group ....

Some of the White middle-class leaders are genuinely loved and respected while others are deeply resented, and some are both loved and resented by the same persons ....

Commonly, groups have factions around support or non-support of the leader and her leadership. These factions often split along the sharp edge of class difference on various issues, with the welfare mothers forming a faction lined up against the middle-class allies.

In most of the organizations, women of color, working-class women, and welfare mothers share a kind of aversion to leadership within the organizations .... [L]ower income women rejected leadership on the grounds of isolation from group solidarity and discomfort with contradictory gender roles that emphasized nurturing. In addition, they often lacked experience operating with power in bureaucracies. They actively supported middle-class women's leadership, and even deferred to it, while at the same time resenting it and complaining privately among themselves that it was classist or elitist.

Often the middle-class women felt they were forced into leadership of the group because of lower income women's deference and reluctance. Some of the middle-class women said they felt "used" and resented being cast into positions of authority ....

The lower income women stick together and present a strong, united front, but are afraid to stand out or above the group and come forward on their own. Sometimes this takes the form of being afraid to compete and confront authority, especially as an individual. On the other hand, low-income women see their middle-class allies, with their more individualistic values, as having a sense of entitlement, but without a strong sense of being able to "walk the walk and talk the talk" of lower-class women or strength in community and consensus building skills .... These criticisms however, are tempered by a deep admiration and respect for their allies' skills and abilities in dealing with and confronting the authority of "the system."

Dottie Stevens

The allies respect and admire the lower income women for the strength of their solidarity and sense of community, but at the same time are critical and impatient with their fear of authority and lack of a sense of entitlement ....

Often in the organizations I studied a tacit agreement is made about the value of keeping the reality of poverty out of sight. Poverty becomes something "out there," something that we write about, talk about, care about, and of course, fight against. But when its victim is sitting right next to you, staring you in the face, it is more comfortable to think of her as your activist peer. While poor women in these groups want to be treated as peers, and are peers, the single strongest message poor women I interviewed want heard is that their middle-class allies have no real idea about what their struggle with poverty is like ....

Poor women come out to get away from their struggles while middle-class allies come out to get involved in 'the struggle'. Poor women say they enjoy the hours of positive support and comfort, of having power and being valued, of learning and sharing with other women something larger than their individual lives ....

Middle-class allies come out to meet needs for making a contribution to the struggle and to be a member of a community with a different, less rigid, and less competitive status system, where they may get more respect than they do from their professional peers. Professional peers often view middle-class allies as involved in a hopeless, unglamorous cause. While some middle-class allies take a lot of flak for their activism, others clearly benefit emotionally and some even gain professionally .... Those in academia and the social work field are professionally trained to separate themselves from their clients and students as a matter of ethics.

Although middle-class women usually have control of the finances, money-handling styles ranged from outright stinginess to large-scale largesse. Even the most generous, non-materialistic middle-class allies could not comprehend or accept the welfare mothers' preoccupation with their need for money. Some middle-class allies viewed this with suspicion, secretly resenting the welfare mothers and at times referring to them as "con artists" ....

Allies quietly contribute money to poor women's needs from their own personal funds on a consistent basis. Welfare mothers and poor women constantly help each other out as well .... One interesting thing I found is that welfare mothers share childcare with each other, but not with allies. Allies push organizations to reimburse welfare mothers for childcare, but in general, they don't offer to do any actual childcare ....

Most of the middle-class allies, whether or not they control [the group's] money, feel that welfare mothers should earn or deserve the monies they receive. This attitude is pervasive among the middle-class allies as well as among many welfare mothers themselves. Giving poor women money "for nothing" is not seen as acceptable yet stands in stark contradiction to welfare rights advocates' consistent criticism of the term "undeserving poor"....

The lower income women reported that middle-class women talked more, demanded more space, more attention, and more control ....

[V]ery few women shared close personal friendships outside the organizations. More specifically, the women seldom invited each other to their parties, vacations, out to lunch, to dinner, or important social gatherings.

[A]llies referred to the welfare mothers as "them" when speaking to each other, and they practiced social distancing outside of the organizations. They could not bear to see or deal with the welfare mothers' poverty situations ....

At the same time that being at the center of poverty is painful, there were benefits in terms of the culture of resistance it creates. In the same way that blindness accentuates hearing, class oppression generates particular strengths ... creating spaces for resistance and in creating alliances in cross-class coalitions for social change. They call themselves "Warriors" and they fight with and for each other against great odds ....

Dottie Stevens

I really value middle-class activists when they could buy their way with their money or education out of the problems most people face, but they stick it out and really work hard. — **Brenda Carter**

Obstacles to Alliances?

Cross-class coalitions founder or fail to materialize for many reasons, but there are some predictable patterns to be aware of:

- Middle-class activists can step on working-class toes.
- Internalized classism can hold working-class activists back.
- Cultural and political differences can drive people apart, and bridging skills are needed, especially when there are socially conservative working-class activists or counterculture middle-class people in the mix.
- Conflict can be based in concrete differences in resources and power.
- Logistical differences can put up invisible walls that keep working-class people out.
- Working-class activists can react to middle-class activists with deep-seated rage and mistrust.
- Middle-class conditioning can make it hard for middle-class allies to build bridges.

While most of this book focuses on the dynamics between middle-class and working-class or low-income activists, this "Obstacles to Allicances" section also includes a chapter about dynamics with owning-class activists.

Classism
from Our Mouths

blw

We've all learned classist prejudices, and none of us has completely eradicated them from our minds.

Few middle-class people would say we have prejudices against working-class or low-income people, of course. Our classism is often disguised in the form of disdain for Southerners or Midwesterners, religious people, patriotic people, employees of big corporations, fat or non-athletic people, straight people with conventional gender presentation (feminine women wearing makeup, tough burly guys), country music fans, or gun users. This disdain shows in our speech.

And we all make mistakes. There's not a middle-class person alive who hasn't said dumb, insensitive things that step on working-class toes. Hiding our classist mistakes or defending ourselves ("I didn't mean it that way") doesn't do any good. The only thing to do is to 'fess up, apologize, laugh at ourselves, and commit to learning how do better in the future.

As we talk, working-class people notice how oblivious or how aware of class issues we seem, and make decisions about how much to collaborate with us based on those evaluations, among other factors. The goal of reducing the classism in our speech is not to keep ourselves out of trouble by avoiding angering working-class people, and it's not to reach some kind of perfect non-classist purity. The goal is to make ourselves more trustworthy and to alienate working-class people less so that we can work together for economic justice and other common goals.

Barbara Ehrenreich on Classism

While ideas about gender, and even race, have moved, however haltingly, in the direction of greater tolerance and inclusivity, ideas about class remain mired in prejudice and mythology. "Enlightened" people, who might flinch at a racial slur, have no trouble listing the character defects of an ill-defined "underclass," defects which routinely include ignorance, promiscuity, and sloth. There is, if anything, even less inhibition about caricaturing the white or "ethnic" working class: Its tastes are "tacky"; its habits unhealthful; and its views are hopelessly bigoted and parochial. These stereotypes are hurtful in many ways, not least because they imply that nothing can be done. Efforts to help the poor would only increase their fecklessness and childlike dependence; and the working class, as stereotyped, would be hostile to such efforts anyway.

—Barbara Ehrenreich, *Fear of Falling*

Top These!
A Few Classist Things I've Said.
(If I can admit mine, you can admit yours.)

- I came back from college and bumped into a working-class guy I'd known in high school. I asked what he was doing. "Bagging groceries at the supermarket." I said, "Oh, is it interesting?" He just looked at me like I was an idiot.

- In college, I was going door-to-door in the dorms signing people up for an Oxfam fast in which we would all skip eating for a day and donate the money for famine relief. One guy said, "No, this isn't for me; I'm working my way through college. This is for people whose parents pay their tuition." I told him, "No, this is for everyone!" I wouldn't take no for an answer. He actually opened a drawer and showed me those little packages of peanut butter crackers he was eating for meals, and still I badgered him to contribute.

- My friend with an Associates degree said, "I am *so* tired of teaching dental hygiene." I said, "Well, why don't you try teaching something else?" She looked at me like I was clueless and said, "Because I don't know anything else."

Middle-class activists drive me crazy when they ask me what my degree is in — not if, but what! You would not believe how often that happens. **— Linda Stout**

What's the Most **Classist** Thing
You've Heard an Activist Say?

Five interviewees' answers to this question — and mine:

Recently I was facilitating a discussion for an organization that was trying to decide how much severance pay to give a staff person leaving because the organization couldn't afford to keep them full-time. Someone said, "Let's give them a huge party and show them we love them, and they'll remember that a lot longer than any money we give them."

—Paul Kivel

Most of the Homeowners Associations wanted in an icky way to "color up" with racial diversity. They were happy to have people of color at the table as long as they were in the minority and didn't get to make any decisions. At one meeting, this one white homeowner was complaining about "why Latinos won't come to our meetings" and she suggested that maybe people should bring their maids! It was too gross!

—Roxana Tynan

There was a fund-raising event that cost $50 and I heard comments about how "anyone can afford that."

—Pam McMichael

Several times I've heard social welfare professionals say about poor mothers, "We have to speak for them because they can't speak for themselves."

—Theresa Funiciello

There was one guy I worked with, he thought he was the smartest organizer, and he would say things to me like "Can you turn out 500 people for this meeting and then we'll go and do the negotiations for them?" He thought of working-class people as props and their voices as sound bites.

I've heard people patronize, tokenize, and fetishize, like "Let's hear from the welfare recipient now! Isn't she smart?"

—Gilda Haas

A new friend said, "My neighbor wanted to put up a 15-foot fence that would block my view. He's real redneck low-life trailer trash." I told her I was offended by that, and we had a big argument that lasted all day.

—blw

Find the Invisible Working-Class People in These Statements

- Women still have to choose between career success and children.

- I bought some land in Vail and built my dream house.

- Everybody got burned in the stock market crash.

- I run an institute at the university.

- When I was a girl, every family had a cook.

—blw

The First Principle of Movement Building

Anyone who steps out of political passivity to give time to any progressive effort deserves to be honored, appreciated, and treated with complete respect. Disagreements, mistakes, and oppressive behavior call for supportive feedback; they are not justification for abandoning a respectful stance. Solidarity is our only strength.

Overlooking Intelligence

As our [peace] group started growing, more college-educated men came in .... I remember feeling that I was slowly becoming invisible. In a discussion about who should be the speakers in community churches .... I volunteered to speak .... Someone said, "Well, you know, I think Ken might be a better person to speak to this group because people will listen to a doctor more." I felt I wanted to crawl inside myself and disappear. Before this incident, I had been afraid to speak but I had thought I had a lot to contribute to the peace movement. Afterwards I thought I had nothing to say that anyone would want to hear.

—Linda Stout,
Bridging the Class Divide

Growing up, I attached "stupid" to workers and "smart" to executives. This didn't happen because of a weird personal quirk. It resulted from force-fed images and words of TV shows, newspapers, magazines, and movies. Any TV show with working-class characters, first *The Honeymooners* and *I Love Lucy*, then *All in the Family*, covertly and overtly highlighted the stupidity of bus drivers, factory workers, and plumbers. Movies, books, and comics followed suit. At school, middle-class kids called us stupid; we hurled back "stuck up," but never "stupid."

—Joanna Kadi,
Thinking Class

Not long ago, I gave a presentation to an environmental group about simplicity study circles, a small-group, peer-led form of education and social change. When I finished, a man spoke up: "Your ideas are all well and good, but most people out there are intellectually challenged!"....

But to believe in democracy, you need to believe in the power of people to find answers to the problems they're facing. You must commit to the idea that people have the wisdom they need. Our job as activists is to help them discover that wisdom.

—Cecile Andrews, "Study Circle Democracy," *Yes! A Journal of Positive Futures*, Winter 2003

Overlooking Necessity

An activist said that he heard other antinuclear activists say, "Construction workers must hate their babies or they wouldn't work in a nuke."

—David Croteau

A peace activist working to turn defense jobs into nonmilitary manufacturing jobs heard someone at a town meeting say to a member of a defense union, "You guys don't deserve a penny." Some in the peace movement argued that the defense workers shouldn't have taken those jobs, saying, "They should have known that it was wrong and they shouldn't have done it, and we don't owe them anything."

—Fred Rose, *Coalitions Across the Class Divide*

Visitors to the Piedmont Peace Project would talk about vacations and sick days, assuming that everyone gets them, which mill workers didn't.

—Linda Stout

I really value middle-class activists when they can recognize the intelligence in people with less formal education than themselves and in very different styles of communication than their own.
– blw

Internalized Classism

For middle-class people, one of the trickiest things about cross-class bridging is dealing with working-class people's internalized classism, the self-limiting beliefs that mirror society's messages. Hard experience of failure, deprivation, and limited options sometimes gets under someone's skin and keeps hopelessness in place longer than is realistic. Other working-class people can seem like the enemy. Internalized racism and sexism can compound the problem, making internalized classism even harder to struggle free from.

Sometimes it seems anything we do to help just makes things worse, since it leaves us in the "one-up" position of the helper. We can make a difference, but mostly in the context of trusting long-term relationships, and in settings with many incremental leadership opportunities. We need both interpersonal skills and unwavering political understandings of where the negative messages come from.

"Why are you so afraid?" my lovers and friends have asked me the many times I have suddenly seemed a stranger, someone who would not speak to them, would not do the things they believed I should do, simple things like applying for a job or a grant or some award they were sure I could acquire easily. Entitlement, I have told them, is a matter of feeling like "we" rather than "they." You think you have a right to things, a place in the world, and it is so intrinsically a part of you that you cannot imagine people like me, people who seem to live in your world, who don't have it. I have explained what I know over and over, in every way I can, but I have never been able to make clear the degree of my fear, the extent to which I feel myself denied: not only that I am queer in a world that hates queers, but that I was born poor into a world that despises the poor.

—Dorothy Allison,
Skin: Talking About Sex, Class and Literature

My dad worked, and still does, for a propane company. I was proud of him (and am today), but it was hard to tell people he delivered gas when I was younger.

I appreciate many working-class parts of my background, like resourcefulness and resilience. But there were also working-class patterns like chaos and always feeling a shortage of time, running around not taking care of myself, not exercising or eating right that can really frustrate me. My mom ran around like that, and I fall into it too. I feel like I'm lacking in some way; I can't hold enough pride.

Sometimes my internalized oppression makes me think I'm not good enough to talk with anyone, no matter how rich, powerful, or different from me.

—Natalie Reteneller

Barry Mandel

In our cross-class dialogue group, a major issue was the ability to dream. If you come from wealth, it doesn't seem so strange to spend $100,000 all at once. If you're coming from a life where $500 is the biggest amount you've ever spent, it's hard to wrap your brain around a big amount like $50,000.

Entitlement, I have told them, is a matter of feeling like "we" rather than "they." You think you have a right to things, a place in the world, and it is so intrinsically a part of you that you cannot imagine people like me, people who seem to live in your world, who don't have it.   —Dorothy Allison

I've always had the idea of starting a training center for social change activists. But I wouldn't know where to begin. I can dream it up, but I can't sell it. I imagine asking my friends for donations, and they could each give $100. I know of a training center started by one person; he just dreamed it up and rolled it out, and I imagine he knew big donors and felt empowered to ask for major support. Without that empowerment and access to resources, nothing happens. If I was more empowered, I could describe an inspiring vision and get people with resources on board.

The value of cross-class groups for me, coming from the lower end, is opening wider the realm of what's possible. Sometimes other people believe more than I do in my dreams, and they may feel moved to support me with resources.

My biggest "aha" on the impact of internalized classism was when Movement for a New Society members pooled their money to pay the whole national Coordinating Committee stipends so they wouldn't have to do other paid work. It was supposed to jump-start the organization with an infusion of leadership energy. But all of us on the committee were from working-class backgrounds, and collectively we had no vision of what was possible. It fell flat on its face. We all had the mindset that every goal was too

The value of cross-class groups for me, coming from the lower end, is opening wider the realm of what's possible.
—Jerry Koch-Gonzalez

hard, that we were unlikely to succeed. We had no clear image of potential success. With a more mixed group with more vision, it might have done better.

I hate it when I tell my troubles to higher-class people and they ask me, "Why don't you just .... " They're coming from a sense of belief and resources. I hear it as "You're not courageous or smart enough – it's obvious what needs to happen here – why are you so committed to being a victim?" It's good to challenge people acting like a victim, but it doesn't work in that tone.

When I counsel mixed-class couples, I see two sides to their dynamics. The person with more money doesn't see their dominance, how their choices affect the couple. They want the less-privileged partner to take charge and ask for what they want. And invariably, the lower-class person isn't stepping up. The door is open and they're not walking through it. The oppression isn't actually happening anymore, but they continue to act like it is.

For example, I'm thinking of one couple that was stuck about money. One had her huge pot of money, and the other had his small pot of money, and they couldn't talk about their budget. The man wanted a computer and couldn't afford it himself. The idea of asking his partner to buy it, which she could have done with no trouble, was humiliating to him. So he didn't ask, and felt resentful. Time went by and they didn't talk about it. The person with the money wasn't paying attention to this dynamic. I asked them, "There's his pot and her pot – what's in 'our pot'?" They realized that there was no reason not to put certain assets into the common pot. One ended up putting in 30 percent, the other 70 percent, and that joint pot paid for the expenses they agreed to.

—Jerry Koch-Gonzalez

Middle-class activists drive me crazy when they act surprised at how hard it is for some people who aren't like them. — **Pam McMichael**

Internalized Classism

and Solidarity across **Race**

blw

The worst fights I've ever seen among activists – with slaps, swearing, changing locks, and coups – have been between low-income white people and low-income people of color in discouraged, low-budget organizations.

I feel like I'm breaking an activists' code of silence by mentioning these fights. Most accounts of grassroots groups seem sugar-coated compared with what I've seen with my own eyes. In that parallel universe, the problems would always stem from the white activists' racism, all the bad behavior would be theirs, perpetuated against innocent victims of color. And a racism workshop would be the solution.

Of course racism is woven through these conflicts, but not always in the straightforward sense that the white activists have prejudices and so mistreat the activists of color.

Low-income activists burn with righteous rage at the unmet human needs in their communities. Some take their frustration out on fellow activists. When conflicts flare up between activists of the same race, social ties are more likely to calm them down. Sharing a church or a friend, or watching the same TV show and thus having something to joke about, can pull people back from the brink of unforgivable behavior.

Middle-class and employed working-class activists turn against each other too, but have more comfortable places to retreat to that soften the raw edges of conflict: their jobs, their homes, other groups. Linda Stout says she has a photo over her desk of a nest with one egg in it and the words

Most accounts of grassroots groups seem sugar-coated compared with what I've seen with my own eyes.

Low-income activists burn with righteous rage at the unmet human needs in their communities.

"Sometimes you *have* to put all your eggs in one basket." Low-income activists often have enormous investment in a grassroots group: it can serve as workplace, creative outlet, social network – sometimes home and family. When I was on the board of a low-income group, at one point three board members were homeless and sleeping in the office. Some unemployed members spent all day there. In tenant groups I organized, some unemployed leaders belonged to literally nothing else. Advantages that might seem small to an outsider – the right to photocopy, a trip to a conference, a committee slot – were sometimes contested ferociously.

I don't think most middle-class people can imagine an organization becoming that all-encompassing. Even if we had little else in our lives at a particular moment, there would be other imaginary options in our minds. There's a desperation to conflicts within low-income organizations that I doubt middle-class people or stable working-class people are likely to feel.

To resolve racial conflicts would mean first dealing with the shortage of resources for grassroots organizations as well as for their low-income members in crisis. Expressions of respect and appreciation would have to become much more common, from funders and local government, between the staff and board, among volunteers. When both material needs and needs for recognition are minimally met, then prejudice reduction training would stand a better chance of succeeding.

Watching those fights helplessly, I longed to see more working-class solidarity, an all-for-one-and-one-for-all attitude that says, "These are low-income people like me, so everyone better treat them with respect." I see the absence of that ethic as internalized classism – turning society's disrespect for you against others in your class. Successful bridging across race will happen among low-income people to the extent that internalized classism is replaced with working-class solidarity.

Digging out of Internalized Classism
in the Face of **Overt Classism**

"Ellen Smith"
[name changed at her request]

When I tell my story, I start by saying that I was a really smart kid. My mom was a single working parent who was never home. She did her best. I went to nine schools in ten years. I just slipped through the cracks.

The summer before 10th grade, I left home with a 21-year-old family friend. He introduced me to drugs, and it quickly became a big problem. Luckily, when I got pregnant, I stopped using. I went on welfare. After almost two years on welfare, my caseworker gave me the number of a dental office and said, "You need to do an internship, or your food stamps will get cut off." After my internship they hired me, and I ended up working there for eight years.

The job changed my outlook because it made me realize that I had potential. Up until that point I didn't have a vision of anything better. My

> *The job changed my outlook because it made me realize that I had potential. Up until that point I didn't have a vision of anything better.*
> —"Ellen Smith"

mom hadn't had anything better. No one I knew did. It was hard to imagine being independent of my husband, but at the same time extremely dangerous to stay with him. He made all the decisions. He checked the mileage on my car to see if I had gone an extra three blocks. He insisted that I sign my payroll checks over to him and offered me an "allowance." He paid all of the bills and wouldn't allow me to put anything in my name. I left him when I was 21. It was finally too much

to wonder when he would lose control and kill me.

When I enrolled my daughter in the neighborhood school for kindergarten, it happened to be a special focus school and had many privileged people in the community. I heard about parent meetings but didn't go. It seemed overwhelming, like all the parents were wealthy and smarter than me. I didn't see a place for me as a parent in that school. I felt angry and isolated.

Then someone who knew I was involved with a woman invited me to a queer parents' potluck. There was a

---

I really value middle-class activists when they can hear my experiences and learn something and change, and then give me credit. **– Lisa Richards**

referendum to prohibit gay and lesbian issues in schools. The measure failed, just barely. So then my participation in parents meetings increased because I had seen the success of sharing our stories. I became the representative from my school to a local community organization that empowered parent leadership in about ten schools.

Without notice about a year later I had to move because of death threats from my very violent ex-husband. I took my daughter out of her school, and her next school was in an area of high poverty. I was shocked. All the schools are supposed to be the same, but they're not. Kids were being asked to bring toilet paper as part of their school supplies at this new school. That's how bad it was. I begged and pleaded and through a lengthy application process, eventually got her back into the original school the following year. This meant we

I see such a difference between privileged communities and low-income communities. Parents with power feel worthy of calling decision makers and saying "I need an appointment."

—"Ellen Smith"

commuted by bus one hour each way, every day, but it was worth it.

The attitude of parents in privileged communities can be "If parents want something, they should get off their butts and do it." My daughter's school was able to raise over $150,000

Marilyn Humphries

for a covered playground recently. Most school communities simply cannot do that. So that's why I'm passionate about it now, because I see that equity is not practiced in education.

At the school in a high-poverty neighborhood, I was seen as a leader. The move made me realize that I hadn't been seen as a leader before, and I had rarely spoken up before either. Some of my holding back was just perception. I thought that they were all smarter and would never listen to me. After going through leadership trainings, I am now more comfortable.

I see such a difference between privileged communities and low-income communities. Parents with power feel worthy of calling decision makers and saying, "I need an appointment." Our leadership training includes understanding the dynamics of power: who holds it and

how to get to the table where decisions are made.

I brought up the idea of evening meetings because I, for example, work 7AM to 6 PM and couldn't make their 5:30 meetings. At one meeting I said, "Parents who can't be in the building feel left out. I'm glad you stay-at-home moms can put in lots of hours, but it feels like you don't want to accommodate other parents." One mother said, "I'm so sick of this. I volunteered 30 hours in that school last week, and if you want something done, then you come do it." I thought, "Exactly. I don't need to say anything. You just made my point." She had such a chip on her shoulder and was angry at me because I physically could not be there. Working parents deserve to be valued too.

The other schools don't have so many super-active parents. I met with a principal to talk about parent involvement once, and he said, "Well, our parents can't be like the parents in other schools. We make these decisions for them because they are not in a position to speak for themselves." I was blown away by his idea that parents are not capable of making positive decisions.

So I'm invested in parents realizing their potential to make the school what they want. Community organizations can help them do it. Our organizational model is to empower and mentor parents. For example, one apartment complex was 9/10ths of a mile from the school, and the policy was that students could only ride the bus if they lived over a mile away from school. The kids were taking the bus, but then someone found out they were too close and kicked them off. So 30 Latino families were now walking on unsafe roads. One mom went with someone from our organization to the administrator's office and said, "Will you walk that route with me?" The administrator said, "Are you kidding? It's cold and raining out there." They got their kids back on the bus with good negotiation and organizing. Not only that, they had a safer stop added to the route. Parents made this happen, but with the help of a community organization that could support them as leaders.

Personal stories are a big piece of how we empower people. More powerful people get impatient with that. But if you are going to involve people, then you need to be patient enough to know where they are coming from. That's why our model starts with "relational meetings" [one-to-one discussions based on personal experience]. They come out of these meetings amazed at what the other person is dealing with. Parents who don't have to worry about transportation or lunch money see a real human and get friendlier. I get hellos in the hallway now. And because people recognize me, I feel like I have a role in the school.

I think middle-class people are uncomfortable hearing my story. When I talk about dropping out, teenage pregnancy, drug addiction, and a crazy husband, they are thinking, "Whoa! I don't know what to say." To be an ally, someone has to be willing to hear these social issues.

When I was being mentored for leadership roles, it happened slowly at first. When I talk about patience, that's what I mean. You have to build a relationship; otherwise, people are just too scared.

I want parents to understand that if enough of us speak up, people in power have to listen. They can't ignore it if it happens in a critical mass. Everybody has to be brave enough to tell their story.

And that's when people realize they are not so isolated. Even in that basic step, they are networking and getting support. When I tell people about the pressures in my life, people start saying, "What can I do to make it easier for you?" Until you tell your story, nobody knows.

And it needs to emerge within yourself that your story matters and that you have a contribution to make.

When I was in poverty day in and day out, I often heard people say things like, "Just pull yourself up by your bootstraps." It's such a ridiculous image – if you actually lean down and pull on your bootstraps, nothing happens. It often leads to more frustration if the boot simply doesn't fit or the straps were weak in the first place. We need to remember what that struggle is like for people.

I believed I was less worthy than other people because I wasn't able to decide, "I'm going to get a job, leave this asshole, and find a new life." It didn't seem possible, but I still felt like it was my fault. It's not possible for a lot of people because of the way our society is set up. The people in power need to understand what that life is like. I want everyone to imagine how alone you really feel until a connection is made and you realize that your story is not unique.

For example, even after having a decent job for seven years, I was still spending 50 percent of my income on housing. Before, I was always looking at my budget thinking, "Why can't I just catch up?" I was buying groceries on my credit card because I spent all my money on rent. There's nothing that you can do until you realize the problem is not unique to you. I now realize that there are thousands of others in the same position. So instead of feeling ashamed, I am angry. You have to find some outlet to take action collectively.

When I was in poverty day in and day out, I often heard people say things like, "Just pull yourself up by your bootstraps." It's such a ridiculous image – if you actually lean down and pull on your bootstraps, nothing happens.

—"Ellen Smith"

I really value white middle-class activists when they acknowledge what they don't know. It's endearing to hear "I don't know what you're talking about, but I would love to find out. Can you help me?" – **Barbara Smith**

Working with Socially Conservative,
Economically Progressive People

blw

The stereotype that working-class and low-income people (especially white people) are all right-wing on social issues is harmful because it masks the real diversity of opinions. No middle-class activist should be surprised to meet impoverished socialists or blue-collar pro-choice advocates. (See the "Occupation, Not Income" box below for polling data about this.)

Occupation, Not Income, Correlates with Politics

[Cornell] Professor [David B.] Grusky and Kim Weeden, an assistant professor of sociology at Cornell, turned to 30 years of data collected by the federal government and the National Opinion Research Center, affiliated with the University of Chicago. Together, the two surveys contained information on a representative group of about 760,000 Americans, from their political attitudes to their reading and television habits.

The professors concluded that lumping people into big groups like the "working" or "middle" class on the basis of their incomes ultimately had little to do with what they bought, what they watched, or whom they voted for. Rather, cultural and political similarities are more likely to be found among people who are in the same profession or do the same type of work, reinforced first by educational training and then by work experiences.

Sociologists, for instance, are mostly politically liberal while economists are mostly conservative, they said.

Even big occupation groupings can hide differences, Professor Grusky said. Consider an issue like abortion. Among service workers, bartenders tended to support legalized abortion while cooks and cleaners tended to oppose it.

—Felicia Lee, "Does Class Count in Today's Land of Opportunity?", *New York Times*, January 18, 2003

But when millions of people are surveyed, there is an actual correlation between opinions and class. On economic issues, people with less class privilege tend on average to be more progressive. On foreign policy and on social issues such as abortion, gender roles, gay rights, sex education, gun control, prayer in schools, and the role of religion in government, people with more formal education and higher incomes tend to be more liberal.

Americans who are progressive on economic issues but more conservative on social and military issues tend to include Catholics; white rural low-income people; Latinos and recent immigrants from conservative areas; and senior citizens of all races. (See the "Political Polling of Latinos" box on p. 99 for data about this.)

Those who are conservative on economic issues and liberal on social issues tend to include WASPs, white middle-class suburban dwellers, yuppies, and a significant minority of upper-middle-class African Americans and Jews.

This difference is slowly eroding as young working-class people ditch the conservatism of their elders and as more middle-class and owning-class people take up economic justice causes. But there's still enough of a correlation to affect national politics. And there's still enough of a correlation to create tension in some coalitions.

When I was an organizer of low-income and working-class tenants, social and moral issues sometimes seemed like a minefield. Some tenants with previous activist experience had gotten it in anti-abortion groups. Others were pro-choice. Coming out as a lesbian to tenant leaders was scary. I got some warm and friendly reactions. But I also got some unfriendly reactions – from white and black tenants, young and old – including one from a previously active member who dropped out of the group and never spoke to me again. Tensions arose sometimes between Christian tenants who saw sex as sin and others who saw it as a good time. And it was sometimes touchy to try to empower women when that might mean disrupting traditional family gender roles.

It's a core competency of a middle-class alliance builder to have respectful conversations with socially conservative people about areas of disagreement. Another essential skill is to be able to build a coalition on economic issues that includes people with different viewpoints on social issues.

Ellen Shub

Working-Class Left-Wing Tendencies

[L]eft-wing tendencies as defined by working-class people ... differ from the middle-class white left wing with its pro-peace, pro-disarmament, anti-gun stance that is for the most part neutral towards capitalism, that favors feminism in which the women gain footholds in "respectable," middle-class professions, that holds a romanticized view of Mother Earth, and that encourages sensitivity among (middle-class) men. This analysis, while progressive and useful in some ways, is a class-bound ideology lacking an understanding not only of class issues but of race.

Left-wing tendencies among working-class people differ markedly. The antiwar and anti-military position is usually absent because the military provides benefits and job security. Added to the pro-military position is a strong anti-police and anti-government sentiment. A critique of the capitalist system runs through this ideology.

—Joanna Kadi, *Thinking Class*

Political Polling of Latinos

According to the survey data [Pew and Kaiser polls in 2003], Latinos are, in fact, more conservative than whites on social issues such as divorce, homosexuality, abortion, and extramarital sex. But they're not much more socially conservative than blacks (in fact, less so on some issues) ....

Latino voters [are] only half as likely as white voters to mention moral values and abortion as voting issues. Indeed, by a wide margin, Latinos' top three voting issues are education, the economy, and Social Security — three issues that have little to do with social conservatism. Moreover, Latinos, in contrast to both whites and blacks, declare themselves willing to pay higher taxes to support a larger government that provides more services (55 percent) rather than to pay lower taxes for a smaller government with fewer services (38 percent). So Latinos not only lean strongly Democratic, they say they're even willing to pay for the services they expect Democrats in government to provide!

—Ruy Teixeira, *Public Opinion Watch*, June 16-22, 2003

I really value middle-class activists when they are conscious of their class identity.
– Ellen Smith

Unequal Control over
Information and Money

The point of cross-class work is not so much how people can be nice to each other in the same room, but how people can share economic resources across class. Just changing interpersonal relationships doesn't challenge organizational practices.

I know that there are some organizations – like *Bridges*, the Jewish feminist magazine – that have explicitly tried to share resources and develop policies on contributions and compensations of time and money that take into account people's economic situations.

The class dynamics I see are when more privileged people come into a low-income community with an agenda of what's the issue and where the money will go. Whether it's AIDS prevention or domestic violence, outsiders are making the decisions. I know organizations that have done a lot to circumvent that and keep class on the table. There's a housing program, Berkeley Oakland Support Services, which has hired homeless people to run the shelters. The woman who runs that group moves comfortably across classes and keeps people's attention on empowerment of the local community.

—Paul Kivel

Paul Kivel

Power differences are most dramatic when the middle-class people in a coalition represent huge, wealthy institutions, as these next two stories show:

Research or Results?
Sam Grant

In 1988, I worked on lead abatement with a group of residents of the Phillips neighborhood in south Minneapolis, which had the highest lead levels of any part of the city. Back then the lead laws weren't as rigid, and landlords could paint over lead paint in most cases. We met with our state representative and folks from the university. Right from the beginning, there was tension about priorities. Neighborhood residents wanted to get the lead out of the housing while the university wanted to do research to test the effectiveness of a lead education intervention. They wanted to do a study where some people are a control group and don't get any information about the fact that their children are going to be poisoned. And others would

get information, to see what difference the information would make in reducing lead poisoning. Their goal was to test the efficacy of this public education model. What they would not pay attention to was the lifelong consequences of lead poisoning for those who did not benefit from their study.

The university raised about $2.5 million for their study, and the question asked by residents was, "What do we get out of this?" Given the cost of lead abatement – $8000 to $10,000 a unit at that time – some residents argued that instead of doing this study, we should do full lead abatement for 250 homes. Residents advocating lead abatement were not able to raise resources to do it, while the funded lead education study proceeded. As a carrot to win the participation of residents in the lead education study, the university proposed to include training and skill-building opportunities for residents – which were expected to increase their economic opportunities.

When it became clear to me that we were going to do lead education but we weren't going to resolve the problem, I walked out of the group. And I went home, and I tried to figure out how this happened. I call it a situation of class, manifested through serious institutional privilege, in a political climate that does not include the poor in decision-making. When a major institution works with low-income people, they have a very substantive amount of hidden power. The money went back into the university. It helped the university bring more white, soon-to-be medical professionals into the community to get field experience. What did it leave the community? A few people got some certificates and some travel, and a few people got some education. It wasn't the worst fiasco in medical science history, not like the [Tuskegee] syphilis experiments. But it reminded me of that.

Community Control, Community Roles
Attieno Davis

In the 1990s, a number of people in the [Boston] community were taking up the issue of asthma. The environmental justice group ACE [Alternative for Community and Environment], some housing groups, a neighborhood health clinic, and a lot of community people of color were all looking at why so many more people had asthma, especially colored youth. I got involved as an organizer for the Boston Health Access Project

Marilyn Humphries

of Health Care for All. Tenants organized by the Committee for Boston Public Housing were also meeting regularly around asthma. And these various projects actually mobilized people in the community.

We linked asthma to the use of neighborhoods of color as dumping grounds for toxics. And we looked at the lack of inspection of buildings for mold and dust mites.

The Boston Medical Center was involved, which added some oomph because they had lawyers to challenge landlords on tenant rights, that kind of thing. And the Boston Public Health Commission got involved in defining asthma as part of public health. And behind those organiza-

tions were the universities: the Harvard, Boston University, and Tufts schools of public health.

And what happened was particularly painful. Federal money started to be available. A decision was made to pull together all the groups working on asthma into one coalition, the Urban Asthma Coalition. And there was jockeying around who was in control. We organizers started pulling together community people to talk about the possibility of this money and what it could be used for. And before we knew it, we realized that the Boston Public Health Commission (BPHC) was already applying for the money. So our discussion meeting turns into a meeting to pressure the BPHC to let us in. We told them, "You can't just come in and write up this grant without community involvement."

And out of that grant came something called Healthy Homes. Every agency got a little piece of money to do this or that. But the community piece, with meetings about what was needed to take out asthma and tenants actually fighting with landlords about better housing, that's all gone. The Urban Asthma Coalition has one organizer, and none of the other groups have asthma organizers any more. If the community groups with a more independent stance, like ACE and City Life/Vida Urbana, had been more in control, I feel it would have been different.

Those more connected with city agencies stuck with the agenda set by the city. That agenda included trying to reduce the cost of emergency room visits due to asthma. The issue got narrowed down and quieted down.

The domination of the big institutions meant the activism petered out. For example, the Committee for Boston Public Housing had done a research project on asthma with the BU School of Public Health, and they used community health advocates trained from each housing development. People became lobbyists, they became peer educators in their own community, and they gained expertise – but no more.

I really value middle-class activists when they know how to step back and support emerging leadership. – **Brenda Carter**

Marilyn Humphries

ACE had youth who measured air quality, and they wrote a little book documenting what they learned, and they started putting out daily air quality flags from the window of ACE's office, until the landlord stopped them. And they started challenging the Transit Authority about letting diesel buses idle. Now look at all the things those kids participated in: they did research, they organized and led demonstrations, they made presentations to the community.

As opposed to what happens now with Boston University, where health advocates go to people's homes and help them figure out if their kids have asthma and teach them to measure what the kid is reacting to. It's an important piece, but why were community people reduced to just that role? It's racist and classist when your role is reduced down to just being the subject. The loss of the movement reduced the roles, took out the creativity, and took out the social justice, antiracist frame and made it just a health issue: "We're dealing with this, so you don't have to worry about it anymore."

So there was a struggle across race and class lines over balancing whose interest would remain at the center, and it actually changed the course of the alliance.

Clarity about Coalition Ground Rules
Penn Loh

ACE (Alternatives for Community and Environment) has never lost control of a coalition. We've never been on the short end of the stick. We make it very clear in ground rules from the beginning that this is a community-led campaign. We ask partner groups to sign on to a position statement.

For example, the campaign against the bio-terror lab [proposed to be sited in Roxbury, MA]. Lots of antiwar folks from the well-off suburbs have gotten involved, such as United for Justice and Peace. We asked them to acknowledge ACE's leadership and to include economic gentrification as well as the health and safety risks. And another ground rule concerns funding: if any of the groups in the coalition seek funding on this issue, they have to coordinate with the others. We're not getting into a situation where a group with the ability to raise more funds gets funding without sharing in a joint manner that lifts all the partners.

Working-Class
Rage and Mistrust

Listening to Rage and Mistrust

blw

Hearing the rage and mistrust of working-class people – it goes with the territory of doing cross-class social change work. In my mind I understand that, but in practice it's been painful.

When I was a tenant organizer knocking on doors, most people met me with distrust, assuming I was more likely to threaten them in some way than to help them. Some figured I might be a bill collector, parole officer, truant officer, child welfare worker, or building management. Others recognized that I was an earnest do-gooder, but they didn't have good associations with earnest do-gooders.

Rage is even more difficult to hear. We middle-class Anglo women in particular tend to have been raised as hot-house flowers, with norms of politeness and feelings that are easily hurt. The first few times working-class people yelled at me or accused me of being classist, or people of color angrily accused me of being racist, I felt devastated, defensive, and critical of the messy or inaccurate way they communicated. I still have those feelings, but I've toughened up. If I hadn't had middle-class caucuses and supportive middle-class friends to turn to, I wouldn't have lasted long in the movement.

Here's one situation when low-income people yelled at me. Once when I was on the board of a low-income group, I was one of only three out of 15 board members who had been to college. A foundation had just awarded a grant big enough for a full-time position. Because there had been fights in the past over which members got stipends and grant-funded positions, usually divvied up informally, the board decided to create a hiring committee and take applications more formally. Two of the three hiring committee members were college graduates. The two finalists for the job were both white women, one a beloved insider member, the other an outside college-educated candidate. The hiring committee chose the outside candidate for reasons that seemed solid to us, like better people skills and more experience with antiracism and community organizing. We told the candidates our decision. That evening I walked into a kitchen full of low-income board members, friends of the rejected woman, who were fuming about the decision. They all started yelling at me at once, saying that I had no loyalty to longtime members, that I'd betrayed the organization, that they never should have let middle-class people into the organization in the first place. It was really hard to hear.

I feel okay about how I handled the situation. I sat and listened for two hours. One guy started swearing and insulting me, and I said it wasn't okay with me to be abused, and he

The first few times working-class people yelled at me or accused me of being classist, or people of color angrily accused me of being racist, I felt devastated, defensive, and critical of the messy or inaccurate way they communicated.

Middle-class activists drive me crazy when they think the only problem is that people are not voting.
– Penn Loh

backed off. I couldn't really process their words or my reactions, so I filed them away in my mind to think about later.

Over the following months and years I thought a lot about insider and outsider hiring, formal and informal hiring processes, and the pros and cons of each. I did start to see some strengths of informal decisions and insider hires; previously I had only seen the positive side of formal, criteria-based hiring. I learned about the centrality of personal loyalty in working-class culture and about the centrality of "objective" standards and rules in professional middle-class culture. The full board did ultimately ratify our initial hiring choice. So it was a learning experience.

But the hard feelings between me and those low-income board members never completely dissolved. One was my friend, and we were less close after that day. Others remained wary around me. I never again felt safe with the guy who swore at me. The incident highlighted our class differences and drove a wedge between us.

I learned about the centrality of personal loyalty in working-class culture and about the centrality of "objective" standards and rules in professional middle-class culture.

What to do
when a working-class person is raging at you:

- Listen.
- Hold an attitude of caring and learning.
- Don't assume it's about you. There may be years of built-up rage in what you're hearing.
- Don't assume it's not about you. Stay open to challenges to your attitudes and behavior.
- Don't let the style of the delivery stop you from hearing the message.
- Apologize if you see something you did wrong.
- Agree if you hear something that rings true.
- Empathize with the pain.
- Clarify your side of the story, but not necessarily immediately. Some activists would advise never arguing back. I think such passivity is condescending and lacking in respect both for your own thinking and for the other person's ability to see reason. However, clarifying your side of the story will only help if the person is calm enough to hear you. Consider waiting to put out your point of view later (unless there's an obvious factual clarification that might clear things up immediately).

- Don't let yourself be abused. Be clear about your bottom line on how you're willing to be treated (for example, no sexual insults) and object firmly if it's violated. Walk out if it's violated repeatedly or if you feel in danger.
- Afterwards, get support from someone you trust (ideally someone not connected to the situation) to listen to your feelings. Don't try to make your feelings conform to what you think you *should* feel. Don't try to figure out or solve the situation right away. Give yourself time to recover first.
- Don't drop out of the group, and don't avoid the person. Make contact later, reflect back what you heard, and ask to talk about it more. Put forward your version of the story with confident humility and openness: "Here's how I saw it. How did you see it?"
- Investigate whether there's something oppressive in the current situation, and if so, work to change it.
- Stay engaged. Keep listening, caring, and learning.

The Deep Roots of **Mistrust**

In The Tyranny of Kindness, *Theresa Funiciello tells story after story of social service providers and anti-poverty activists taking control away from low-income women and making things worse for them. Middle-class activists bewildered by the degree of mistrust they encounter in working-class and poor communities would do well to read her story of how she started out trusting "do-gooders" to do good, felt repeatedly burned, and ended up mistrustful. When I interviewed her, she was even more blunt:*

Poor people usually can't win in coalitions. We've been colonized, and the colonizers are not the "bad guys" [i.e., not officials, but advocates]. Cross-class coalitions mean using low-income people for the ends of the middle-class people. It never works unless it starts with a goal that cannot bypass poor folks. It's the big tent theory. Go for something everyone stands to gain from and don't kid yourself.

Never in my history has there been a movement that actually benefited poor people. The movement against redlining screwed poor people by bringing gentrification. I suppose you could say that the Civil Rights and women's lib movements of the 60s and 70s were cross-class and had extraordinary levels of success. However, neither poor blacks and other minorities nor poor women of all races/ethnicities benefited where it counts most: in the pocket book or at the theoretical level to change the way most non-poor people think about poor ones. Neither of these mainstream movements ever seriously addressed poverty per se. What that says to me is that they never really set out to include poor people either in the strategy or the organizing phases. They didn't know how, no-one put in the effort to be more than token-inclusive, etc.

Though poor women were token-courted by the mainstream women's movement also, it was never to the former's benefit.

It is possible for things to be done together to benefit all, but it only works if you're cautious, have your antennae up very high to see if you're being manipulated to betray the people you're organizing.

Theresa Funiciello

Never in my history has there been a movement that actually benefited poor people. The movement against redlining screwed poor people by bringing gentrification. What that says to me is that they never really set out to include poor people either in the strategy or the organizing phases.

—Theresa Funiciello

Middle-class activists drive me crazy when they think they "get it," and then retreat to the comforts of their home when the going gets tough. **—Susan Remmers**

Counterculture
Lifestyle Clashes

Not all middle-class activists make counterculture lifestyle choices, but the majority of countercultural people are either middle-class or owning-class.

To eat vegetarian or organic, to prefer natural fiber clothes, to watch no TV, to not smoke — these are not in themselves signs of classism. But if you think these choices make you better than someone else, the odds are that there's classism in your superior attitude. And using our influence to push our lifestyle choices onto uninterested working-class people is a misuse of class privilege.

It used to make me laugh to see the clothing at these Boston coalition meetings. The low-income women on welfare would turn out dressed as if they were going to the Sunday social, and all these middle-class activists from Harvard and Boston College would turn out in Salvation Army clothes, having invested very little in personal hygiene products. That's something that used to annoy me about middle-class folks, who dressed down because they didn't want anybody to think they were rich, while the poor folks dressed up because they wanted to be taken seriously.

—John Anner

Some people, in their attempts to be anti-establishment, pay little or no attention to personal grooming, not washing on a regular basis, not using deodorant. I find this highly offensive.

It first came to our attention during organizing around the Amadou Diallo trial, which was moved from New York City to Albany to escape protest, but we made sure there was protest. My friend, who was the point person for

Ellen Shub

Diallo organizing, said, "I just can't stand it when younger people don't wash, it's just so unpleasant to be in a closed space with them."

We organized buses from Albany to the April 20 anti-war rally in Washington. A Puerto Rican sister in Stand for Peace said, "My husband won't ride those buses because he can't stand the smell." That doesn't help the cause, when a family of color won't take the bus because some people are so committed to not washing.

I think it's an act of hostility to be unpleasant to be around on a physical level if one can make a choice about personal hygiene. I don't believe that soap or deodorant is a capitalist plot.

I find it insulting that they think the way to be down with the people is not to take care of personal hygiene. It's an old and inaccurate stereotype that Black people are dirty. My aunt and my grandmother raised us not to leave the house without looking impeccable. They made their own soap from lye – not just growing up in the South, but in Cleveland in the 1950s – and ironed everything, right to our hair ribbons.

—Barbara Smith

Many women and men of color do not want to have many dealings with white people. It takes too much time and energy to explain to the downwardly mobile white middle-class women that it's okay for us to want to own "possessions," never having had any nice furniture on our dirt floors or "luxuries" like washing machines.

—Gloria Anzaldúa, *Making Face, Making Soul = Hacienda Caras: Creative and Critical Perspectives by Feminists of Color*

An Interview with
Barbara Ehrenreich

"Don't be too preachy about the goddamn health issues"

BLW: You describe in your book Fear of Falling: The Inner Life of the Middle Class *how middle-class people are molded by long professional apprenticeships and by their parents' anxiety about whether they'll make it into the professional middle class as adults. In the context of cross-class coalitions, how might this middle-class conditioning cause miscommunications or conflicts?*

Barbara Ehrenreich: A lot of the professional middle-class ethos is related to the kind of Protestant ethic Weber wrote about. You need that Protestant ethic to defer gratification while you become a mature member of the class, while you get that degree and move up to a certain position. So that there is a psychology of deferred gratification. I see this so much among academic friends I have who are such total workaholics that they really can't do anything else. They are anxious and unhappy if they are not accomplishing enough, even relatively late in their careers when they are well-known and established. There continues to be kind of Puritanism about life. Not that people in nonprofessional jobs don't have to be very disciplined. But I don't think it pervades the whole psyche as much as it does in the professional middle class.

BLW: I have noticed something along the same lines: that there is a difference by class in what percentage of your attention is goal-oriented. It rings true to me for my own life, being molded by that pressure and anxiety: are you going to make it or not? It also rang true when I generalize about middle-class activists. It is not always the best attitude to bring into a coalition setting.

BE: I think the worst kind of extreme of this was Lenin himself, who saw the revolutionary process as all about deferred gratification. Leninists would think of themselves almost as soldiers. It was a very grim, pleasureless approach. In the antiwar movement, and

the Civil Rights movements of the 60s, on the other hand, people built community, had a good time together, danced all night. There was sort of a countercultural overlap that was hedonistic in good ways.

BLW: How did it play out between activists of different classes?

BE: In the 70s, the left was full of youngish college-educated people who became very concerned with building cross-class and cross-race organizations. One kind of problem had to do with stereotypes of what working-class people were like. I remember there was a funny story of a couple of leftist guys who went to work at a factory. And to

Barbara Ehrenreich

Sigrid Estrada

People with resources drive me crazy when they pretend they don't have resources in order to fake a class solidarity with those less well-off. — John Anner

prepare themselves, they cut their hair real short and donned flannel shirts and did what they could to look "working-class." And then they found they were being avoided by other young workers because they thought these guys were narcs. And they were shocked to find that many young workers had long hair and smoked dope. That's where a stereotype gets in the way.

I had friends who were young doctors in residence in Chicago, and they had been organizing hospital workers for better care. They decided to have a party, to bring everybody together and socialize. But they were absolutely stymied by certain things like workers smoking and bringing hard liquor. The young doctors were nonsmoking non-

drinking vegetarians, which is fine, but they couldn't figure out how to celebrate in the same space. I just cracked up. I thought, "Well, I am going to be the only one left on the left who can go out into the workforce."

And that kind of issue actually became extremely divisive in Minneapolis in the mid-70s, where there was something called the Twinkie wars. The food co-op typically offered up organic vegetables and grains, and a Marxist group insisted that the food co-op start offering things like Twinkies because they were presumably what other people would like.

BLW: *There's a story like that in the PBS special about* class, People Like Us, *about people wanting the food co-op to*

carry white bread, but in that case it was actual local work-ing-class people, not a particular group.

BE: Yeah, that is just beautiful. I love that part of that documentary.

And another problem is that people with col-lege educations have a certain expectation of how a large group of peo-ple should interact, based really on the academic world. Conferences, for example, will be pre-dictably based on plena-ries and break-out ses-sions, just like a sociolog-ical meeting would be. The whole idea that a coming together of peo-ple on the left should be something like an aca-demic learning experi-ence is not good, I think.

BLW: What style would you contrast it with?

BE: I think there need to be many more possibilities for discussion, not so much resting on a few expert or big-name speakers. There should be a lot of possibilities for conviviality, people talking informally and having a good time. And one person who has really worked on this is Jim Hightower, with his Rolling Thunder Review. They do have perpetual speakers, but there are also all kinds of things going on at the same time, like music, events for children, and booths selling things.

BLW: I like the way you use quotes from your father in Fear of Falling *to illustrate the "ancient antagonism" with which some working-class people regard profession-als. When we're together in a coalition, there is still some-*

times mistrust. We're supposedly on the same side, but there is still wariness there.

BE: Well, it's quite possible that a working-class person has only encountered highly educated professionals in positions of power over them, from social work-ers, judges, and lawyers to teachers (although teach-ers are not a very privi-leged group). That's why there isn't much trust, I would say. If you associate a certain style of speaking or style of dress with peo-ple who didn't serve you well and were actually antagonistic bosses, you're not going to suddenly warm up to that style when you're in a political group. And especially if those people are kind of behaving in subtly obnox-ious ways, like thinking they are the experts and acting like they know much more than anybody else about how to do things.

BLW: You wrote in Fear of Falling, *"The dilemma we so often read about today, over whether women can combine careers with child raising, is freighted with implicit class assumptions: that women have careers, as opposed to mere jobs, and that they have the wherewithal to abandon these careers without condemning their children to penury." Can you com-ment on the class makeup of the women's movement?*

BE: Well, given that it started with middle-class women, and upper-class women in some cases, I think it's amazing how rapidly the feminist con-sciousness spread to poorer and working-class women. Maybe they were waiting for some way to articulate

> *The whole idea that a coming together of people on the left should be something like an academic learning experience is not good.*
>
> —Barbara Ehrenreich

I am not sorry to be in the professional middle class. My extended family and ancestors toiled in all these miserable ways, in the mines, or being migrant agriculture workers. I think I owe it to them to be an intellectual.

—Barbara Ehrenreich

their concerns, and the middle-class women's movement provided new words like "sexism." So I think that is very impressive, and in my experience, some of the strongest feminists are blue-collar or pink-collar women who face a male-dominated hierarchy everyday. I don't see why we shouldn't be working together, and I see that happening now, in little bits, here or there. At some college I was recently, the Women's Studies women had a lunch for me, and half the women there were staff, clerical workers. And I said, "This is new, this is better." I think that some of the academic women are feeling self-confident enough to reach out, and also there is much more awareness on campuses now of campus workers.

BLW: To write Nickel and Dimed, *you went and got low-wage jobs. The coworkers you describe had little or no free time, and no slack to think about anything besides day-to-day survival. Can you imagine a movement for economic justice that would involve them or seem relevant to them?*

BE: This is such a hard question, for all classes except the very rich. Because in the upper-middle class, it's people caught up in being "crazed," as they like to put it, with their work. And for the working class, it's now two jobs each. I think that the issue of time and leisure has to be promoted. How can you be a citizen in any kind of involved sense if you don't have time to read or think about issues and talk to other people? People have to be paid enough for an eight-hour day to support them.

BLW: What classist questions did you get on the book tour for Nickel and Dimed?

BE: On the more conservative side, it was "Well, why can't they just pull themselves up? Why can't they just go to school at night?" The implication is that these things would be so easy to do, and you have to be pretty lazy not to.

On the more liberal side, I think the question I got in about every other bookstore – and this always amuses me – was "Couldn't the people you were working with tell you were different? Couldn't they tell you were well educated?" I just had to laugh and say I wish I could say that just one person somewhere said, 'You're so special and wonderful!" In fact, I was always the new person who was learning.

BLW: The world is full of people without formal education who read, think, talk, make up theories.

BE: Right, that is my ancestral experience. I think of some people in my family as real intellectuals – they love to read, love to discuss – but they were miners and nurses' aides. And of course it was well known that the paternal side of my family were all geniuses; they just happened to be working for a railroad. There was this great confidence in how smart this family was, how we could do anything. So it never would enter my head for a minute that the intellectuals were all in the middle class.

BLW: I used to love that when I was going door-to-door as a low-income tenant organizer, discovering some guy who had every book about the Civil War ever written. There would just be these pockets of expertise. I just treasured arguing politics around a kitchen table. Not all the thinking is going on in schools.

BE: I just spent a week with a nephew who was long-lost to the family due to teenage births and all those kind of things. He showed up one day, and he's a delivery truck driver, and his wife is a retail clerk, but he's an extremely bright person. He knows everything about practical science, the natural world, and electronics.

BLW: What class would you describe yourself as?

BE: With the amount of money I can earn now, with a PhD, I fit the demographics of professional middle-class. But that's not what I was born into.

The way I personally feel about it is I kind of feel awkward sometimes. I don't know which class I am more comfortable in. I am not entirely comfortable in either one. And I thought about this for a long time, and I thought it's okay to be divided like that. Why should I make an emotional adjustment to a class-divided society? I am torn, torn by things that should not be pulls at all.

I feel a certain kind of basic comfort with my blue-collar relatives. And there are a sort of spontaneity and a lot of good things there. I enjoy a lot of my academic friends who are burbling with their new article ideas.

I am not sorry to be in the professional middle class. My extended family and ancestors toiled in all these miserable ways, in the mines, or being migrant agriculture workers. I think I owe it to them to be an intellectual. I have so much they couldn't have had in terms of opportunities to think and meet with people and read, and I treasure that.

BLW: Do you think there's any grain of truth to the stereotype that white working-class people are more racist than white professionals – or at least more outspoken about their racism?

BE: There's political correctness that working-class people may not have been tuned into. I have relatives that say things on the edge. A working-class person in my family said something about how "African Americans have an attitude problem. They can be really hard to work with unless you get past that." Now I don't think an upper-middle-class person, like an academic, would say that, although he or she might have a similar feeling. There is just a kind of a censorship: "Well now, wait a minute, before I say this, what kind of a generalization am I committing myself to?"

But there was a recent study of racism in hiring practices, where in response to help-wanted ads for professional and managerial jobs, you were 50 percent more likely to get a call back if you had a more white-sounding name. If your name was Latisha or Tyrone, you were not going to get the call back. And these decisions were not being made by blue-collar workers, but by managers.

BLW: How is bridging across class lines similar to and different from bridging across race lines?

BE: I think in both cases there are two mistakes a person can make, whether it's a white person relating to black people or an upper-middle-class person relating to working-class people. The first mistake is to assume that the "other" people are entirely different from yourself, that they must have had some tragic problem like drugs that has prevented them from getting anywhere. But the other mistake is to assume that everybody is the same. There is vast similarity, we have the very same loves and issues about family and kids, but also we need to be open to the differences. Let me find out, let me not just assume you come from the exact same background. It's a matter of learning.

BLW: If you were advising middle-class activists on how to be allies to working-class or poor people, what tips would you give them?

BE: Be aware of the way the culture puts down working-class people. A wonderful title of a book that came out in the 70s was *The Hidden Injuries of Class*.

And I would also say, "Don't be too preachy about the goddamn health issues." That's not saying it's unimportant. Maybe people shouldn't smoke, shouldn't eat cheeseburgers. But it's not your business. You'll find plenty of working-class people who do yoga and eat whole grain stuff.

The whole yuppie food explosion – the low fat and all that – is expensive, so that's part of it. But there is definitely a class correlation with smoking. Most people will agree to not smoke in the meeting as long as there's some place they can retreat to, walk out a door and puff and come back.

One of the most important tips is to be aware that there can be kinds of hostility that don't have to do with you personally, but that come out of people's experience. If your only experiences with people with a Master's degree in the past have been with people who were judging you or punishing you or scolding you in some way, you might get nervous every time you see them, you might get anxious or hostile. So be aware of that.

Middle-class activists drive me crazy when they are willing to endlessly analyze and critique but are not willing to act. I've seen people who are paralyzed by their class and race privilege.
– Brenda Choresi Carter

Invisible Walls

Linda Stout grew up in North Carolina, daughter of a "mill-town girl" and a tenant farmer, later a mill worker. She was a 13th generation Quaker who grew up inspired by the Quakers' tradition of speaking up for their beliefs. Her home had no indoor water or plumbing. Other kids were told not to play with her because she was "white trash." A devastating car accident disabled her mother, who became confined to their trailer because she lacked a wheelchair, not even leaving it to go to Linda's high school graduation. Linda figured out on her own how to apply for college and scholarships, then had to drop out when college costs rose and her scholarship didn't. She worked in a hosiery mill, then in offices. She started the Piedmont Peace Project in North Carolina in 1984, and with others slowly built it into one of the strongest multiracial, multi-issue low-income organizations in the state. It won the National Grassroots Peace Award. In a very conservative area, they gradually swayed their Congressman's votes until he supported limiting the military budget and expanding domestic spending. They were banned from meeting places, had their office vandalized, and received threats from the KKK. After ten years at PPP, she moved on in search of how to build power and do movement building at the national level. She moved to Massachusetts and directed a foundation, the Peace Development Fund, before starting a new organization, Spirit in Action, where she is now the director.

Bridging the Class Divide

Excerpts from Linda Stout, *Bridging the Class Divide and Other Lessons for Grassroots Organizing*

Why haven't we yet learned to build more effective multiracial, multiclass organizations in the United States? We'll begin to find some answers if we look closely at the invisible walls, or barriers, that low-income people and people of color often encounter when joining primarily middle-class and white organizations ....

The wall of language:

I speak two languages: one I use in my own community and family and one I have had to learn in order to communicate with formally educated middle-class people .... We must begin to honor each other's languages and accept different voices if we are going to build a winning movement ....

The wall of assumptions of knowledge:

People often wrongly assume that others have the same understanding and information about a problem or issue that they do .... When I first became active in the peace movement, I always left meetings feeling stupid because the group seemed to share information that I did not have ....

The wall of simple logistics:

Physical accessibility ... transportation ... child care ... time of meetings ... membership fees ...

The wall of meeting format and organizational structure:

Structure is critical to people's ability to participate and feel included .... In many groups, a lack of explicit structure means that only those people who feel comfortable talking (usually people with privilege) will do so. It's not that low-income people have nothing to say, we just feel that we don't have a way in ....

An Interview with
Linda Stout

Reaching Across the Walls

BLW: You've written about how different language and ways of communicating can be for people of different classes. What's an example of these different uses of language?

Linda Stout: I used to start my classism workshops for white middle-class people by playing a piece of rap music by Public Enemy. They would say, "Turn it down" and "That's not music!" I would ask them, "What's this music talking about?" They would answer, "He's advocating murder and killing." I asked them what feelings came up when they heard the music, and they talked about being scared and angry and frustrated. Then I told them that the song is about a guy upset at being drafted and determined to be a conscientious objector even if it means going to jail. I used that to talk about how we all speak different languages.

When people came into our rural North Carolina community trying to organize, it was like that music. You heard words, but you weren't sure of their meaning. The way they're presented makes them hard to understand. Middle-class, college-educated people would ask me, "If I try to speak like them, isn't that patronizing?" My answer was that it's only patronizing if you think it is. It's like going to

Linda Stout

Mexico and saying your few words of Spanish. People appreciate an honest attempt to communicate.

The other thing is not to assume that if someone has a third grade reading level, they are like a third grader. Someone asked me, "Why don't you get third graders to help you write the materials so your members can read them?" I just looked at this person like they were out of their mind, which they were, because they didn't understand that these were highly intelligent people with a lifetime of experience behind them, who understood the problems at a deeper level than many middle-class people.

BLW: Can you give some examples of logistics as an invisible wall?

LS: One barrier is fees. Sliding scales are helpful, but not when the form says "low-income member" for the lower price. I refuse to be a "low-income member." I'll be a regular member who's low on the sliding scale.

Because so many low-income people are disabled, handicapped accessibility is a class issue. I can't tell you how many events I've gone to that are not physically accessible. The National Network of Grantmakers had a big celebration downstairs, not wheelchair accessible, and I was using a walker and couldn't get there.

Middle-class activists drive me crazy when they exclude people based on time issues or daycare issues. Also when they talk over my head, and when I ask them to explain something, they get a tone.
— Ellen Smith

Examples of Invisible Walls

I've seen lots of ways in which in organizational cultures, people from poor and working-class backgrounds were less enfranchised in the organization, and therefore they didn't contribute as much. They felt resentful and withdrew, left, and it's not often that that is voiced in a clear way.

Often it is not safe to voice it because the people that are most likely to be management level in organizations are well-educated and white and usually have access to money. So I think it's a constant issue. It's rare that it comes up as an explicit class issue, and often because it is overlaid with race, it's more likely to be seen as a racial issue than a class issue. When issues do come up around class, if they are divisive, like around benefits and hiring, they're often referred up to a board which is even more privileged in terms of class.

Often the tension is around who makes decisions, and the other part of that has to do with the culture of power within the organization. Who's comfortable and who isn't? The fact that people of color who are successful in non-profits are usually middle-class or have attained some middle-class status or education or something to make them less vulnerable means that it's hard for class issues to remain visible.

—Paul Kivel

How you run meetings can set up invisible walls too. People are moving away from Roberts Rules of Order, which is good. But even consensus decision-making can get twisted. For people not used to speaking out, it becomes a barrier. It's not true consensus if some people's voices weren't heard or honored.

I want to be clear on process versus storytelling. Storytelling is telling our individual stories. I have no patience for discussing the agenda for an hour.

—Linda Stout

BLW: In a mixed-class setting, do you have to get more formal because no one class' style of communicating can be assumed?

LS: Yes, but not too formal – there's a balance there.

BLW: What would a movement that really worked for low-income people look like?

LS: Resources would be shared in a healthy way. I've seen the power to decide on funding put into low-income hands, who then become totally powerless. They don't do it any better, because they bring in issues of powerlessness and internalized oppression, just as a wealthy person might bring in issues from being an oppressor. It doesn't automatically work just to switch decision makers. We have to figure out how to put resources in a pot and make group decisions. There needs to be some experimentation.

There would always be time for telling stories. There would be time for caucuses around class. We would pay attention to how we build relationships and trust as we do political work. I believe you get more done when you take the time to build trust and relationships.

BLW: I'm confused about what you're saying about class and group process. Say you created 100 groups, each composed half of middle-class women and half of working-class men and gave them a project to do. After three months, the men in at least 75 groups would be complaining, "Too much group process is driving us nuts!" Part of that is gender, but part is class.

LS: I want to be clear on process versus storytelling. Storytelling is telling our individual stories. I have no patience for discussing the agenda for an hour.

It's important to working-class people not to waste time, but to get the work done. There needs to be a balance. Not all working-class people are comfortable telling stories, especially men, but it is incredibly life-changing, again especially for men. It's less theoretical than a workshop, more personal and dramatic. For example, we'll ask, "Tell a story about when you really mattered."

There's a story I love to tell about Andrew Young, the ambassador to the UN under President Carter. The first thing he did when he arrived was to visit every UN representative, and he had a strict Southern rule of no business without eating. He was the first US ambassador to the UN who was never vetoed.

That's different than process work. I've been learning this method called Appreciative Inquiry, which works better in working-class communities because it uses storytelling and is less critical.

For working-class people to be part of a movement – I believe this very strongly – we have to have a vision. To constantly talk about what we're against doesn't build an organization. To counter internalized oppression and hopelessness, we have to hold up a vision of what we're building. It's harder for middle-class activists. Movement culture has too much cynicism; it's critical and negative.

BLW: In your book, you tell a number of stories in which PPP decides to put forward its own point of view rather than following what the community wants. For example, you assigned readings to the literacy class rather than letting them choose what to read, and you asserted anti-homophobia values unpopular with some members. It's always a strategic choice whether to push your own ideas or to follow your constituency's lead. Do you think that choice is different for a low-income organizer than it is for a middle-class organizer in a low-income community?

LS: Yes, it's different. This is one place where Alinsky organizers [those in the tradition of Saul Alinsky, founder of the Midwest Academy] criticized us, said, "You can't do that." We said, "But we're from the community."

A middle-class outsider has to build alliances carefully. First, assume that the visible leaders – for example, ministers – aren't necessarily the ones who really make things happen. Start by talking with people and listening. For example, in a new community, we would ask people, "Who helps you decide who to vote for?" Maybe it's the elderly woman down the street, not the minister. Find the real leaders, and follow your heart. Listen both outside and inside.

Movement culture has too much cynicism; it's critical and negative.

—Linda Stout

Examples of Invisible Walls

In the Alliance Against Women's Oppression, a mixed-race women's group here in Louisville, one woman didn't have a car. We took it on as an organizational problem because we wanted her there. It wasn't Jackie's individual problem, so at each meeting we would talk about who's Jackie's transportation next time. Jackie's responsibility was to let the person know where she'd be and to call if she couldn't come. During a workshop at a statewide women's conference about our cross-race organizing, we shared that story, and a white woman in the front row started crying. Afterwards she came up and said, "I can't tell you what it meant to hear that story, because I don't have a car, it's hard for me to get to things, and the attitude is, 'That's your problem. If you just worked hard enough, you'd have a car!'"

—Pam McMichael

The black community was overwhelmingly opposed to the war. Representative Barbara Lee of California was the only vote in Congress opposing the decision to invade Afghanistan in 2001. But the antiwar movement, for some reason, couldn't seem to find a way to intersect with the issues then motivating the black community, which was more tied into budget cuts. The antiwar movement was concentrated in the white middle-class. They didn't have much of an outreach plan and concentrated on e-mail outreach, with no leaflets. That's not very effective at reaching out beyond those groups who use the internet/e-mail, so for those groups that don't use it, it's almost like writing them off.

The antiwar movement's banner was peace and justice. And while folks speaking at antiwar events would talk about the impact the budget cuts would have on the social programs, the organizers couldn't figure out how to reach those people involved in that movement. It was some of the poorest organizing work I've ever seen.

—Attieno Davis

Middle-class activists drive me crazy when they assume I know certain information. It makes me feel small and insignificant. In my rural region, we didn't have NPR [National Public Radio], and the only newspaper was owned by the textile mill. Or when they assume I've had certain kinds of experiences, like visiting Europe. — **Linda Stout**

Inner Barriers
for Middle-Class Activists

blw

It's hard for us middle-class people to see our own class conditioning. Our lives are supposed to be the ideal to which low-income and working-class people should aspire. Get an education, work hard, play by the rules, and you'll get to be middle class. This makes the particular nature of middle-class conditioning, especially the harmful parts, invisible.

It's helpful to see our own class conditioning more clearly for two reasons. Some of our conditioning holds us back, limits the tools we have in our toolbox for working towards social change. Seeing it helps us change it. In other ways our conditioning strengthens us as activists, and it's helpful to hang on to it, but it may seem strange and foreign to working-class people, and

we need to understand how we are perceived in order to be able better to communicate across differences.

The path to becoming better allies to working-class people is also a path to personal growth. Much of what we feel is missing in our lives – community, support, relief from time pressure and performance anxiety – can be found through loosening our class conditioning and bridging to working-class people and movements.

Middle-class conditioning squelches people as much as working-class conditioning does, and in some ways more so. What Paolo Freire calls "the project of humanization" is not any easier for us than it is for less class-privileged people.

Some working-class people report that the most reliable allies are those who understand their own

self-interest in changing the class system. If we see what's in it for us, we'll have better motivation for the struggle.

I'm presenting in this section six directions for middle-class people to grow, to become both better allies and healthier people. Because middle-class people's lives are varied – for example, depending on race and gender, depending on our place on the spectrum from upper middle to lower middle class, and depending on our particular family – all six won't ring true for everyone. And I don't mean to imply that some people of other classes don't get similar conditioning and sometimes face the same issues. But there's a core of similarity in middle-class lives that points us in some common directions.

Illustrations by Matt Wuerker

1) Moving from pretense to authenticity

Professional middle-class people are the class group most likely to repress our honest reactions. Some of us were taught to speak and write competently to fulfill someone else's expectations. Even when our hearts are burning at the injustice of the current class system, some of us will find ourselves tongue-tied and unable to speak or write in our authentic voice. We marvel at the boldness of some gutsy working-class people and at the elo-

quence of some smooth and confident owning-class people.

And because of this reserve, because we put our authentic selves behind a screen, others tend to find us boring and/or untrustworthy. Working-class people looking for allies gravitate to the more flamboyant or charming owning-class people, or to the middle-class people who escaped being repressed, sometimes because of an ethnic heritage that kept the conditioning at bay.

Working-class academic David Green says that when he was growing up, his friends and family divided the world into real people and "fake" people. The real people were their working-class community. The "fake" people were kids who liked school, teachers, landlords, employers, and other middle-class people.

The term "fake" resonates with me. As a child, much of what I said to adults was fake politeness. This is less true of other ethnic groups, but becoming middle-class sometimes means taking on those WASP norms.

Pretense is a big turn-off in cross-class alliances, especially in some working-class subcultures that have "no bullshit" directness as a core value.

In the 1970s, I saw some middle-class left-sectarians pretend to be working class. They cut their hair short, dressed in jeans and plaid flannel shirts, and got factory jobs. They introduced themselves by their new occupations, as in "Hi, I'm Joe. I'm a steelworker," never mentioning that they'd gone to the steel mill from Yale by way of the Revolutionary Communist Party (RCP).

Once I saw four RCP members get out of the same car, then enter the meeting room and pretend to introduce themselves to each other: "Hi, I'm Doreen and I'm from the United Auto Workers" – "Hi, Doreen, I'm Al and I'm from the United Mine Workers." At the antinuclear coalition meeting where I saw this, they were regarded with eye-rolling scorn, and I imagine they got a similar reception at their plants and union meetings. The scorn was not for the fact that they were middle-class people joining working-class organizations in the hopes of strengthening them; many activists have done that and been respected for their work. The problem was that they were fake.

We don't have to pretend to be anyone besides who we are. It's better if we don't hide our privilege; people's negative reactions to it will sometimes start honest dialogues that can build bonds of trust.

As middle-class people, we may think that being non-classist is a mask we need to put on, a studied behavior. It won't work. Pretense is inconsistent with being an ally. Our real mistakes, our real classist thoughts, will get us in trouble, but it's a kind of trouble others can help dig us out of, while pretending cuts us off.

Getting in touch with our feelings and boldly speaking up with our authentic voice – these sound like tasks for the therapist's couch, not for coalition meetings. But a little bit of getting ourselves unstuck from pretense will go a long way in cross-class work.

2) Moving from politeness and caution to openness and humor

In some of our families, anger itself was considered bad manners, and it's hard to imagine we could learn anything from a scary and badly behaved angry person. Working-class people's anger makes us want to retreat somewhere invisible, huddle quietly in the middle of the pack so we won't be targeted. After we retreat, we debrief with other middle-class people, who reinforce each other's judgment that the angry working-class person was "inappropriate." Several times after loud blowups, I've seen professional middle-class people simply and quietly disappear from an organization.

I'd say my biggest inner barrier to being a bridge person is in regards to humor. I don't know what to say when teased. I'm not very comfortable telling jokes. When I try, sometimes working-class people look at me with pity. Joking around is a social lubricant, especially for most working-class communities. But styles of humor can vary between classes and cultures, so people attempting to be humorous can also step on toes.

One of my favorite stories of Saul Alinsky, pioneer of community organizing methods, is the one about him being at a Mexican community banquet and saying, "How can you eat this crap? This is almost as bad as the Jewish food they fed me as a child." Apparently the group around him cracked up. Can you imagine risking such impoliteness? I can't.

I come across as earnest – a dead giveaway of being a middle-class do-gooder. I used to hang around with a working-class white woman and a woman of color, and they lovingly called me their "stiff white girl."

Once I met a group of cool working-class people and really wanted to make friends, but asking about their lives and listening wasn't getting me anywhere. One day one of them said something about sex being as good as great chocolate. I quipped, "Yeah, well, I've had some sex that was about like your average Sarah Lee." They laughed. One woman warmed right up to me then, and a couple weeks later she said, "I knew you were okay when you said that thing about the Sarah Lee cake." Unfortunately, I can't be funny like that at will.

When I look at times that I've successfully built bridges across class and race, what I did right was project down-to-earth warmth, friendliness, and respect. Then some very prickly working-class people, quick to see snobby disrespect in every college-educated person, decided I was okay.

FINALLY! I'VE MADE IT TO THE TOP OF MY PROFESSION!

SINGER

Andy Singer: http://www.andysinger.com/

Success was defined as being set off from the common fate of working people.

As activists, we may have renounced conventional definitions of success – but in renouncing them, we may have recreated them in a new form. Some of us flipped "keeping up with the Joneses" over into its mirror image of "being less consumerist and more simple-living than the Joneses." We still fall into the trap of thinking we're set off as superior.

This one-upmanship is a major obstacle to cross-class alliance building. When I asked 20 working-class activists how they saw middle-class activists, many described arrogant know-it-alls who think they're so smart.

One form of arrogance is thinking of ourselves as missionaries helping the less fortunate. We can fall into the trap of thinking less-privileged people need us to save them, while not seeing the resources they have to give.

Once I was in a wonderful support group about unlearning class conditioning, connected with Re-evaluation Co-Counseling. We would try to come up with provocative statements to get us to laugh, cry, and see things in a new way. This is the statement that stirred up the middle-class people the most: "I am no better and no worse than anyone else, and I will never again pretend otherwise."

3) Moving from competition and superiority to confident humility

Middle-class conditioning taught us that our worth is conditional on accomplishments, winning competitions, being right, and being "smart." Somewhere along the way, as we competed with other kids to get into college, someone told us we were superior to those who didn't make it.

From this moment forth, I promise to always remember my inherent goodness and value as a human being, and to give up all reliance on superiority, being right, and competition for my sense of worth." Try saying it out loud and see how it feels. Personally I went through stages of crying too much to finish it, arguing with it, laughing at it, and ultimately feeling like it reconnected me with a lost birthright of being part of the human race.

Growing up, some of us were continuously tested and judged, both at home and at school. It can be hard to turn off the inner judge and jury. Sometimes our arrogant judgments come out as classism towards people with less formal education. I've noticed that if I judge someone's behavior negatively, even if I think I'm carefully hiding it, the person often gets hostile towards me. As soon as I have thoughts like, "Look how she mistreats her kids!" or "He never lets anyone else get a word in edgewise," hostility sometimes comes back at me in waves, especially from working-class people and people of color. I must leak disapproval in some alienating way, but it's hard for me to see it. I think of my parents — my dad's harsh self-righteousness, my mom's sniffing disapproval — and I think I must have a shadow side with their faults. I haven't fully learned how to deal with critical thoughts so they don't push people away.

Middle-class people are not only critical of less privileged people but also of each other. In fact, among leftists, we often politely avoid criticizing poor people, lest we seem classist (and if we're white, we avoid criticizing people of color lest we seem racist). Our most arrogant criticisms are often turned on activists with our amount of privilege or more, sometimes in less-oppressive-than-thou pissing contests.

Sometimes we confuse rejecting classism with despising middle-class people. Our middle-class brothers and sisters did not create the oppressive aspects of US society, nor are they the primary beneficiaries of it. The fact that they benefit from relatively more class privilege than working-class folks does not make it progressive to despise them.

Another way that arrogant superiority is expressed is in attacking people in leadership roles. Instead of "Question authority," some activists' bumper stickers must read "Trash authority"! It's not a coincidence that extreme anti-hierarchy ideas arise mostly from middle-class activist culture. If you think you know it all (or you're supposed to pretend to), then there's no reason anyone else should have a role of expert or leader. Out of overconfidence, some middle-class activists confuse appropriate deference with submission. In *Doing Democracy*, the late Bill Moyer writes

There are certain traps I'm trying to avoid. The first one is telling on other people from my [middle-class] class background, so you'll know for sure how much less classist I am than they are. Several years ago when I came out to a straight guy, he went on and on about how virulently homophobic his father was, as if to let me know how enlightened he was in comparison. I thought of brilliant retorts long after the conversation was over, but it showed me what it's like to be on the other end of someone with privilege telling on their peers to someone who's oppressed. It made me realize that if I tell on my queer middle- and upper-middle-class peers (or other people who I share some kind of privilege with), I get to be Not Like Them. It's so delicious to be Unique. But the problem is, unique is alone, and even though femmes do have special powers, I can't dismantle class oppression all by myself. So we (middle- and upper-middle-class queers) have to work together, and that is hard. Things get personal, and we all want to tell on each other because it's too painful to see ourselves reflected in each other's mistakes. I can point out the classist thing you said yesterday, but I'll oppress someone tomorrow and not even know it. I can honestly say that I've lost middle- and upper-middle-class friends because of classism, and how hard it is to talk to each other about values we were raised with that are oppressive to other people.

—Mary Davies, on www.butchdykeboy.com

The First Principle of Movement Building — Round Two

Anyone who steps out of political passivity to give time to any progressive effort deserves to be honored, appreciated, and treated with complete respect. Disagreements, mistakes, and oppressive behavior call for supportive feedback; they are not justification for abandoning a respectful stance. Solidarity is our only strength.

Middle-class activists drive me crazy when they think you just need that right argument. The best information won't win the day! **– James Spady**

The professional middle class is based on control of information. It should come as no surprise, then, that social movements made up primarily of members of the middle class are preoccupied with the issue of knowledge, information, and expertise ....

A certain amount of information and expertise is, of course, necessary for social-movement efforts. But it is problematic to make the dissemination of information the primary focus of political action. First, the middle-class emphasis on political information is akin to what workers often refer to as "book learning" .... The information that activists offer often appears to be of little use to workers, since it explains problems but usually does not offer practical or realistic solutions ....

Second, the emphasis on education — no matter how well intentioned — ends up contributing to workers' perception that they are not qualified to take part in public life ....

Third, through their emphasis on information, [middle-class] activists undervalue the kind of understanding that arises from daily life. Workers have as much to teach activists about the realities of this country's social and political life as activists have to teach workers.

—David Croteau, *Politics and the Class Divide*

Some people say there should be no middle-class people in low-income people's movements: "The grassroots can solve its own problems." But middle-class intellectuals have had the privilege of learning theory, and we're looking for a fusion of grassroots experience with theory.

—Manuel Criollo

We had a retreat, and one of the things we were talking about was the Environmental Justice (EJ) movement and where it came from, and the seventeen principles developed at the EJ Summit. And somebody said, "You know, those principles are really fuzzy. The labor movement had very clear goals — an eight-hour day — but this is not the blueprint for a movement." And he said that in the presence of somebody who was part of the drafting committee, and he meant it as constructive criticism, with good intentions for moving things forward. But it wasn't just the fact that there was somebody who had been involved in drafting the principles in the room, it was also that he wasn't thinking it was a result of real people struggling to put something together. He was ruminating about it and putting it out in stark terms, turning it into something abstract. I thought that was classist. From a position of privilege, you can play with all kinds of issues like that, like academics do, and criticize people for this or that strategic move. But the principles came out of some real struggle. There was a history to it, and he wouldn't criticize if he knew it. The fact that people agreed on something was an amazing achievement.

— Penn Loh

about the "negative rebel," someone stuck in the rebellious role both when it's helpful and when it's unhelpful.

Leadership is needed to build an effective movement. Those who stick their necks out to take leadership roles are, of course, imperfect human beings who make mistakes. But someone with an appropriate balance of confidence and humility will give feedback with appreciation, respect, and tentativeness about how accurate it may be.

4) Moving from excessive abstraction to groundedness

There are strengths in having our knowledge based more on book learning than on direct experience. Chuck Collins told me that a gift many professional middle-class people bring to movements is "the sociological imagination": that is, the wide scope of comparing different times and places and seeing themes emerge.

But there are weaknesses as well. When I interviewed class-privileged activists, a couple of them could make abstract statements about class – but no matter how many times I asked for examples, they couldn't come up with even one story about particular people, groups, or events.

Contrast me with a working-class guy I worked with in an anti-nuclear-power group (the man in the story on page 60), and the differences in how we each got involved. I read about nuclear power in the book *Small Is Beautiful* and committed myself to opposing it based on ideals of decentralized appropriate technology. I had no idea where the nearest proposed nuclear plant was at the time. He saw a flyer on a telephone pole with a bulls-eye over his neighborhood; he committed himself to opposing a particular plant when he learned how close it was to his neighborhood. Which of us would be more compelling in convincing someone in the neighborhood to speak out against the nuclear plant? Overall, movements grow best when the concrete knowledge of the problem as understood by the people personally affected is combined with the theoretical and technical knowledge of people who have studied the problem.

Can't say I'm comfortable up here with you all being so squished down there.

That makes two of us!

John Lapham

Both families and schools tend to foster a sense of independence and autonomy for middle-class people, although many jobs increasingly deny it. This emphasis on autonomy ... creates considerable confusion about the role and importance of community and support. It becomes difficult for those who are born and brought up middle-class to ask for help from others — or, sometimes, even to give it — because, ideally, each of us is supposed to be able to manage on our own. To ask for help seems to call into question one's autonomy — and, therefore, one's dignity as a person.

This constellation also leads to guilt and paralysis in a social/political context. Middle-class people do not, after all, have enough money either to change things dramatically in the society as a whole or to feel completely secure in their own position. They are also aware of the arbitrariness of it all. Consequently they may feel guilty for their own success, even at the same time that they are unable to take full responsibility for it. Thus, middle-class people, too, suffer from a sense of alienation, isolation, and powerlessness ... feelings that probably help explain why so many middle-class people prefer not to have to think about class, or about their monetary situation, at all .... This feeling has an important connection with spirituality, or wholeness — which, as I understand it, means being in touch with the sources of power, integrity, and capacity within each of us, and in connection with each other .... [I]f we are divided from one another — and even from ourselves — by class differences, then we are unable to experience that wholeness. Further, if those same divisions block our ability to act — and in particular, to act in concert with others — then they disempower us and undermine our ability to do the work of tikkun olam [repairing the world]."

—Martha Ackelsberg, in Lawrence Bush and Jeffrey Dekro, *Jews, Money, and Social Responsibility*

Among some middle-class progressives, one downside of abstract knowledge can be an excessive emphasis on ideology. Theory and ideology can be helpful tools, but if too rigid or too unrooted in concrete reality, they can get in the way.

For example, at a meeting of an anti-corporate-globalization group, I heard one college-educated leftist say, "Before we can plan any action, we have to decide whether our coalition opposes capitalism in all its forms." There was an audible sigh in the room. I have never encountered this kind of ideological barrier to action in a working-class activist. I have known working-class leftists with strong ideological positions, but they've had a pragmatic understanding that the work can proceed without everyone's theoretical agreement.

5) Moving from guilt to balanced responsibility

As progressive activists, we have an endless list of things to feel guilty about.

Particular guilt for our own harmful behavior can spark us to helpful restitution. But generalized guilt can be immobilizing and distracting. To escape guilt's dreadful undertow we can turn away from activism altogether, or turn to unappealing extremes of self-denial, such as wearing torn and smelly clothes that may be offensive to those in whose name we have supposedly sacrificed our self-care. It can keep us self-centered, endlessly critiquing our own behavior instead of

Black middle-class activists drive me crazy when they seem to have a belief that great speeches will be all it takes to win justice. — **Dorian Warren**

responding to other people. Because it keeps us focused on "me, me, me," guilt is a form of narcissism.

Our guilty feelings can mislead us. Not every failure of a cross-class alliance is our fault. Sometimes we build our half of the bridge, but the other half isn't there. If our middle-class guilt leads us to assume all fault is ours, we can miss learning a lesson from a more realistic assessment of the experience. Yes, our actions have effects, but it's helpful to keep in perspective just how much we *didn't* cause.

None of us middle-class people designed or lead the major institutions that perpetuate class oppression. We are responsible for our choices, for rectifying our mistakes, and for what we do with the privileges we've been handed. We are not responsible for the whole capitalist system and how it hurts people, just for making one person's-worth of effort to change it.

6) Moving from individual achievement anxiety to community interdependence

It's almost impossible for some of us to escape our middle-class conditioning enough to recognize the importance of putting energy into cross-class relationships. Most of us were raised to see individual achievement as the purpose of life. Doing well on the test, in the class, on the job; getting a good grade, a degree, a promotion – isn't that our goal?

Every day I arrive at work anxious about completing the tasks on my to-do list. This anxiety and task-focus serve as blinders to keep me from looking around at the big picture. If we put our time and heart into connecting with working-class social change agents and collaborating with them on their efforts for economic justice, it is quite possible we will achieve less individual success (in the conventional sense), earn less, and displease authorities.

In *Fear of Falling: The Inner Life of the Middle Class*, Barbara Ehrenreich describes the role of advanced education in professional middle-class culture:

The professional and managerial occupations have a guildlike quality. They are open, for the most part, only to people who have completed a lengthy education and attained certain credentials. The period of study and apprenticeship – which may extend nearly to mid-life – is essential to the social cohesion of the middle class. It is in college or graduate school that the young often find their future spouses and life-long friends. Much more than an extended childhood, however, this long training period requires the discipline and self-direction that are essential to the adult occupational life of the class.

Unlike in other classes in the US and throughout history, Ehrenreich says, parents in the US professional/managerial class don't see an automatic route for their children to remain in the same class as adults. Rich parents can pass wealth to their children, and working-class parents can usually assume that their kids can take up working-class occupations or rise to better-paid ones. But only if the "lengthy study and apprenticeship" are successfully completed will the children of the professional/managerial class remain in that class. This fact creates a signature element of middle-class culture: parental anxiety and pressure to succeed, sometimes starting before kindergarten.

I felt a click of recognition when I read Ehrenreich's description of parental anxiety as a formative experience for professional middle-class kids. My father framed most experiences in his kids' lives as challenges and opportunities to rise to excellence – or fail and face his scorn. I remember a fun opportunity to weed the patio for the thrilling sum of 50 cents turning into an anxiety-wracked ordeal when he announced halfway through my weeding that he would pay double or nothing – double if the patio was perfect and nothing if it wasn't. I kept weeding smaller and smaller bits of grass until it got too dark to see them. I don't remember if I got my dollar. When I was in high school, most of my conversations

M. WUERKER

with my father were about how prestigious a college I might get into.

Of course, low-income and working-class kids also sense anxiety in their parents, and some of them get pushed to excel in school and become upwardly mobile. But the cultural flavor of "fear of falling" seems different than the cultural flavor of being pushed up and out. For one thing, the great majority of upper-middle-class kids, and many middle-middle-class kids, get intense pressure to be disciplined enough to get into a good college, while only some working-class kids experience intense upward-mobility pressure. For another, worth and approval, sometimes even affection, are conditional on achievement in some middle-class families in a way that seems rare in working-class families. So staying on track and pleasing authority figures can feel like a life-or-death mandate to us, even to those of us who have dropped out of the rat race and outwardly chosen another path.

In our tunnel vision on our own tasks, we miss out on building relationships, noticing group dynamics, and supporting others. I remember when I was on a board with low-income people, and I would come to the office on my lunch hour for committee meetings. Some of the other members were unemployed people who hung out at the office all day. It would take us forever to start the meeting, and then it would drift off the tasks at hand into long rambling conversations about personal lives or the inner politics of the organization. I would be so impatient to get back on topic that my crabby impulse was to dismiss them as a bunch of undisciplined flakes. They thought I was a cold, humorless person who only saw tasks, not people. Later I went on a long car trip with one of them, and she was so surprised that I could laugh and gossip like a normal person. She opened up to me, and I realized that I'd been overlooking what we had in common as well as the strengths she could give the organization.

It's not that we need to give up our individual goals and accomplishments, or our to-do lists. Disciplined task orientation and even driven ambition are in fact gifts to the movement. Without them less social change would have happened. But it's a matter of balance. To build better cross-class alliances, we need to put more of our attention on relationships.

To avoid hurting our eyes during long bouts at the computer, they say, we should look up every 20 minutes and refocus our eyes farther away than our computer screen. To avoid getting stuck in the individualistic middle-class accomplishment trap, we need to lift our eyes frequently from the task in front of us and shift our focus to the web of human connections in which our work is embedded.

When it comes to the issues addressed by most middle-class movements, workers have neither the guilt nor the sense of responsibility that seem to be associated with many middle-class-value-based actions. For example, appeals from the peace or Central America anti-intervention movements have often played on the idea that citizens must stop actions that are carried out in our names .... Since they often do not vote and since they see themselves as having virtually no input into government decision-making, most workers find rather incomprehensible the suggestion that they are responsible for the actions of their government – a theme often sounded by many middle-class activists. In addition, most middle-class movements clearly have more than a kernel of guilt associated with them. This approach, too, needs a sense of privilege in order to be effective.

—David Croteau, *Politics and the Class Divide*

The middle class teaches its children individualism and a focus on personal development to prepare them for professional work .... They learn to be "object oriented," that is, motivated by the achievement of some moral, material, or cultural goal that they adhere to for personal reasons .... They must internalize a sense of striving to accomplish, so that personal self-worth depends on their ability to perform at work. Because middle-class members define themselves through their accomplishments and activities, they have a strong stake in the projects they get involved in .... Middle-class movements thus tend to advance broad or even universal goals and values that can inspire a sense of mission.

—Fred Rose, *Coalitions across the Class Divide*

Black middle-class activists drive me crazy when they think they should be in leadership.
– Preston Smith

Integrating the Best
of All Class Cultures

Barbara Jensen
from "Becoming Versus Belonging"

I suspect that the inhibiting sense of self-consciousness that many middle-class people are plagued with may well be born of the close parental monitoring of children through verbal exchanges. It can also lead to the

Barbara Jensen

development of a constant internal censor or critic of speech and behavior. An example that comes to mind is the teaching of middle-class table manners ....

It may also be the case that excessive emphasis on children to translate impulses and feelings into speech, and

formal speech at that, may obscure other kinds of experiences. The inculcation of the ego-heavy "I" may have ramifications for how much empathy one will feel with others .... I remember the few lower-middle-class kids who lived, briefly, in the working-class neighborhood I grew up in. They were not very able to relate to the other children. They were always trying to get the teacher's attention and it seemed to the rest of us that they were missing out on the best part. They didn't like recess. They seemed awkward and lonely on the playground, almost like they didn't know how to be children ....

Middle-class culture, through its emphasis on means and ends, which are placed further apart as a child ages, creates a psychology based on delayed gratification, which has its rewards in education and in professional work. Working class people enjoy a larger and roomier sense of "now."

Relatively free of pressures to prove one's originality or cleverness, working-class people enjoy a more unmediated "being there" – in just "hanging out" with friends and family ... This directness is also an attitude toward life itself and, as such, preserves something essential in human

experience: an unearned sense of oneself as part of other people, part of the world we live in, part of life – a foundational sense of belonging.

I am trying to imagine a society that could integrate the best aspects of each of these cultures. The fact that these cultures exist in opposition to each other makes imagining their integration difficult. And yet all of these things – the capacity to "tune in" to non-verbal systems, the capacity to use and enjoy words and concepts, the ability to feel that one "belongs" with other people, the desire to respect one's own particular self and psyche – are all part of the human potential, they are things we all contain. What would it be like to focus on developing one's personal talents if it did not mean "proving oneself" and competing for scarce resources (scholarships, jobs, etc.)? What would it be like to enjoy a silent sense of communion with something while also learning to play with words and build intriguing theories about it? How might those theories be different if the person thinking them up lived in a close relation to the physical world and regularly worked with his hands? How might these human qualities reconfigure if they were not constructed by society as mutually exclusive; if they were not constrained by a society committed to privileging some people over others, some aspects of the human spirit over the other ones? How might society itself look different if all these qualities were available to all of its members?

What Middle-Class Activists
Give Up

blw

When I interviewed Linda Stout, she said something that moved me:

I don't use the words "power" or "privilege" any more with middle-class people. They don't reflect people's actual experience well enough, especially activists'. People don't feel powerful and can't grasp the concept of privilege.

I led a yearlong classism workshop with monthly weekends. I got to know these middle-class and owning-class activists' stories really well. I learned how people get punished for being allies. Often their families step away from them, and sometimes they get actually cut off. It's the same as what happens in the rural South when white people get ostracized for working with people of color. It helped me understand the real costs to them, how painful their struggles are.

Hearing that made me reflect on how rarely I tell anyone about my father's reaction to my activism.

My father was an ideologically impassioned Republican. It was unacceptable to him that his daughters have any other worldview. Once I became a liberal in high school, he spoke to me mostly to bait me with attacks on liberals. He got colder as my politics moved leftward.

A recurring theme of our arguments was his belief that anyone could make it in America, and that therefore poor people, in particular black people, just hadn't disciplined themselves, versus my belief that the rules were rigged against some people.

When I dropped out of Princeton to be a full-time activist, my dad went from cold to hostile. He threatened to disinherit me. Since his will was not anything I'd ever considered before, I took this proclamation as not about future money, but as an attempt to manipulate my behavior. I only heard from him when he mailed me clippings from the *Wall Street Journal* with mocking notes.

Other upper-middle-class 22-year-olds got help from their families, but I struggled through dental crises by extra dishwashing shifts and long waits in dental clinics. My mom, who didn't control the purse strings, snuck me help in the form of practical Christmas presents, but the overall message was that I was on my own.

When I went back to college, my dad declined to help pay because I didn't return to the Ivy League. I supported myself by loans and cleaning houses, sometimes working 30 hours a week or more – similar to how working-class people go to college.

Now when I see middle-class people eased into adulthood by parents who help them fly off – giving them an old family car or lending them the security deposit for an apartment – it occurs to me what I might have had. Quite tangibly, being an activist meant not getting those privileges.

And Linda's right, sometimes when people describe class privilege, it doesn't ring true to my experience. I wouldn't trade my 20s for anything; total movement immersion was transformative. But they weren't easy years, financially or in terms of family dynamics.

Now as I work with other middle-class activists on uprooting classism, I try to connect to our real experience, not to some idealized concept of what a "privileged" life must be like.

Betsy, age 16, on left

I really value middle-class activists when they live a simpler life even though their full potential could give them houses and yachts and cars. **– Lisa Richards**

Dynamics with
Owning-Class Activists

blw

Many social change groups include owning-class activists – more than we think, since some of them are closeted. Some people who grew up middle-class or even working-class now have millions of dollars, from investments, inheriting, or marrying into money. Some people grew up owning-class but no longer have money, either because they were cut off by their families or because they gave it all away. And there are rich activists from owning-class backgrounds.

It can seem progressive to trash owning-class individuals. It's a short distance from critiquing the structural inequities that favor the rich to mocking the human beings with the privileges. And it's an easy way for working-class and middle-class activists to bond because of course most of us are jealous of rich people's money and free time.

Why shouldn't we trash rich people? Not just for ethical reasons, and not just because more of them will be activists if they are welcomed. Trashing them fits into a pernicious right-wing philosophy.

In *Right-Wing Populism in America*, Chip Berlet and Matthew Lyons talk about a "producerist" philosophy that foments hate for the "nonproductive"

people at the top and bottom of the economy. White working people and businessmen are seen as the hard-working "real Americans" who carry everyone else on their backs. Hate for the unemployed is woven together with racism (against low-income "parasites," presumed to be people of color) and anti-Semitism (against owning-class "parasites," presumed to be Jewish). White supremacist groups claim to be speaking for working people, protecting them from the rabble below and the conspiracy above.

Responsible Wealth lobby day to preserve the estate tax on multi-millionaires.

You can see a version of this world-view in Disney animated films. In *Aladdin*, *Pocahontas*, and *The Lion King*, the villains are ostentatiously rich and greedy. Some can be read as Jewish or Arab (hooked noses and olive skin), some can be read as gay (effete British-type accents, limp wrists). Dumb, low-life villains serve

the evil rich. The heroes are plucky, hard-working – and always WASP-looking, no matter their supposed ethnicity.

Even some of us who cringe at the race and gender stereotypes in Disney movies cheer at the downfall of these greedy villains – without thinking that these stereotypes of the rich buy into a right-wing producerist ideology.

Progressives need to affirm that it's not a job that gives a person worth. And we need to distinguish between fighting systems of privilege and fighting privileged individuals.

Ruling-class people, who have real power over major institutions, are the subset of the owning class most likely to act as enemies to our causes. Even with them, we will succeed better if we remember that particular human beings are at the helm, who respond in human ways to threats and incentives. But most owning-class people have decision-making power only over their own investments, professional behavior, and lifestyle choices. They need challenging on classist attitudes and behavior, as we middle-class people do, but personal hostility dooms such challenges to failure.

Power Dynamics with
Owning-Class Activists

As a radical person who grew up wealthy, I always feel like I'm actively upholding the same system of inequality that I'm trying to fight against. It feels impossible, so my first tendency is to disassociate from where I'm coming from. It feels like my background can't coexist with my politics, that one's got to go and I'm not willing to give up my values.

But then that feeds into the power dynamics in cross-class organizing. It's not fair when working-class people lay their shit out on the table and I'm being dishonest and keeping my shit behind locked doors. Plus then I'm not tapping into circles that I have access to.

I end up protesting outside buildings when I could be inside sitting at the table. I end up feeling like I'm raging against myself because the two sides are so polarized that they're at war with each other. It's much scarier to demand that the two parts of me have a voice and work together. But that's what needs to happen for anything to change.

—Molly, in Courtney Young, ed., *Protest and Privilege: Young People with Wealth Talk about Class and Activism*

One foundation has gone through various ways of having donors and activists work together, and that's been

more and less successful at different times. The donors didn't want to monopolize the decision-making around grants, so they set up a system of a donor board and an activist board. They split the money into two pots. It wasn't effective because it didn't build an organization or a culture that was actually dealing with class issues. And the communication back and forth was hard. And there were still the issues of resentment because half the money was under the donors'

Members of Resource Generation

control, without any accountability around that. So then they tried to do a grant-making board that was mixed, or balanced. In some ways the donors were seen not as activists, even though many of them were.

—Paul Kivel

At one point, there was an organization that certainly needed some

resources in the very immediate term. I said, "What if I were able to provide the resources that are needed here in the very short term?" Suddenly the group of people said, "Are you sure? Are you sure you want to give us that money? How do you feel about that? …. Do we really want to be taking money from you?" ….

As soon as the personal relationship entered the scene, the people who were sitting around the table all of a sudden had a whole different set of criteria about whether or not they even wanted to accept the money. They weren't really sure, and did they want to have somebody so close to the organization who would also be a major donor, and as a major donor might exert some demands for accountability that might result in agenda setting? ….

To find an activist in their midst who was suddenly crossing the line toward major donorism, and having these extremely inconsistent rule books for how you treat volunteers in your organization and how you treat major donors, left some of my colleagues who are organizers in this funny place, like "Hm, how do we treat you? Do we treat you like a major donor, do we treat you like an activist?"

—Holmes, in Courtney Young, ed., *Protest and Privilege*

I love activists who don't have to fight so hard, but they do the work anyway. — **Gilda Haas**

The World Looks **Different**
from an Owning-Class Perspective

blw

Sometimes tensions between middle-class and owning-class activists fall along the dreamy/pragmatic class-cultural spectrum. Here's a composite conversation I've had repeatedly with owning-class activists:

Them: "If it could be this way, that would be ideal."

Me: "Well, here's why it can't be that way."

Them: "But I really think it should be this way."

Me: "That's impossible. Let's move on to a realistic idea."

Them: "But if it could be this way …"

To me it seems very frustrating when they can't see a ceiling. I imagine that to them it seems very frustrating when I can't stop fixating on the ceiling when the organization has broken through many ceilings before.

Here's a classic story: There's a progressive foundation in which wealthy donors collectively decide where the money goes. In 1991, this donor-controlled foundation gave a grant to a low-income group whose board I served on. I wrote a grant proposal for the next year, 1992, focused on the group's urgent campaign to prevent health care budget cuts that would devastate the community. They turned us down. The reason? They had decided to give 100 percent of their grants to the next year's Columbus quincentennial counter-events. Important work, educating people on the devastation caused by the "discovery" of America 500 years before – but hardly the most pressing concern of low-income communities. Every foundation makes bad decisions sometimes, but in my considered opinion, this particular flavor of idealistic disconnect would have been very unlikely in a foundation controlled by people from any other class.

I feel like I've been groping my way for years towards understanding how best to collaborate with owning-class activists. I know there must be ways to include their big-picture worldview and their ability to dream in our organizations without giving them more than their share of power, and ways to ground them to earth without squelching them. I know there must be ways to partner with major donors with honesty and without always doing things their way. I know that having people with a sense of entitlement should be able to make our organizations more powerful and well-connected without disempowering the less privileged people in the group.

Owning-class people in Jobs with Peace tended to think the most macro, the most systemically. They were brought up to think macro. The bigger forces we mobilize, the more important it is to think big. And the more likely we are to collide with power-holders who are owning-class, so it's important to know how they think.

—George Lakey

[I]t was easier for me to make the choice to take on these jobs, to put my ideals in the workplace and accept a lower salary, because I don't have any loans, and I do know that in a couple years, I have a big chunk of money coming to me. While I'm not relying on that, it's nice to know that there's that cushion. So I know my class status has affected my level of activism.

—Ariana, in Courtney Young, ed., *Protest and Privilege*

TRICKLE DOWN ECONOMICS
AND THE EROSION OF THE AMERICAN MIDDLE CLASS

Upper Class
Middle Class
Working Class
1970

Trickle Down Action
1980

Trickle Down
1990

Middle Class
Working Class
2000

M. WUERKER

Isolation, Secrecy and Others' Reactions
to **Owning-Class People**

It's easy to say sarcastically, "I'd like to have those problems!" But in fact wealthy activists face difficulties that make me count my blessings for not facing them. The money is like the elephant under the carpet wherever they go. They have to question why someone is interested in them. And it takes guts to come out as owning-class, especially in movements full of angry working-class people and socialists. The following quotations evoke some of these uncomfortable dynamics:

A few people in my small nonprofit office gathered for lunch and a couple minutes after settling into our respective egg salad and tuna sandwiches, my coworker casually dropped the loaded question, "Do you consider yourself wealthy?"

Even though we worked at a social justice fund that supported progressive grassroots work, we never talked about our class differences, so her question felt somewhat abrupt. But the conversation seemed to be waiting for my answer. I thought for a minute, weighing the implications, anxieties, and realities, and answered, "Yes, I guess so." I cringed internally (and quite possibly externally) as I waited for the backlash and cold shoulders I feared. But none materialized. What did come up, though, were the conflicts and questions surrounding my class background ....

What did it mean that I worked during the week for a social justice organization, but I spent a weekend on my parents' yacht in Florida over the winter? What did it mean that nobody at the struggling community center where I volunteered knew I could also be a major donor? And what stopped me from being a donor anyway? What did it mean that I wanted to fight against an unjust economic system when I was one of the few benefiting from it?"

—Courtney Young, *Protest and Privilege*

In Food Not Bombs in California, half the people are broke or scraping by, and half have inherited money or

Billy Wimsatt

trust funds, and people don't really talk about it. I interviewed someone who grew up on the streets squatting and then found out she has family money. At first she renounced it, and now she's dealing with it. She has a secret PO box to get the statements, and she uses the money to fund projects anonymously. She lives in a dilapidated house and has a set of stories to explain how she gets by, like that her sister helps her. Another person in a similar situation finally came out as having money and caught a lot of hell for it.

Another friend who does social justice philanthropy raises money from wealthy people, and she gets so frustrated and angry at them. They're so unaccountable and unconscious of their privilege, and so defensive. Sometimes she speaks up to challenge them and sometimes she bites her tongue. They can always just pick up and leave, stop returning her calls.

There's a *Charlie and the Chocolate Factory* worldview that says, "Poor people were noble. Rich people were spoiled. Poor people were warm, caring, and experienced in life. Rich people were cold, sheltered, and materialistic ...." Stereotypes of any kind dehumanize us, both the stereotyper and stereotypee. The sickness of our society damages us each in different and complicated ways, and we sometimes forget that rich people get damaged too.

—Billy Wimsatt

As a funder I was feeling objectified as a source of money. I felt invisible, and I yearned to have more authentic and genuine relationships and to find how to talk about it.

—Carolyn Cavalier

I really value privileged activists when they put themselves in the trenches and take risks to stand up and learn. **– Pam McMichael**

Class Prejudice:
A Two-Way Street

Joanie Bronfman, in More than Money, *Winter/Spring 1998, adapted from her dissertation "The Experience of Inherited Wealth":*

In the process of building successful cross-class relationships, many wealthy people have to confront their own misconceptions and prejudices about others. Wealthy children are likely to receive many overt and subtle messages about the inferiority of people from the "lower classes." Some are discouraged or even forbidden to associate with people from other classes. They are taught to assume that others are only interested in their money. [These] beliefs form an obstacle to the development of trusting, close relationships.

Another obstacle to satisfying cross-class relationships is the resentment, hostility, and negative stereotypes many working and middle-class people project onto their wealthy friends, lovers, and acquaintances. Although hostility towards the rich is socially acceptable in this culture, stereotypes about anyone, including rich people, are unproductive. There are wealthy people who are stingy and only concerned with themselves, but there are also many generous rich people.

Throughout history, many rich people have lived productive lives and given their time, money, and even their lives for the common good. Julia, the wealthy friend portrayed in Lillian Hellman's *Pentimento*, and Raol Wallenberg, the wealthy Swedish diplomat, both died during World War II fighting fascism. Many other wealthy people have worked for social change. Blanket, negative stereotyping ignores and obscures this important tradition among the wealthy.

While money can provide benefits like good health care, excellent education, luxury vacations, and a nice place to live, the rich still get cancer, have children who die, experience physical, social, or mental abuse, get divorced, and are still subjected to oppression as members of other groups, such as Jews, women, or gays. Denying the suffering of wealthy people dehumanizes them.

Overcoming obstacles in a cross-class relationship is hard work and requires ongoing dialogue and challenge. For wealthy people, it also requires becoming clearer about who they are, separating themselves from the common stereotypes of the rich and developing enough self-esteem to challenge their own prejudices while knowing they don't deserve mistreatment.

The First Principle of Movement Building
— Round Three

Anyone who steps out of political passivity to give time to any progressive effort deserves to be honored, appreciated, and treated with complete respect. Disagreements, mistakes, and oppressive behavior call for supportive feedback; they are not justification for abandoning a respectful stance. Solidarity is our only strength.

Many rich people have lived productive lives and given their time, money, and even their lives for the common good.

—Joanie Bronfman

Steps towards Building Alliances

What should middle-class activists do if we want to do better at cross-class collaboration?

Up to this point in the book, implicit (and occasionally explicit) lessons for alliance building have appeared in the form of activists' stories. This section adds concrete advice, perspectives on being an ally, and stories of deliberate cross-class dialogue.

Tips from Working-Class Activists

PUT RELATIONSHIPS FIRST

Middle-class people are often not in the room except on their own issues. A sense of community is not a priority, just whatever their goal is. That's a different perspective than my experience with low-income people who think the community is the main thing, that you're always there for each other.

People always told us that if you spend all this time telling stories and doing class caucuses, you won't have time to get anything done. But skipping that part is a big mistake. Always make time for telling stories. Piedmont Peace Project was successful because we built relationships and trust as we did political work.

—Linda Stout

Whether in Puerto Rico or the US, the more educated someone is, the more they tend to be educated in white culture, logical and linear, and the more they move away from indigenous and African ways of thinking. So the models of struggle tend to be "What's the strategy, get down to the tasks," with less attention to relationships and less tolerance for circular thinking.

—Raúl Quiñones Rosado

It's all about relationship building. Until you start reaching out to people very different from you, until we reach outside comfort zones, nothing's going to change. We can't afford to assume anyone is our enemy. People can grow and change.

—Natalie Reteneller

TALK LESS, LISTEN MORE

The Bus Riders Union has some white members who were always the first to put their hands up. They had opinions on everything. Someone took them aside and asked them to consider the implications of talking so much, the connection between privilege and feeling so sure of your voice.

—Manuel Criollo

At a peace festival in a working-class area of Philadelphia, the Veterans for Peace were there. This working-class guy brought up the subject of antiwar coalition meetings. "They're getting worse and worse, less and less practical. They must think verbosity makes peace. They exhaust me. I have to go home and get up to get the kids to school and go to work. I can't stay as long as people who

Training for Change

George Lakey

have more discretion in when to get up. I have to stop going to these meetings."

—George Lakey

There's a woman who I think of as one of my best allies. But when I would say to her, "So and so said this to me," and I wanted her to be my ally about classism, she'd say, "She didn't really mean it that way." One time I said, "I know she didn't mean it that way, but I need you to understand that I'm feeling hurt and to listen and be a friend and not try to fix it." After that, she got it, and we became really close.

—Linda Stout

In many organizations I've been part of, decision-making is hard. Middle-class people with more education are just faster and more articulate. Others are silenced because they can't keep up with the style of arguing.

—Barbara Willer

DON'T LET GUILT MAKE YOU FOOLISH

Middle-class white activists always see the best in everyone, so they get scammed. I see through people's bullshit and I tell my coworkers, and then some of them get upset because they think I'm being judgmental. They say I'm seeing the glass half-empty: "We should believe that people can change." But others are also jumping up and down saying they see the same warning signs, and then it turns out that someone really was taking advantage of the organization. Money gets lent, and some people have a different excuse every week on why they can't pay it back. But my middle-class coworker says, "But they're really hurting," and I say, "That's why they talked with you and not me, they know you're the softy."

—Lisa Richards

White middle-class activists go to one of two extremes on black experiences. Either they think they already know all about black experiences, or they assume they don't know anything and rely on any black spokesperson to be their interpreter. There's a middle position, not relying on a racial spokesperson, but also not making assumptions without investigating to learn more about particular black experiences. It shouldn't be "whatever you say" to a black person. They have to bring their critical faculties and their own experiences to bear.

Sometimes they have a well-meaning impulse to include people of color in a coalition, but they sometimes primarily choose a person on the basis of their race and not their politics, and they sometimes get someone with politics contradictory to the organization's. All black people experience racism, but we respond differently to it, some in individualistic ways. If you don't look at politics, not just on racial issues but on class issues, you are going to get into trouble. If instead whites approach coalition politics by simply saying "I need one of these and one of those," then that's problematic.

—Preston Smith

HANG IN

Low-income folks believe that middle-class folks won't stick around. When the going gets tough, they'll leave. It's a vicious cycle: it happens so much that there's no trust, so middle-class people wonder why they should stick around if they're not trusted. The key is to stick with it even if pushed away. You'll be tested. Like when [civil rights pioneer] Septima Clark sent me as a white person to a black church meeting, and I came back saying they didn't want me there. She asked "What did you expect? Now, next time you go …" She kept sending me back to that group until I had built trust.

I really value middle-class activists when they're willing to stick it through hard times – and I say that coming out of an area where doing this work meant Klan harassment and threats.

—Linda Stout

Middle-class activists drive me crazy when they believe that just speaking truth to power will change the minds of the powerful. **—George Lakey**

Latino middle-class activists drive me crazy when they wimp out. When they engage only if it's convenient and fits into their schedule, and then if it gets uncomfortable, they withdraw. During the Vieques struggle, I saw some folks who have relative comfort and status, who are very committed in their hearts, but who said, "I'm really burned out here, I know you're struggling but see you later." We all need vacations, but some withdrew on a long-term basis. I respect someone's need for sanity and well-being in their lives, but they have the privilege to be able to take a break. They don't have to deal with the issues.

—Raúl Quiñones Rosado

I organized a classism course with an owning-class woman, and she did a good job at hanging in with me. When I got angry, she'd try to understand and not get mad back. I asked her, "What are you doing here? Why aren't you walking away?" She said, "I'm committed to supporting you." She listened to me, asked about my life.

But sometimes she fell through, like dropping a conference workshop we were planning, leaving all the work to me, because "I'm feeling overwhelmed and can't handle it." I think she was oblivious to what really being overwhelmed is like.

—Rachel Rybaczuk

SUPPORT WORKING-CLASS ISSUES

Last year the police shot a black man, James Taylor, while he was handcuffed. There were demonstrations about it every weekend. This was before the Iraq war. Not many of the white middle-class antiwar activists had been involved in the James Taylor organizing. One weekend there was a march for peace, and some people attempted to bring the two groups together, with speakers from each group on stage. But then the demonstrators left separately. The deep community building didn't happen.

—Natalie Reteneller

Want to be an ally? Honor boycotts, buy union, use union printers, don't cross picket lines, pay a living wage, and give family leave and good benefits.

—Felice Yeskel

In the 1980s in my city, the Nuclear Freeze campaign put a referendum on the ballot, and 60 percent of the voters supported a freeze on nuclear weapons. Then Jobs with Peace proposed a followup referendum calling for more jobs through peace conversion, which had the potential for even more public and labor support. But most of the Freeze people just faded away, uninterested.

I was asked to speak at a statewide Freeze convention, and I made a strong pitch for reaching out to labor and working-class people. Afterwards, in the hallway, a number of working-class people came up to me and said it made a big difference to them; they hadn't had the nerve to raise it themselves.

Sometimes peace activists kind of raise their noses, as if it's more pure to be against war for idealistic reasons, as if it's a bit tawdry to be concerned with jobs and self-interest.

—George Lakey

WATCH YOUR LANGUAGE

The Rainbow Party and Green Party were merging. Our meetings with the white middle-class guys from the Green Party were challenging, to say the least. The Rainbow Party thought it was going to whip them into shape – but it needed to deal with its own internal racism and classism. A man on the board of Rainbow Party said a "$25,000 word." I said, "Do you have a dictionary for that word?" He

laughed and went on. I said, "No, really, I need to know what that word means," and he went on. So I stopped the meeting and said, "This is the problem, the Rainbow Party is trying to influence the Green Party, and we can't even talk among ourselves." Turns out he had made up the word. He was laughing because everybody but me knew it didn't exist.

—Lisa Richards

When I was a college undergrad, I went to a Socialist Party meeting. They went on and on, talking in a way that was abstract, competitive, abstract, unrelated to my life experience – and did I mention abstract? I concluded, "That's interesting, but it's not for a working-class guy like me." It was years before I realized the irony of a socialist group not being relevant to working-class people.

—George Lakey

Language has been one of the larger barriers I've seen. In materials written for college-educated people, the educational level is greater than, for example, members of the Piedmont Peace Project could relate to. It's not just the words, it's the whole context of the way things are written.

When we had built a strong base of power so national groups wanted to work in coalition with us, they would say "Give this to your members." But the material was absolutely impossible. So the only way we could work in coalition was to take the materials and translate them into our own language. So if the peace movement called up and said there's this big effort against the MX missile, we would have to say, "Give us all the information, how much it costs," and then we'd have to think how much housing that money would buy. We'd have to make the links to things that made it important to our community. We'd beg them to do the translation, but they didn't see the need, or they couldn't quite do it because they could only see it from their perspectives.

It's not about avoiding all big words. We brought an economist in from New York who used big words, but she was able to explain them to us so we understood.

—Linda Stout

USE YOUR PRIVILEGE

If you have privilege, have a conversation with low-income leaders about how you could use it strategically. If you have a country house, maybe we could have a retreat there. It's not just your money, it's who you know, what you know, how you talk.

We were organizing a conference on homelessness, and members of our group who were homeless were going to speak. There was a woman who had a lot of classism. She said, "How are you going to find homeless people to ask to speak? Would they know enough? How could you find homeless people who can talk well enough?" I was going to debate someone on the Governor's Council, and she said, "Do you know how to debate? Do you know enough information to debate? Would you be able to keep up with him?" I asked my owning-class coworker to talk with her, and she persuaded her. Now this woman points out classism when it happens. That's the fastest turn-around I've seen. My coworker was able because of her similar background to explain how things sounded. It was a strategic use of privilege.

—Lisa Richards

People with more privilege need to figure out how to equalize things, which doesn't mean to empty out their bank accounts. But it's the responsibility of activists to be generous and to figure out how to support things they care about materially if they possibly can.

—Barbara Smith

I resent people who try to pass as someone like me. I met an upper-middle-class woman who said, "I'm on welfare so I can be a full-time activist with youth." That's not what welfare's there for. I hate it when people hide their privilege and don't acknowledge it.

—Rachel Rybaczuk

Middle-class activists drive me crazy when they see race and class issues being brought up as being divisive, not realizing that the race and class differences themselves are divisive. **– Paul Kivel**

HAVE A LITTLE HUMILITY

Constant critiquing and challenging drains me. I think people learn it in college. Say you put up on the wall a proposed mission. Instead of discussing the content, people say "That word's not exactly right." Or they spend an hour arguing over the agenda. It's a big issue because it shuts people down.

It's a piece of movement culture, and working-class people learn to do it too, but I believe it comes from a middle-class perspective.

—Linda Stout

I don't know if you've ever heard this term "Miss Ann" but the Miss Ann attitude needs to be dispensed with. I'm talking about white middle-class arrogance. Sometimes the slightest comment sets our teeth on edge, and it's like, "Later for you! I don't need to be dealing with THAT mess, life's hard enough as it is."

—Barbara Smith

If grassroots people have attitudes of racism or anti-immigrant prejudice, a negative approach isn't productive. Nobody likes to be told they are wrong, especially by a more privileged person. Instead, ask questions and help someone learn. Hold fast to principles, but let go of ideology. Equity is a principle, but "only one way to get there" is ideology.

—Barbara Willer

When some middle-class male activists start expounding, they turn into know-it-all gasbags. I wish I had the self-confidence of some of these guys who can talk on and on and on as if they were absolutely right about everything.

—Barbara Ehrenreich

My pet peeve is a technique for interrupting racism called "calling out." Say if you say something that's sexist, I say "Betsy, that's sexist" right there in the group. That's what some young middle-class people do, and they see it as a mighty blow for freedom. It's the norm in some groups, calling out. It chills the groups' environments; people are more scared, have less trust.

It comes from academia, where middle-class people are trained to maintain hierarchy in the society. Even if working-class children start out thinking they're equal, the teachers' and preachers' job is to remind them that they're not. So rating people on scales is common in schools. And it is brought to diversity work by college-educated people. In middle-class families, too, people are tested and found wanting, and sometimes excluded. Working-class people at our best are about acceptance, not testing each other.

I asked [working-class diversity trainer] Felice Yeskel about it. She said that if your goal is ranking people, calling people out works, but if your goal is helping people learn and grow, it's dysfunctional.

I had five people from the calling-out subculture in a workshop. They sat warily, waiting for someone to say something wrong so they could call them out, or waiting to be called out. It was day 14 of a 17-day training before they could relax enough to learn anything. If we're aiming to build a movement able to take on the greatest empire the world's ever known, we need people who can put their attention on learning.

I know that when someone is inviting me to change my behavior about something, what works is when they approach me as a friend and I know they're caring about me rather than only about some political point they're trying to make. The missionary stuff reminds me of fundamentalists trying to save me, so I react defensively. I'd rather that a comrade simply approach me with the attitude of a friend who knows that we teach each other and give each other a hand.

—George Lakey

LET GO OF CONTROL

I've seen this pattern over and over. A cross-class alliance is formed to deal with a problem. A group with resources offers to sponsor it. They staff it, they control the funding, they control the information …. Next thing you know, we have our own class divide internally. We build power just to give it away, without knowing it's been given away until it's gone.

—Sam Grant

I helped start a community development corporation that created affordable housing. The board was all professionals, and all of us in the houses were neighborhood people. There was so much tension over decision-making and who had the control. We argued over what color paint to use. The middle-class folks didn't get the concerns about power and why the working-class folks were so frustrated. We had no language for it, because everyone was white, so weren't we all the same?

—Barbara Willer

RECOGNIZE WORKING-CLASS PEOPLE'S CONSTRAINTS

I remember going to a national women's group conference. They wanted low-income people and people of color there, so we said sure, Piedmont Peace Project would bring a group of folks in. First, they didn't do a sliding scale, which was shocking enough. But the worst thing was, we came with kids in tow, and we got there and there was no childcare. We had to turn around and go home. We were so used to providing childcare, we assumed there would be childcare.

Some groups have meetings in the middle of the day, and then wonder why no working people come. Ridiculous! We used to plan meetings taking people's work hours into consideration. In farm communities, we'd meet after dark. With millworkers, we'd have meetings in shifts, one in the morning and one at 6 p.m. You've got to know your constituency.

—Linda Stout

Who gets to be the gatekeeper for resources? In a poor community, when one organization has some access to, say, scholarship money for a training program, who decides? This woman controlled a pot of money to send people to our community organizing programs, and she wanted to give only partial scholarships so that participants would have to make some effort, do some fundraising. And I agree with that, because if something is given away, people don't value it, they're more likely to drop out. But I'm also aware of a barrier she's setting up, which is a class dynamic, and a classic example of gatekeeping.

—Raúl Quiñones Rosado

Middle-class kids of color disappoint me when they want to get involved in communities of color but don't last long. We want to create long-distance runners, not sprinters. **– Manuel Criollo**

I hate it when middle-class advocates go to conferences themselves without taking low-income activists with them and without raising money to fund low-income people to be able to go. No conference on poverty should happen without someone living in poverty. But also, don't send a low-income person by themselves! I went to DC by myself for a NOW [National Organization for Women] conference, I didn't know where I was going, and they wanted more money from me than I was supposed to pay. You need someone else with you at a conference, like a buddy system. If you haven't been to enough conferences and aren't empowered enough to speak up, you need someone to have a conversation about what happened.

—Lisa Richards

In Southerners on New Ground, we always budgeted money to bring people who couldn't afford the travel to our weekend retreats. We bought plane tickets for people. We didn't make them fill out a fancy form to prove their need. We only got burned once.

—Pam McMichael

Sharing Resources and Control

Creating cross-class alliances means not only changing our interpersonal behavior, but actually sharing the money and decision-making power that flows more easily to middle-class and owning-class groups. This is not easy to do. Foundations and government agencies may find professionally run organizations more worthy of funding than low-income organizations. Technical expertise actually is crucial to many social change projects, and having it gives clout. Institutional backing gives some organizations a stability that few grassroots groups have.

Explicit discussion about decision-making and funding can strengthen community groups' clout and prevent coalitions from being shattered. Here are a few examples:

- *Some coalitions have made agreements that no member group will write funding proposals for the coalition's area of work for themselves alone, but only on behalf of the coalition.*

- *One-person-one-vote rules let bigger groups pack meetings and dominate coalitions. One-group-one-vote decision-making rules prevent Goliaths from out-voting Davids. Some coalitions go further and make the people affected by the issue the sole decision makers; but rarely will organizations commit scarce resources to a coalition in which they have no say over the strategy.*

- *Coalition procedures can be set up to suit the least funded member groups. For example, money for travel expenses can be fronted instead of reimbursed.*

- *Some coalitions have put technical experts at the disposal of grassroots groups.*

- *Training in technical information as well as in public speaking and media can empower working-class and low-income people to play a wider range of roles in the coalition.*

I have a commitment to turning resources outward. If as a professional I develop relationships, I need to turn those relationships over to the organization, over to people from other backgrounds.

I teach at UCLA, and I developed a community scholars program in which organizers can come work on whatever they're interested in. That's one way of turning resources outward, using the university's resources to help build an infrastructure for economic justice.

—Gilda Haas

Two neighborhood residents mobilized a team of residents to examine race and class disparities in financial institutions in the city of St. Paul. This project, the Community Banking and Economic OpporClusive Project, worked with poor people on economic literacy and access to financial credit. We did workshops on how the economy works and on financial sobriety, so poor people would understand what part of their poverty came from own actions and which part came from structures of the economy. We wanted to create a model of non-racist access to financial institutions.

We brought bankers and businesses together with the community to talk about the opportunity gap and the part each has to play.

One woman came to the group because she was about to lose her house, and only a loan from a known predatory lender could save it. We gave her names of bankers who would go over the deal with her, and two people gave her an hour each. She managed to get a loan at 10 percent instead of 24 percent. The group was there for her.

—Sam Grant

Middle-class activists drive me crazy when they lack a deeper consciousness that class work isn't just being nicer to people who have less than you, it's economic justice work, restructuring resources so they're not so concentrated in the hands of a few. – Pam McMichael

The Ally's Balancing Act

blw

Sometimes when we first realize how class-biased our thinking is, we have an impulse to throw out everything we've ever thought. We start to believe that only working-class and low-income people have the answers to how to make social change. The pendulum swings from an oblivious middle-class-only worldview to blindly following working-class activists, with a rejection of all book learning. This is an unnecessary narrowing of our minds. Our own life experience gives us valid perspectives, and useful ideas can be found in books and in other middle-class people's thinking as well as in working-class people's thinking.

I have been very influenced by the Gandhian idea of truth. Every person has a piece of the truth, but no-one has the whole truth. The first step to a broader truth is to take a stand strongly for our own piece of the truth, and then to engage in principled struggle with those who disagree. If we listen, more truth emerges from the struggle.

When I apply this theory to cross-class alliances for social change, I think that middle-class activists have useful perspectives that can help the struggle move forward, but we only have a portion of what's needed. Our working-class and low-income coalition partners have crucial pieces that we need to learn. And there are other pieces that none of us yet have, but that we need to discover together – and that discovery takes trust and good communication across differences.

The working-class and low-income points of view we need to hear are not handed to us on a silver platter. Few working-class people have official platforms like published articles and books, talk shows, and speeches at conferences through which to disseminate their ideas. Our starting point is not just ignorance, but a head full of negative images. It takes a lot of effort, consistently over years, to hear working-class voices and get our perspectives balanced enough so

that in our minds middle-class points of view don't drown out working-class ones.

But sometimes middle-class activists have thoughtlessly subsumed themselves into movements led by working-class or poor people. To put our energy into a working-class-led group because we believe in the effort and we want to help can be a self-respecting and sensible move. But I get nervous when I hear declarations that all middle-class thinking

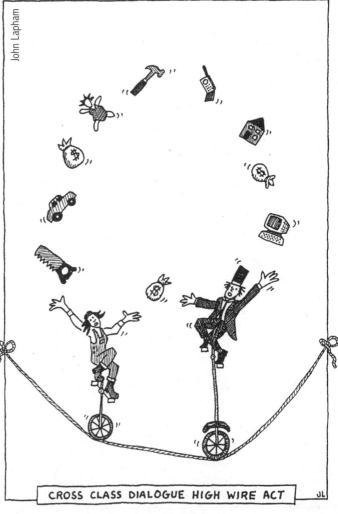

John Lapham

CROSS CLASS DIALOGUE HIGH WIRE ACT   JL

is bullshit, that only low-income people's analysis and leadership will bring about social change.

I heard the great labor historian Staughton Lynd speak, and I had a negative reaction to his description of himself as an "accompanist," meaning that his career has been accompanying working-class-led organizing efforts. It didn't seem honest, for one thing. He clearly has created his own ideas about union organizing, not just passively followed union ideas. And I'm not sure working-class efforts would benefit from middle-class people doing nothing but accompanying them.

Similarly, I've had a negative reaction when I heard middle-class staff of low-income organizations describe themselves as tools in the hands of the members. Again, this seems like a necessary corrective swung too far, from professional domination to professional passivity.

It's not easy to contribute our skills and ideas without dominating. It's not easy to find a balance between over-emphasizing middle-class worldviews and over-relying on other people's thinking just because they are working-class. We find the balance when we listen more to working-class people and to our own best judgment as well.

To me the key to finding the balance is being well informed about the particular nature of class oppression, and for those of us who are white, about the particular kinds of racism each ethnic group faces. Well-meaning people who don't learn enough aren't very useful, nor are people who turn their minds off and become passive followers.

Let me give examples from the oppression I know best from the down side: sexism. There's a kind of man, let's call him the Clueless Humanist, whom I've met so often that I can quote him from memory: "I don't have any problem with women! I treat everyone alike, woman or man. Some of my best friends are women." Meanwhile he's missing every sexist thing going on around him because he doesn't know the first thing about it.

And as bad as the Clueless Humanist is the Wannabe-Feminist Wimp: "We men can't know what women go through. I follow women's lead." He has learned chapter and verse about sexism in the abstract, but he's too weak to actually help in real situations. It's easy for unscrupulous women to push him around or manipulate him into backing their side of a feud by implying that it would be sexist not to. He can't stand other men because they are so sexist, so he berates them, but he never sits humbly down with them to unlearn sexism together.

And then there's the Informed Ally. He has taken it upon himself to learn about sexism and feminist theory, from books and by listening to women. He keeps his antennae up for sexism and takes initiative to do something about it, experimenting with different approaches to being helpful. He keeps his mind turned on, not automatically agreeing with anything any woman says. There are feminist women he trusts, with whom he checks out his decisions. He is accountable to them, but doesn't follow them like a puppy-dog.

For example, say a meeting happens across a dark park from the bus stop. Because he has gone to the trouble of learning about violence against women, the Informed Ally notices the situation without any woman saying anything.

Middle-class activists drive me crazy when they romanticize the working class,
saying they'll have all the solutions spontaneously. — **Barbara Ehrenreich**

Maybe he speaks up and says, "Let's all walk across the park together" or "Next time let's hold the meeting in a better-lighted place." Or maybe he proposes a petition to the city to add a bus stop on this side of the park. The Clueless Humanist leaves early and wanders over to the bus alone. The Wimpy Wannabe says something rhetorical about violence against women and calls the group sexist for meeting there, but says it's up to the women to decide what to do about it – which means he does nothing.

As a woman, I prefer an Informed Ally because he has specific knowledge of how sexism works and he proactively acts on it. He may make mistakes and step on women's toes, but by hearing feedback and learning from mistakes, he steadily becomes a more effective anti-sexist.

(I am dramatizing the contrast between the three types here, of course. In fact, sometimes one guy played each of the three roles at different times.)

I want to be an Informed Ally against classism and racism, but I'm afraid I still sometimes do things that fall on the Clueless Humanist end of the spectrum. I treasure the bits of specific knowledge that let me pick up what's going on and be effective as an ally. For example, because I've learned that some people live paycheck to paycheck, I've raced to get payroll checks cut early in the day, before the banks close, without being asked.

But for every issue I *am* aware of, there are hundreds I don't know enough about to help. I don't want to give up and be a Wannabe-Working-Class Wimp, saying that I can't possibly know anything about working class people's experience, so I should just step back and do whatever they tell me to.

For example, I've been a newsletter editor considering articles by working-class people with limited formal education, and I've been all over the spectrum, made every possible mistake. As a Clueless Humanist, I marked up drafts with a red pen just as I would with a college-educated author and was surprised to get a negative reaction based on bad experiences with high-school teachers, sometimes as

Marilyn Humphries

Arrest at sit-in against Central America intervention.

extreme as quitting the group. As a Wimpy Wannabe, I let things be published that were such a mess that the intended readers couldn't make sense of them. And occasionally I've managed to be a supportive Informed Ally, listening to inexperienced writers' past stories about writing, encouraging them and drawing them out, and holding up high standards while discussing what edits would help the readers understand. I don't find it easy to strike the right balance.

I had a working-class African American friend (who has since passed away) with a job at a nonprofit warehouse distributing furniture and other household goods to formerly homeless people. She told me, "You couldn't do my job. You're too soft. A lot of people got a scam, and I can see through them, but you couldn't." My Wimpy Wannabe side did not command her respect.

I see Wimpy Wannabe behavior all over the economic justice movement. Why? Our attraction towards acting on our inner Wimpy Wannabe is partly because it's "cool" to be connected with an oppressed group, and because we're avoiding facing our dominant role. The most eye-catching manifestation of this is clothes and hair that literally try to imitate low-income people, sometimes with unintended condescending parody. And partly we give in to our inner Wimpy Wannabes because we are afraid of being called classist or racist, and it's easier to silence our principled disagreements and lower our standards. Finally, as beginner allies, we don't know enough to be Informed Allies, so the best we can figure out to do is to be nice and deferential to working-class people, so we are Wimps by default.

> *I see Wimpy Wannabe behavior all over the economic justice movement. Why? Our attraction towards acting on our inner Wimpy Wannabe is partly because it's "cool" to be connected with an oppressed group, and because we're avoiding facing our dominant role.*

Patronized by the Left

When I share my experiences of growing up poor with folks whose political views are left of center, I often receive unmerited respect and become someone who cannot be challenged or contradicted. As patronizing as I find this, I realize it has its advantages.

—Scot Nakagawa, in *Queerly Classed: Gay Men and Lesbians Write about Class*

Sometimes attempts at championing anticlassist or antiracist causes have the effect of casting actual working-class people or people of color as helpless victims, reinforcing stereotypes. For example, one white coworker at a nonprofit regularly proclaimed righteously, "Staff of color have never gotten enough support here to be able to do their jobs," which patronized and dismissed colleagues of color who had in fact accomplished impressive things for the organization.

One kind of Wimpy Wannabe assumes that the most apolitical or conservative members of a community speak for the whole community, and so doesn't see potential for change. For example, in my antinuclear group, when we did outreach in new neighborhoods, one middle-class organizer came back from a working-class neighborhood saying righteously, "No-one there cares about nuclear power. They're too busy struggling to survive." In fact, a thriving chapter was organized there; only a handful of people who did care were needed to start it, not the whole neighborhood. By having an attitude of passively following the lead of grassroots working-class people and refusing to put forth an issue that doesn't arise spontaneously from them, people can miss opportunities for progress.

The opposite type of Wimpy Wannabe assumes that the most radical voices in a community are typical of the whole community. They become mindless followers of the most militant faction, accusing skeptical people of being

Middle-class activists drive me crazy when they fail to listen. — **Theresa Funiciello** classist or racist, when in fact most of the community in question shares a similar skepticism. They pick up and use rhetoric that leaves most of the community cold, thinking they're being culturally appropriate. For example, some white middle-class activists took up the cause of the group MOVE and anointed them Philadelphia's black leadership at a time when in fact almost everyone in the surrounding African American neighborhood objected to the group's violence, squalor, and noisy disruptions (without, of course, condoning the police violence against them). In the 1970s, I saw white activists use the phrase "Third World" to refer to people of color (then leftists' preferred term) in front of mixed-race grassroots audiences who had never heard the term before.

The late 60s saw an extreme form of this trend in the Weathermen and other violent groups of mostly college-educated white young people. Some thought they were imitating the Black Panthers, not seeing that they didn't have the same realistic concerns about self-defense. Some of them explained their bank robberies and bombings by saying, "We're taking on ourselves the same risks black people face on the streets every day." I imagine an African American person of the day thinking, "Don't do me any favors!" Contrast this pointless imitation with the white Freedom Riders, who risked beatings to desegregate buses in the South. They were thoughtful allies who listened to people before championing them, and who took risks strategically.

Once I saw Wimpy Wannabes endanger someone's life. On the 50th anniversary of the 1929 stock market crash, about 1,000 of us, mostly white college-educated activists, tried to shut down the New York Stock Exchange to protest nuclear investments. Because heavy police reaction was expected, we had strict rules: that everyone had to go through non-violence training to participate, and that everyone had to be part of an "affinity group" – a small group that would look after each other. Several untrained and unaffiliated people approached my affinity group the

morning of the action and were told no, it was too late to join. Then a middle-aged black woman, with an accent that made us guess she was a low-income Southerner, begged us to join. We caucused. I thought we should say no, but I was outvoted by the other members. One of them said, "She's probably done more civil disobedience than all of us put together," presuming that she had been active in the Civil Rights movement. She joined us as we sat in before a door to the Stock Exchange. When the police charged their horses at us, she screamed, clutched her heart, and said she had chest pains. The police carried her out through the crowd as a medical emergency. It turned out she had never done civil disobedience before, nor had she done any role-playing trainings to prepare for such confrontations. My affinity group members abandoned their better judgment in the face of someone with less privilege than them – the essence of being a Wimpy Wannabe.

Building a cross-class movement requires those of us in "dominant" groups to be savvy and tuned in, to look for

Building a cross-class movement requires those of us in "dominant" groups to be savvy and tuned in, to look for the best thinking both in less privileged people and in ourselves and other more privileged people.

the best thinking both in less privileged people and in ourselves and other more privileged people. We need to get systematic in our efforts to raise our own consciousness by hearing the life experience of working-class people or people of color and drawing lessons about how to be more informed allies.

Steps to Becoming a More Informed Ally
to Working-Class and Low-Income People

blw

1) Read Howard Zinn's *The People's History of the United States* and other books about low-income revolts, labor struggles, and working-class life stories.

2) Join Jobs with Justice (www.jwj.org) and read their alerts about local labor struggles that need support. Act on them when you can.

3) Subscribe to the newsletter of a local low-income-led group. (If you can't find one locally, subscribe to *Survival News* [102 Anawan Ave, West Roxbury, MA 02132].) (www.survivorsinc.org).

4) Attend conferences where working-class and low-income people speak, for example Labor Notes (www.labornotes.org).

5) Don't cross picket lines. Stop and ask why they're picketing.

6) Donate money to organizations working for a stronger social safety net and decent wages, for example the Kensington Welfare Rights Union (www.kwru.org) and the Coalition of Immokalee Workers (www.ciw-online.org).

7) Be a loyal and supportive friend to low-income and working-class people in your personal life. Ask them how they see various political and interpersonal situations. (Remember, people who work for you in any capacity may never tell you their honest opinions.)

8) In organizations you're associated with, ask the lowest people on the totem pole, and anyone from a working-class background, how they see the organization. Keep asking and listening, as the first answer you hear may not be their whole story.

Balancing Acts

A running argument I've had with one group in Philadelphia is over the line that "movements should always be led by the poorest." That overlooks the contributions of other classes. And it's not true that you can't co-opt working-class people — look at War on Poverty! Its major purpose was to hire activist leaders and take them away from the front lines, and, sadly, it often worked.

—George Lakey

I have seen some really bad organizers whose attitude is "Well, we know what's best for the workers, so we need to show them that this is the best thing for them." The other approach would be that we need to develop and train workers to decide for themselves. They know what's best, more than anybody. So it's just a matter of making it possible for them to collectively demand what they already know is best for them.

It's a tricky balance. I don't think middle-class people should be silent, because if we do have some skills or insights or strategies, I think we should put them on the table. That doesn't mean our way is what will happen. But we should be able to contribute, and say, "What about this, what about that?" But I do think it's a hard balance to use our skills, but in a way that is ethical and that is not exercising power by virtue of our class status.

It's a balancing act to believe that people can decide for themselves, to critically interrogate your power relations, and not to lose your critical faculties.

—Dorian Warren

I really value middle-class activists when they risk not knowing. — **Ellen Smith**

Reducing Classism
in Nonprofit Organizations

The following checklist from the corporate sector seems useful for nonprofit organizations as well. Just mentally substitute "organization" for "company."

Excerpts from an article by Indra Lahiri, Workforce Development Group, and Kimberlee Jensen, Isis Eye Media, published on the Diversity Central website (www.diversityhotwire.com)

Classism shows up in the workplace. Consider your own organization. From what class are most of your managers and executives? How about your janitorial staff? Who is treated with more respect? Who has more opportunities to gain income and power? How about access to education (consider educational assistance, time to attend courses, and training opportunities)? Does it vary by level?

Recruitment

Does your company seek alternative recruitment channels for those who did not attend college but are qualified for various positions? Conversely, does your company consider college-educated people for jobs traditionally held by those who did not attend college?

Many talented potential employees may be overlooked if your organization holds a strong preference either for college-educated or for non-college-educated people. Instead, help hiring managers to look at the person's ability to do the job.

Are those with extensive unpaid internships given preference over those with lots of paid work experience?

Internships ... can provide excellent training opportunities for students. However, it must be recognized that unpaid internships require a time investment that many people cannot afford.

Job expenses

Does the company ask employees to use their own laptops or their own automobiles?

Do positions involve business travel that requires employees to spend their own money upfront and be reimbursed later?

Even company credit cards may pose problems for people who have bad credit histories.

Weekend and off-hours events

Are required team-building or training events scheduled during off-hours, such as weekends or nights for weekday employees?

Does the company offer assistance for child or elder care when employees are required to attend events or work beyond their normal schedule?

Jokes and slurs

Do employees use classist terms such as "trailer trash" or "rich b_ _ ch"? Even uttered as jokes, these are as offensive and as intolerable as racial slurs.

External communities

Do your company's charitable contributions include organizations that serve lower-income households?

Location

Is your company accessible via public transportation? If not, is transportation from major cities to the work site provided for employees who cannot afford an automobile?

Levelism

Does your company have different rules, or application of rules, for employees at higher levels in the organization? What perks are offered only at certain levels?

Do people only speak to, or know the names of, "important" people?

The leadership of the company can and should set an example by making sure that members of all levels of the organization are recognized. This practice reinforces the idea that all employees, regardless of their position, should be treated with dignity, and fosters a sense of humanity and decency in the workplace.

Sustaining Staff for the Long Haul

At Alternatives for Community and Environment (ACE), we've thought about what wellness means and how you sustain people's involvement in this work by the salaries you pay and the benefits you provide. We've thought about being able to support single-parent households. We know our salaries are not yet sufficient; there are still places we need to make up. There's a middle-class mentality that working in the nonprofit sector means taking a pay break, accepting less salary because it's something you believe in. But if we want to have staff who are not in it because it is a luxury or a lifestyle choice, but because it is work they have to do, then you have to figure out how to create a working environment that enables them. We try to make sure that people of equal value to the organization are at equivalent amounts of pay, so the salary for someone with a law degree isn't driven by the market for lawyers. We joined the National Organizers Alliance pension plan, and we cover all health benefits.

—Penn Loh

Marilyn Humphries

I really value middle-class activists who respect everyone's different contributions. – **Gilda Haas**

Walking the Talk
in Our Individual Lives

Simple Living
as Solidarity with the Poor

bell hooks, from *Where We Stand: Class Matters*:

At church we were taught to identify with the poor. This was the spoken narrative of class that dominated my growing-up years. The poor were chosen and closer to the heart of the divine because their lives embodied the wisdom of living simply ....

Solidarity with the poor .... was to be expressed not just by treating the poor well and with generosity but by living as simply as one could. If you were well off, choosing to live simply meant you had more to share with those who were not as fortunate ....

As a nation, a shift in attitudes toward the poor began to happen in the seventies. Suddenly notions of communalism were replaced with notions of self-interest ....

While new age spiritual thought gathered momentum, it too tended to "blame" the poor for their plight and exonerate the rich. Much new age thought actually reversed traditional Christian condemnation of the hoarding of wealth by stressing not only that the poor had freely chosen to be poor (since we live many lives and choose our status and fate), but that economic prosperity was a sign of divine blessing ....

To stand in solidarity with the poor is no easy gesture at a time when individuals of all classes are encouraged to fear for their economic well-being .... As the gap between rich and poor intensifies in this society, those voices that urge solidarity with the poor are often drowned out by mainstream conservatives that deride, degrade, and devalue the poor ....

Constant vigilance (that includes a principled practice of sharing my resources) has been the only stance that keeps me from falling into the hedonistic consumerism that so quickly can lead individuals with class privilege to live beyond their means and therefore to feel they are in a constant state of "lack," thus having no reason to identify with those less fortunate or to be accountable for improving their lot.

Growing up on a tobacco farm, I learned a good value that has stayed with me. Everyone would pitch in to plant the tobacco, and no-one would rest until everyone had their crop in the ground. It wasn't done for pay. It was trading favors, not measured like "I worked eight hours for you today so you owe me eight hours." There was a sense of community. This relates to how I do my political work today.

—Pam McMichael

I think of giving money away as redistribution instead of charity. For ten years there have been redistribution networks among Bay Area lesbians. Dykes with resources pool their money and give it away. There are no forms to fill out, nothing to prove. You have to know someone in the group. If you're a lesbian and poor, you call someone. There's a garage sale each year to raise money for one of these networks. These networks keep it as anonymous as possible. I know one woman who gave a disabled woman an ATM card to a bank account.

—Laura Stern

Housing Betrayals

blw

The touchiest personal class issue, in my experience, is housing.

Becoming cross-class allies means widening our circle of concern to include all the people affected by our personal financial decisions, even our real estate decisions. But making a profit from real estate is considered a God-given right in the United States. Even progressive people bristle at the idea of incorporating any values into their property decisions. I have close friends to whom I would say anything about sex, body odor, even income levels, but not about their real estate decisions, which I fear would be friendship-shattering.

Gentrification often begins when a few white middle-class activists and gay people move into a previously all-working-class neighborhood. We are the "wedge people," followed a few years later by hordes of yuppies. Our very eagerness to live near poor people endangers them. Huddling in the suburbs won't prevent gentrification. We have to do something proactive, like organize for permanently affordable housing.

Here's one example where "wedge people" found a way to be allies. In the late 70s I lived in a group house of white counter-culture activists on an otherwise almost all-black, all-working-class block. Two blocks away were streets recently bought up by white professionals, whose presence made their blocks unaffordable for long-time African American families. From black families on the block we got frosty stares, and from white professionals we got friendly smiles of welcome. The time came to paint the house, which was a somber green. A light bulb went off. We painted the house garish yellow with bright orange trim. Several neighbors stopped by: low-income black folks full of smiles and painting advice, and yuppies sputtering in protest over our choice of colors. Twenty-five years later, the block is still majority working-class African American. I like to think our paint job helped make that happen.

When property values rise, individual homeowners can profit from the "social appreciation," that is, the price increase in excess of the inflation rate and in addition to the value of any improvements. This enriches the sellers, but makes the house unaffordable to people at the class level the sellers were when they moved in. A speculative market can make instant millionaires, push established professionals into small, formerly starter homes, keep working-class and young families stuck in rental apartments, push low-income renters into substandard apartments and doubled-up situations, and leave the lowest-income families homeless. I watched this happen in Boston in the 1980s and 1990s. I was a community organizer in the Jamaica Plain neighborhood when it set a national record for rapid rise of property values. Every

Patrick Gagne

tenement and flophouse was turned into condominiums, and thousands of people had to leave the neighborhood or double up.

Middle-class homeowners drive me crazy when they have a NIMBY [Not In My Back Yard] attitude to good stuff we want to make happen. — **Roxana Tynan**

Usually we don't see the faces of both the speculative profiteers and the people pushed down the housing ladder, but in one case both were my friends. Our former neighbors (call them the Seaborns) bought their four-bedroom condo for $150,000 and lived in it for six years. Their daughters were best friends with the girl across the street, whose family (call them the Bests) was squished into a too-small two-bedroom apartment. The neighborhood was gentrifying

Instead they put the house on the market for $350,000 and took away $200,000 profit. Their new home is on four acres and has a pool. The Bests had another baby, so they now live with four people in a small two-bedroom apartment. Their rent went up again. It was hard for me to look the Seaborns in the eye after they sold their condo. I didn't know what to say. They were good people who didn't see an ethical problem with making housing unaffordable for someone else.

tion, plus any improvements we make on our condo – that's a fair price. Much more and we're ripping someone off. If our home was affordable to a pair of 40-year-olds with master's degrees when we bought it, it should be affordable to a pair of 40-year-olds with masters degrees when we sell it – not just to people with big trust funds. This won't necessarily work for us if we need to move in an inflated market. At Gail's common-sense request, I've agreed that we will take some social appreciation profit if not doing so would jeopardize our ability to meet our basic needs for food, shelter, and health care. But if, like millions of Americans, we don't need to move to an expensive home, but can stay put or retire to a smaller home, then we'll take the social appreciation and donate it to an affordable housing group.

Members of City Life/Vida Urbana

rapidly, and it seemed likely that if the Bests didn't buy a home soon, they wouldn't be able to rent or buy nearby. They were beloved members of the community, hosts of picnics and tag sales. As long as a home cost under $250,000, they could swing it. Mr. Seaborn got a job in a cheaper part of the country. Several neighbors suggested that they sell to the Bests. At a price of $250,000, they would have made $100,000 profit on their condo.

I've heard of efforts to give individual property owners the option of keeping housing affordable. The Equity Trust used to ask homeowners to pledge that when they sell their house, they will give some or all of the social appreciation to a fund invested in permanently affordable housing. Before I would buy a home with my partner, I asked her to agree to take that pledge with me. Our down payment and equity payments, plus infla-

In the Jamaica Plain neighborhood of Boston, the local groups City Life/Vida Urbana and JP Neighborhood Development Corporation organized a "Campaign of Conscience for Housing Justice." Landlords sign a pledge to help keep the neighborhood affordable. For example, landlords might promise to raise rents based on their costs instead of on market trends, or to give current tenants the right of first refusal before a sale, or to donate part of the profits from a sale to a fund for legal expenses of tenants fighting eviction. Through tenant organizing, mediation, and negotiation, these groups have prevented thousands of evictions and other displacements.

Being Served, Respectfully

How many times a week does a service worker do something for you? Pump your gas, drive your bus, make your cappuccino, show you to your table, ring up your purchases, spray for ants, mow your lawn, deliver your pizza, clean your office, dry-clean your pants, cut your hair, feed your kids lunch?

Especially with wages low and new immigrants looking for any work at all, some of us have started to take for granted an abundance of people serving us at every turn.

The progressive response to being served can be challenging to figure out. If we all did everything ourselves to avoid exploiting service workers, it would just mean fewer jobs for people who need them. And in the absence of an organized campaign, it wouldn't accomplish much to say to the Wal-Mart manager, "I'm not buying this toothpaste until you start paying your workers more." Out of discomfort, some people try to personalize relationships in an unwelcome way, like telling their house cleaner she's part of the family. What else can we do?

- Tip as generously as you can afford.

- When you comparison-shop for a service, such as a caterer or dry cleaner, ask the management how much their workers are paid, choose one with decent pay, and tell others you rejected them for their low pay.

- Don't make unnecessary messes and leave them for service workers to clean up.

- Make a habit of noticing service people, making friendly contact, and remembering that they have other interests in life besides serving you. Say thank you.

- Honor boycotts and strikes, join Jobs with Justice, and support service worker union organizing.

Cross-Class Friendships

Without friendship among all the different kinds of people who are unhappy with the current system … progressive organizing is impossible and progressive principles are empty. Social justice grows out of your social circle …. I count on my close female friends and friends from the ghetto to constantly remind me how spoiled I am, how sheltered I am, how off is my sense of proportion, how selfish are my instincts, how dull is my character, how weak and how cowardly I am. These are routine lessons that I need to constantly learn.

—Billy Wimsatt,
No More Prisons

It's offensive to me when people set out to make poor and working-class friends to seem cool. Natural friendships are good, but a premeditated mission to make diverse friends is patronizing and tokenizing.

—Rachel Rybaczuk

Middle-class people drive me crazy when I'm embarrassed by something they're doing and I recognize it as something I also do. When I see myself in their patronizing, ignorant behaviors. **– Gilda Haas**

Fire and Frost:
Shaking up Class Conflict Styles

blw

Years ago I was in a romantic relationship with a wonderful working-class woman I'll call Susan. Gradually tensions and conflicts eroded our good times. The hardest part for me was my usually warm and supportive lover screaming at me, slamming doors, and saying melodramatic things like "I do so much for you and you never do anything for me!" I was miserable.

I had never in my middle-class life been screamed at before. In the face of what seemed like a very extreme situation, I acted as I would in a building on fire: I put aside my own feelings and tried to stay calm and do sensible things to help everyone survive.

Friends and therapists kept reminding me that "it takes two to tango," that every dynamic is created by both people in it. They kept saying there must be things I was doing to keep us stuck, and so things I could do to change the dynamic. I took their advice to mean that I should be more understanding and tolerant, look for creative solutions that would meet both our needs. I tried this approach for months. The more understanding I was and the more I proposed reasonable compromises, the more dramatically emotional Susan acted. I felt more and more resentful, thinking, "I'm not making her be crazy; she's just being crazy on her own."

Finally we had a conversation with a working-class friend trained as a therapist. We described Susan's attempts to control her outbursts and my attempts to find compromises. She said to me, "It sounds like you're managing Susan and the relationship." I asked, "What do you mean?" She said I was pushing away my own personal reactions and stepping outside, like it was my role to be in charge and come up with solutions for both of us, treating Susan as a problem instead of a resource. She asked Susan if she felt like I was "managing" her. "Yes," she said. "Would you like Betsy to stop managing?" "Yes." "Would you

rather hear her real reactions and feelings than her efforts to put those aside and manage things?" "Yes!"

I was stunned. Growing up, suppressing emotions and being reasonable had been good behavior. Susan and I were stuck in a classist dynamic, acting out the communication patterns of our class culture of origin. My efforts to resolve our conflicts were in fact oppressive to her.

For Susan, just at the moments when she started to feel upset, her lover would start acting like every cool distant privileged authority figure she had ever known, so she reacted by feeling enraged and self-hating.

Once we got this insight, we experimented with ways to shift our dynamics. I tried to be more real, more direct, more expressive of my reactions in the moment and my uncertainty. I tried saying, "Shut up! You're being an asshole," which Susan said made her feel loved. Or I would cry and say, "I don't like this and I don't know how to change it." She was more able to call upon her strong interpersonal skills once she heard how much I was hurting. (To my surprise, she hadn't known how unhappy I was when I didn't express it loudly.) Sometimes the tension was broken just because she burst into laughter at the sight of her stiff middle-class girlfriend yelling rude things. She nicknamed us "Born to Manage" and "Born to Hustle," and when the "manager" voice came out of my mouth, we could both name it instead of getting hooked by it.

CLVU

Cross-Class Dialogue

Diversity Training
and **Classism**

Felice Yeskel

Felice Yeskel

Among diversity trainers, a lack of attention to class becomes problematic. Here's an example. I was called in to a college that had a racial incident, and the campus police had responded in a way that exacerbated the problem. So the police force was mandated to do antiracist training. A diversity consultant trained these mostly white, mostly male working-class police who were in resistance. It didn't go well, they were labeled racist, and I was called in to clean up the mess afterwards. It's useful in helping people with any diversity issue to build empathic bridges to people different from themselves, by helping them understand their own experience. In the case of the police group, how they had been on the receiving end of unfairness was on class. If I could validate their experience of classism, of how they were treated, and say, "Yes, you have a legitimate beef," they would be more open to understanding how they were creating dynamics hurtful to other people based on race.

So I find it hard to understand how diversity trainers and consultants can be effective without including class, unless they work exclusively with middle-class or higher groups, which is where most diversity training takes place. But if you want to work with ordinary people, and if you want to get diversity training out of the ivory tower, into popular culture, you're not going to be successful unless you include class.

I first participated in classism workshops in Movement for a New Society in the 1970s, where we tackled class not only in the structural sense, but on the interpersonal and group level. So when I went to graduate school at the University of Massachusetts at Amherst Social Justice Education Program, I was astounded that these people who knew so much about oppression trainings were doing workshops on sexism, racism, anti-Semitism, ableism, and heterosexism – but not classism. They thought they were doing complete anti-oppression training. When I raised it, I got resistance, partly out of confusion about what I meant by

I really value white middle-class activists when they're honest and have done thorough
self-examination of all their positions of privilege and oppression, and when they're
self-aware and can articulate that. **– Dorian Warren**

> *There is acknowledgement that most colleges have a dominant white Euro-centric culture, but not necessarily an awareness of the dominant middle- or higher-class culture.*
>
> —Felice Yeskel

"classism." We started a study group of faculty and graduate students to read some of the classics, like *Worlds of Pain* and *The Hidden Injuries of Class*. We got the go-ahead to develop and teach a course, first for undergraduates and then for graduate students, and I've been teaching it now for over ten years. Betsy Leondar-Wright and I revised the curriculum for a chapter in *Teaching for Diversity and Social Justice*.

I was in a collective of diversity consultants called "Diversity Works" in the 1980s and 1990s, and unlike almost everyone else in the diversity field before or since, we included classism as an oppression and class as part of multiculturalism.

Diversity training on college campuses is problematic without classism because education itself functions as a primary access channel for transitioning across class. Through [the nonprofit group] Class Action, I have co-facilitated support groups for students raised poor or working-class who attend the four elite private colleges in Western Massachusetts (Smith, Mt. Holyoke, Amherst, and Hampshire). If you're white and you come from a poor or working-class background, you show up on these campuses and you are having your mind blown hundreds of times a day, and your reality is never noticed or validated by anyone.

If you are a student of color at these colleges, your experience of being different and in the minority is recognized. There are support services available. You get to be with peers who are also encountering a difference. For some it's a racial or ethnic difference; for some it's both a racial/ethnic *and* a class difference. But you are in a support system that says to you, "Look, we know this must be strange for you. You may be the first generation of your family to go to college. Let us help you." But if you are white and you're having a similar experience, there is absolutely no-one who notices or validates that. You can't find other people like yourself very easily. There is acknowledgement that most colleges have a dominant white Euro-centric culture, but not necessarily an awareness of the dominant middle- or higher-class culture.

I remember one woman who said, "My mom works at the Dunkin Donuts in Holyoke [a very poor city nearby], and I'm a student at Mt. Holyoke." She couldn't even find the words to describe her disorientation. She was transversing cultural worlds that were miles apart, but since she was white, she looked like the typical Mt. Holyoke student, and no-one knew she was freaking out. The students are dealing with major issues like loyalty and disloyalty to the families they left behind, and not knowing how to act.

So when they go to a diversity training and hear about multicultural this and diversity that, and their experience is never noticed, they feel like, "What about me?"

The Power of Telling Our Stories

The heart of our organizing is building relationships. We have working-class and middle-class parents, black, white, and Latino parents, and we do it through telling stories. At every meeting we pair up and share a story from our lives, on a question like "What was your experience of school?" or "What's the history of your family's migration to this state?" It's harder for men, but once they do it, they start to open up.

—Barbara Willer

Piedmont Peace Project began to build relations with wealthy people, and the way we did it was to make sure wealthy people told their stories too. We did not sit down and do a workshop on classism with them. People would come visit PPP once a year during our community celebrations and get a tour of our communities. As part of that we sat down with them and the board and staff and tell our stories. For many of these wealthy people, it was their first time to say the turning points of their lives that brought them to where they were today.

I saw people make life-changing shifts, much more than in any workshops I ever led, just from hearing each other's stories. One man, a doctor at a university, after visiting PPP, left and started a clinic at a project for elderly people.

It was those experiences that allowed us to build trust with people, much deeper than a workshop might have done.

—Linda Stout

Stories
from a **Cross-Class Women's Group**

For Carolyn's 45th birthday, she didn't want to be in isolation as a funder any more. Four of us dropped $4000 in coins and bills on the floor and spent the afternoon reacting to it. We each took a turn. One person didn't have enough money for the rent. People cried. The three women there that day are now in our cross-class group. Carolyn has sometimes shared decision-making over giving her money away with the group.

Carolyn, Gloria, and I wanted to bring up class at this progressive elementary school where our kids went. Of course there are hidden class issues in such a socio-economically diverse community. For instance, pitching in on group gifts for teachers. For some families having to come up with that extra $10 was very stressful, for other families it was not noticeable. Or when the kids made sandwiches to give to the hungry, when some families in our school were struggling (in a hidden way) with their own grocery bills. The work we did there provided some of the ground out of which the cross-class group grew.

—Ahbi Vernon

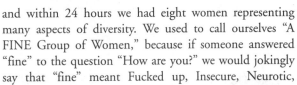

How did the group start? I did an Equity Institute Dismantling Classism workshop, and I found myself yearning for more conversations on class. Since I had grown up in a cross-class family and was in a cross-class relationship, there was something deep I needed to explore. Then in 1997, I was in a workshop led by Lillie Allen, of Be Present, Inc., and I had a vision of a cross-class group, to have genuine, authentic relationships across differences. I knew women who also wanted to talk about class, so I talked with Ahbi and several others, and they in turn knew others,

and within 24 hours we had eight women representing many aspects of diversity. We used to call ourselves "A FINE Group of Women," because if someone answered "fine" to the question "How are you?" we would jokingly say that "fine" meant Fucked up, Insecure, Neurotic, Emotional. What we really wanted to do was to invite each other to be truly present with whatever was going on in our lives as well as inside ourselves at that moment, as we were sitting in the room together. It's been difficult at times, but we continue to try to stay connected even as we work our way through painful feelings.

—Carolyn Cavalier

The cross-class group has been a journey. It's been a process of being able to examine my relationship with money. What do I value, what counts, how do the answers to those questions impact me and my relationship with others. For me it was not just a dialogue, which is an exchange of ideas, but an alliance, an exchange of ideas that leads to an action of some kind. I've never been in a group with that much diversity of class in it, and the concrete alliance work has been amazing. We're enriched not only by each other's stories and lives, but by the concrete actions of allies. For example, Carolyn and another member of the group wrote checks so we could buy our house. I feel tremendous gratitude at that gift. We all shared our wealth … knowledge, wisdom, love, time, as well as money.

Joy and sorrow come into the lives of all the women in the circle, but what money does is open options to deal with sorrows.

—Nell Myhand

I really value middle-class activists that ask me how I feel. **— Ellen Smith**

A Gold Mine of **Class Insights**

Jenny Ladd, with other members of "Cross-Class Dialogue Group" of Western Massachusetts, in Turning Wheel, *January 2000*

One of us has several million dollars for personal use; one of us is in debt with absolutely no financial cushion. One of us grew up with an indoor swimming pool; one of us grew up being called "white trash." Half of us can live on inherited money, and half of us have to work to support ourselves.

We are a group of six men and women from different class backgrounds who have been meeting over the past three years to talk intimately about our experiences with class and money .... We are a laboratory group for one another, doing research on ourselves in hopes of being better organizers in our social-change work and sharing what we learn about bridging the class divide with others down the road ....

We have striven to stay on the edge, to follow our fears and resistance, knowing that there is a gold mine of material to work with in those hidden corners ....

During our first year we decided to do a two-day retreat during which time we revealed to each other our total worth — bank accounts, portfolios, cars, houses, debt, and potential inheritances: all our assets and debts. This was a very scary exercise, and we had to do much work to create safety

for this sharing .... The person with the most money had four times more than anyone else and so grappled with a sense of isolation even from fellow wealthy caucus members. A woman from a working-class background, by working multiple jobs, had managed to save a fair amount of money – and another member of the working-class/poor caucus was shocked by the amount. Another woman struggled

with the shame she felt about having so much debt, even though it was her huge health-care bills that had put her in that position ....

One of the important recurring themes has been how to really allow ourselves to dream, to see ourselves within those dreams, and then to actually think it possible and right that those dreams become reality ....

Not surprisingly, the wealthy people have less trouble dreaming, have more resources to follow their dreams, with no-one to be accountable to and lots of support to go forth and mani-

---

Ground Rules of the Cross-Class Dialogue Group

- Honesty
- Understanding about confidentiality
- Commitment to "clean up" things that may come up
- Good listening
- Willingness to go deep while respecting limits
- Curiosity
- Clarity of intention/purpose/agenda
- Room to be emotional without being taken care of
- Respect as a basis for challenging and confronting each other
- Respect for all types of feelings, sadness as well as fear and anger
- Communication about participation (i.e., alert others if we can't come)
- Room for fun, lightness, and singing
- Shared assumption that we are all doing the best we can
- Speaking from our own experiences
- Periodic check-ins about the process
- Affirmation of different realities/respecting others' experience

fest them …. It is important to add, however, that not all the wealthy people feel so entitled or so free to dream sometimes. Having the money, in fact, often feels like an obligation to have a brilliant dream …. A challenge for people of wealth has been to define their self-worth separately from their net worth ….

In order for the group to work to begin with it was important that everyone be clear that the group was not for fundraising; there was no expectation that any of the wealthy people would fund those without money or their projects …. All of us are committed to institutional social change and feel that individual solutions are needed but not at the core of the problem. This does not mean that some of the wealthy members of the group have not supported low-income members of the group outside of the group context. This has happened quite a bit ….

We have been angry with each other. We have felt deep compassion for each other. We have become aware of our projections onto each other. We

> *In our Cross-Class Dialogue Group, one of the most powerful things for me was when people got connected enough to challenge each other's internalized classism.*
>
> —Linda Stout

> *We have been angry with each other. We have felt deep compassion for each other. We have become aware of our projections onto each other. We have been moved by each other's stories and struggles.*
>
> —Jenny Ladd

have been moved by each other's stories and struggles …. Our dialogues have been, in the healthiest ways, both humbling and inspiring.

Another Voice from the Western Massachusetts Group …

In our Cross-Class Dialogue Group, one of the most powerful things for me was when people got connected enough to challenge each other's internalized classism. In the first two years, it was like, "We're here to help the rich people get through their shit and teach them." Then it began to shift to how internalized oppression stopped our dreams. People challenged that inner glass ceiling that low-income people often have.

For me it was on a deep level. I've overcome a lot of internalized oppression, I was able to quit my job and follow my heart, I was able to fundraise. But when people were talking about their parents aging, getting old and how to support parents, I said I

realized I had never thought about that. I had assumed I wouldn't live that long. I have an immune system disease, so do others I know, my friends are starting to die, so I never expected to live. People said, "You can turn it around" and "We'll support you to do that." It was amazing. It has led me on a path towards life and looking forward long-term.

—Linda Stout

… and from a California Middle-Class Support Group

Our middle-class group has been meeting for about 13 years. We made a list of topics to discuss, and we started covering them one by one. We read *Lesbian Ethics* and *Sinister Wisdom*'s journals on class and Joanna Kadi's book *Thinking Class*. We talked about how to interrupt classism while it's happening, one-on-one, with someone you don't know or with someone you do know. If our goal is educating someone, we found it was not helpful to say, "I can't believe how fucked you are about class!"

—Laura Stern

I really value middle-class activists when they welcome dialogue. **— Ellen Smith**

Cost Sharing

blw

When the "working-class revolution" was happening in Movement for a New Society in the late 1970s, one of the hot issues was how to pay for retreats. We used a sliding scale, and while some working-class people would save all year to pay the middle of the sliding scale for the national gatherings, some upper-middle-class recent college grads and future inheritors would arrive, find $11 in their checking accounts, and pay $10.

We developed a method of sharing the costs based on all relevant factors, not just current income: assets, class background, earning potential, family back-up, and family needs. This cost-sharing process became a way to raise our class consciousness as well as a fairer way to cover retreat costs. I use it to this day in other communities. (To get sample agendas and handouts for this process, contact Felice Yeskel or me. Find her contact info at www.ClassActionNet.org)

I was one of those broke and privileged young people, and I got stern feedback never to pay low on a sliding scale because I chose to be poor. The difference between voluntary and involuntary poverty was hammered into me and, more broadly, a mandate never to hide my privilege or pretend to be the same as a working-class person.

The Movement for a New Society cost-sharing method began in November 1978 during a training program for activists. Participants objected to paying the same fees

when their resources were so different. We went through financial disclosure, and I found myself sitting between someone with $500,000 and someone who was $90 in the hole. "How do we work this?" we wondered.

This question just grabbed me. We made it the central issue of the next training program, with a classism workshop and a disclosure process with support and challenge [encouragement to pay a greater or lesser amount]. People clumped by income, made pledges, then came back together. It was totally thrilling.

So much of my later political work grew out of that experience. MNS started looking at financial accountability, which led to building a land trust with seven properties. The Class Suicide Support Group [an owning-class group in which members considered giving away their inheritance] grew out of it, and from that came the work Christopher

Mogil, Anne Slepian, and Chuck Collins have done with owning-class people. I see the thread from MNS to United for a Fair Economy. [Jerry is the president of the UFE board.]

I called a guy classist and he invited me to be on a foundation board. Relationships between wealthy and working-class people grew not just about money but about true alliance.

—Jerry Koch-Gonzalez

Conclusion
Stepping Forward, Building Bridges

blw

Just as specific critiques of American society grow from the lived experience of the jobless inner city, the rust belt town, or the strip-mined Appalachian mountain, so a genuine critique grows out of the lived experience of middle-class suburban lives. Driving everywhere in a sprawling strip-mall landscape leads to an awareness of lack of community, blandness of culture, and loss of connection to the natural environment – which have sparked middle-class movements to seek community, cultural diversity, and environmental healing. These impulses are real and valid, our pieces of the movement puzzle.

Our experience of American society gives us important truths to contribute to a progressive critique. Just as our viewpoints shouldn't dominate, they shouldn't be missing either. Our characteristically middle-class negative experiences – our boredom, our loneliness, our increasing economic insecurity, our estrangement from nature and from diverse community – reveal the lie in the bootstraps myth that working-class pain can be eliminated by individual striving. There is something systemically wrong with our society, not just that some are left out of its prosperity.

Our life experience is a gift to the movement – and will be more valuable as we learn to speak about it more authentically.

Our abstract thinking and knowledge are gifts to the movement – and will be more valuable as we learn to ground them in experience and humbly pair them with others' concrete knowledge.

Our big-picture vision and our values are gifts to the movement –

and will be more valuable as we learn to offer them more respectfully.

Our hard work and goal-oriented discipline are gifts to the movement – and will be more valuable as we learn to balance them with humor and human connections.

The surge in working-class organizing in the last few years – the living wage movement, immigrant worker organizing, the environmental justice movement, service employee union organizing, and academic working-class studies – gives us opportunities to be more active allies.

So many of the positive stories I heard in interviews include one or more bridge builders: determined, warmly connected, class-savvy activists who find ways to bring people together.

Each of us can build some bridges. Our bridge-building muscles may feel too weak for the job, but it can be satisfying how fast a muscle builds up with regular exercise. Just as we have a million excuses for not exercising, all of us middle-class activists can think of a million reasons why we aren't the right person to be a bridge person. But if we take an honest look around our activist lives – looking for working-class individuals and groups, looking for classism, looking for anticlassist middle-class and owning-class allies, looking for our areas of ignorance, looking for openings for more collaboration – steps will occur to us. If we find support explicitly as middle-class activists, we'll more consistently take those steps.

No one step will make classism disappear or make the movement of our dreams appear. But if enough of us build enough cross-class and cross-race alliances, the movements of the 21st century may outshine those of the last century in the transformations they bring.

Our bridge-building muscles may feel too weak for the job, but it can be satisfying how fast a muscle builds up with regular exercise

---

I really value middle-class activists because their life experience can bring a fuller, richer view to the work. – **Barbara Willer**

Resources

Organizations
and Websites

Class Action is a nonprofit that offers training and consulting about the issues of class and money and their impact on our individual lives, our relationships, organizations, institutions, and culture. Find out more at www.classaction net.org.

Training For Change offers weekend workshops on classism. Find out more at www.trainingfor-change.org, 1-215-241-7035.

Center For Study of Working Class Life at Youngstown State University has biannual conferences on working-class history and culture and labor studies. Find out more at www.workingclass.sunysb.edu.

The Center For Study Of Working Class Life at the State University of New York – Stony Brook has biannual "How Class Works" conferences. Find out more at www.workingclass.sunysb.edu, 1-631-632-7536.

More Than Money is an organization for wealthy people that helps them clarify and act on their values about giving, investing, and spending. They publish *More Than Money Journal*. Find out more at www.morethanmoney.org, 1-781-648-0776.

Resource Generation works with young people with financial wealth who are supporting and challenging each other to effect progressive social change through the creative, responsible, and strategic use of financial and other resources. Find out more at www.resourcegeneration.org, 1-617-225-3939.

A Few Great Books on Class

If you only have time to read two books on cross-class alliance building:

- Fred Rose, *Coalitions across the Class Divide*, Cornell University, 2000.

- Linda Stout, *Bridging the Class Divide and Other Lessons for Grassroots Organizing*, Beacon, 1996.

Books on cross-class dynamics:

- David Croteau, *Politics and the Class Divide: Working People and the Middle-class Left*, Temple University Press, 1995.

- Theresa Funiciello, *Tyranny of Kindness: Dismantling the Welfare System to End Poverty in America*, Atlantic Monthly Press, 1993.

Books on the US class system:

- Teresa L. Amott and Julie A. Matthaei, *Race, Gender, and Work: A Multicultural Economic History of Women in the United States*, South End Press, 1991.

- Chip Berlet and Matthew N. Lyons, *Right-Wing Populism in America*, Guildford, 2000.

- Chuck Collins and Felice Yeskel, *Economic Apartheid in America*, New Press, 2000.

- Barbara Ehrenreich, *Fear of Falling: The Inner Life of the Middle Class*, Harper, 1990.

- Paul Kivel, *You Call This a Democracy?: Who Benefits, Who Pays, and Who Really Decides?*, Apex, 2004.

- Michael Zweig, *The Working Class Majority*, Cornell University, 2000.

Books on the personal experience of class:

- Dorothy Allison, *Skin: Talking about Sex, Class & Literature*, Firebrand Books, 1994.

- Diane Dujon and Ann Withorn, eds., *For Crying Out Loud: Women's Poverty in the United States*, South End Press, 1996.

- bell hooks, *Where We Stand: Class Matters*, Routledge, 2000.

- Joanna Kadi, *Thinking Class: Sketches from a Cultural Worker*, South End Press, 1996.

- Alfred Lubrano, *Limbo: Blue-Collar Roots, White-Collar Dreams*, John Wiley & Sons, 2004.

- Susan Raffo, ed., *Queerly Classed: Gay Men and Lesbians Write about Class*, South End Press, 1997.

- Lillian B. Rubin, *Families on the Faultline: America's Working Class Speaks about the Family, the Economy, Race, and Ethnicity*, HarperCollins, 1994.

- Michelle Tea, editor, *Without a Net: The Female Experience of Growing Up Working Class*, Seal Press, 2004

Books on social change strategy:

- Bill Moyer, with Joanne McAllister and Steven Soifer, *Doing Democracy: The MAP Model for Organizing Social Movements*, New Society Publishers, 2001.

- Adolph Reed, Jr., *Class Notes: Posing as Politics and Other Thoughts on the American Scene*, New Press, 2001.

- Barbara Smith, *The Truth That Never Hurts: Writings on Race, Gender, and Freedom*, Rutgers, 1998.

Discussion Questions

for a Six-Session Study Group on *Class Matters*

Week One

Reading: Working Definitions (pp. 2-3), Reality Check (p. 4), How Did I Come to Write *Class Matters?* (pp. 5-7), and The Power of Telling Our Stories (p. 154)

1. How would you define class? Which is most important in your definition: income, wealth, power, position, or status?
2. Thinking of your grandparents' and parents' younger lives, what signs do you see that let you know their class background? What words would they use/have used for their class?
3. What do you feel comfortable sharing about where you and your family today fit into the US class spectrum?

Week Two

Reading: Class and Our Other Identities (pp. 26-63)

1. What identities are important to you? How does each connect to your class background?
2. How have middle-class people and issues over-influenced identity-based movements? What would those movements look like with much more working-class and low-income leadership?
3. Would a stronger movement on class issues mean less emphasis on race, gender, GLBT, and other identities, or more emphasis, or a different kind of emphasis? In the most effective, transformative movement you can imagine, what would be the role of class issues, of working-class and low-income people, of women, of people of color, and of GLBT people?

Week Three

Reading: Why Do We Need Cross-Class Alliances? (pp. 10-12), Two Stories of Cross-Class Alliances (pp. 13-15), and Are There Class Cultures? (pp. 16-25)

1. What social movements have inspired you? What was/is their class composition? What's the most mixed-class activism you've ever seen?
2. Do you think there are class cultures? How do you see them similarly to or differently from *Class Matters*?

Week Four

Reading: Some Places We Meet (pp. 64-87)

1. If you think about elections where you've been unhappy with the results, what support did the various candidates get from each class? Did class divisions affect the results?
2. How can collaborators with different amounts of money and power (e.g. universities or hospitals and community groups, middle-class organizers and low-income people) work together on a more equal footing?
3. Do the stories in this section remind you of any mixed-class situations you've been in?

Week Five

Reading: Obstacles to Alliances (pp. 88-130)

1. What's the most classist thing you've heard anyone say?
2. Do you observe any political or lifestyle differences between people or activists of different classes?
3. If you think about what has prevented cross-class alliances for social change, which of the factors discussed in *Class Matters* seem like the biggest barrier? When have you seen examples of them?

Week Six

Reading: Steps Towards Building Alliances (pp. 131-159)

1. When have you had an ally? When have you been an ally?
2. How does group structure and group process affect cross-class collaboration?
3. What concrete steps against classism can you commit to?
4. Will your group stay in touch for any further learning or action?

Sample Classism Workshop Agenda

Goals of workshop:

- to develop our own class identities and become more aware of our class conditioning
- to discover commonalities with others of similar backgrounds and differences from people of other class backgrounds
- to learn more about organizational class cultures in our own and other organizations
- to strengthen our ability to work with groups based in any class and to enable us to more deliberately create groups in which people of all classes feel comfortable and empowered

Agenda for a three-hour or daylong workshop

1. Introductions
2. Goals of workshop and agenda review
3. Class-Identity Clumping Exercise (see three versions below)
4. Stress that revealing personal information is voluntary and passing is okay.
5. Class caucuses: What was positive and what was hard about your class upbringing? What messages from your class conditioning do you carry into your work today?
6. Report-backs: What do you want people from other classes to know about your group's common experience?
7. Organizational class-cultures exercise (see below)
8. Return to caucuses: What is the class culture of the organization(s) you work with? How could it be made more inclusive of everyone, especially working-class and poor people?
9. Go-around of one thing you learned about making organizations more inclusive

Class-Identity Clumping Exercises

1. FOUR CORNERS VERSION

A. The facilitator says: "Think about when you were growing up, the years between about ages six and 16." (Pointing to four different corners of the room): "Go to this corner ...
   1) if your family rented your home; owned your home; had unstable or substandard housing or were homeless; owned two or more houses

2) if your parents graduated from high school; graduated from college; had less than 12 years of school; went to graduate school or professional school
   3) if your parents' income came primarily from hourly wages; salary or professional fees; public assistance; investment income."

B. Allow a little time for conversation in the corners of the room after each time people go to the four corners. Tell participants to notice who is in the corner with them.

C. Now tell participants to form groups with the people they saw in their corner most often.

2. SPECTRUM VERSION

A. The facilitator asks the group to line up in order of their class background at age 12, pointing to one end of the room for the most privileged and the other end for the least privileged. Explain that they are to ask each other questions to figure out where they should stand in relation to others. The facilitator does not define class or answer any questions about what factors determine the order, explaining that the group will create definitions out of the questions they ask.

B. While people are standing in line, debrief:
   1) "How did that feel? Were you uncomfortable?"
   2) "What questions did you ask that worked to make distinctions?" The facilitator writes indicators on a wall chart. (For example, if someone says they asked if someone's family bought new cars versus used cars, write "New/used cars" or "Transportation.")
   3) When the chart is full, say that this is the definition of class indicators that the group spontaneously came up with.
   4) Ask people to form clumps with people who had similar answers.

3. QUICK AND DIRTY VERSION

(Not recommended for groups who don't know each other well or who haven't done prior work on class and other identities)
A. Give out hand-out of Class Definitions (see pages 2-3) and say definitions aloud.

B. Post four signs in four corners of the room: "Working Class," "Low-income/Poor," "Middle Class," and "Owning Class."

C. Ask participants to stand by the sign that best describes their family's class at age 12.

D. Form five groups, one under each sign, plus one for people whose situations were too mixed or unusual and for those in resistance to dividing up by class background.

Organizational Class-Cultures Exercise

A. Ask people to think of any personal experiences with an organization run by low-income people. Ask them to imagine entering that organization's space and to run through each of the following questions (posted on the wall):
   1) What is the physical space like?
   2) What do your senses experience – sound, sight, smell, taste?
   3) How do the people interact and communicate?
   4) What are the different roles for people? How are decisions made?
   5) What are the mission, goals, activities?

   Ask them to write anything especially striking on a post-it. (For a shorter workshop, have them call answers out while a cofacilitator writes them on the wall, then skip step B.) (Acknowledge that organizations vary in many other ways besides class culture, so they might want to only write things that they see in more than one organization.)

B. Hang a large paper on the wall with "Low-income" on the top, and ask people to come up and post their post-it, saying aloud what it says. (After the paper is full, the group moves on, but a cofacilitator quietly clumps the post-its and writes summary words for themes of multiple post-its. For example, if three people write about kids running around during meetings, write "KIDS" in bold letters and circle those three post-its and the word.)

C. Repeat with any personal experiences with organizations run by and for wealthy owning-class people.

D. Then repeat with organizations run by and for working-class people.

E. Then repeat for professional middle-class organizations. Note that even organizations serving poor people or rich people are often run by middle-class managers. Ask them to focus on organizations that also have a middle-class constituency, to get a less muddy picture of this class culture.

F. Go to each of the four papers on the wall in turn, summarizing the themes written in bold. For example, "It seems that many of you associate lack of noise with owning-class organizational culture." (Don't comment on topics that only one person mentioned, as they could be atypical experiences.)

G. Allow time for discussion. The notion of organizational class culture is foreign to most people.

H. Ask for examples of when participants have seen groups from two different class cultures trying to collaborate. Ask what went well and badly. Draw out and list on wall lessons for respectful cross-class coalitions.

Index

About the Author

BETSY LEONDAR-WRIGHT is a long-time economic justice activist who has seen class tensions cause rifts in the anti-nuclear, feminist, welfare rights and globalization movements, among others. For seven years she has been the Communications Director at United for a Fair Economy. She co-authored *Shifting Fortunes: The Perils of the Growing American Wealth Gap* and the classism chapter in *Teaching for Diversity and Social Justice*. She lives in Arlington, Massachusetts, with her life partner of 14 years, Gail Leondar-Wright.

Marilyn Humpries

If you have enjoyed *Class Matters* you might also enjoy other

BOOKS TO BUILD A NEW SOCIETY

Our books provide positive solutions for people who want to make a difference. We specialize in:

**Sustainable Living • Ecological Design and Planning • Natural Building & Appropriate Technology
New Forestry • Environment and Justice • Conscientious Commerce • Progressive Leadership
Educational and Parenting Resources • Resistance and Community • Nonviolence**

For a full list of NSP's titles, please call 1-800-567-6772 or check out our web site at:

www.newsociety.com

NEW SOCIETY PUBLISHERS